CONSULTANT'S JOURNEY

CONSULTANT'S JOURNEY

A Dance of Work and Spirit

Roger Harrison

Foreword by Peter Block

Jossey-Bass Publishers
San Francisco

Substantial discounts on bulk quantities of Jossey-Bass books are available to corporations, professional associations, and other organizations. For details and discount information, contact the special sales department at Jossey-Bass Inc., Publishers.
(415) 433–1740; Fax (800) 605–2665.

For sales outside the United States, please contact your local Paramount Publishing International Office.

Manufactured in the United States of America. Nearly all Jossey-Bass books and jackets are printed on recycled paper that contains at least 50 percent recycled waste, including 10 percent postconsumer waste. Many of our materials are printed with either soy- or vegetable-based ink; during the printing process these inks emit fewer volatile organic compounds (VOCs) than petroleum-based inks. VOCs contribute to the formation of smog.

Library of Congress Cataloging-in-Publication Data

Harrison, Roger, date
    Consultant's journey : a dance of work and spirit / Roger Harrison; foreword by Peter Block.
        p.   cm.
    Includes bibliographical references and index.
    ISBN 0-7879-0070-2 (alk. paper)
    1. Business consultants.   2. Consultants.   I. Title.
HD69.C6H374   1995
001'.092—dc20   95-3426

FIRST EDITION
HB Printing   10 9 8 7 6 5 4 3 2 1

CONTENTS

FOREWORD

I have always believed that every person's story, told truthfully, is both compelling and universal. *Consultant's Journey* affirms this. It combines the intimacy of a personal journey and the emergence of organization development as a profession. What is engaging about Roger Harrison's story is that it documents the tension of both a person and a profession in crisis—crisis in the best sense, as a continuous search for purpose, for relevance, for some way of giving meaning to a personal life and a vocation. Roger is as unrelenting in his desire to choose a life of service in the face of his love of self-expression, autonomy, economic success, and recognition.

What Is Organization Development?

From day one, the profession of organization development faced an identity crisis that enveloped all of us who had chosen it. In 1960, the profession was new in its exclusive focus on changing institutions and manipulating culture. It was ill-defined, however, and operated on the fringe. Organization development was sensitivity training; it was controversial, a form of therapy for well-functioning people. It asked adult white males to sit in a circle for five days and talk about their feelings. With nonexistent or maddeningly nondirective leadership, the group would spend the first two days selecting and destroying leaders from among the participants, trying to define what a feeling was, and deciding whether to stay in the workshop or to go home. The question would usually come to a vote on Tuesday night, and the group of twelve would most often vote seven to five to stick it out for the duration. Having finally chosen to be there, their last three days would result in some rather strong personal insights and a high feeling at the end. I never knew if our happiness on Friday was due to what we had learned or if it was lifeboat gratitude that we had all simply survived the experience.

Both its focus on the personal side of work and its fringe quality were what made the endeavor exciting, dramatic, and filled with anxiety. The problem facing the profession was its need for legitimacy: how did you sell a process that functioned on the margins, turned out differently each time you did it, and asked people to abandon their rational, technical training and enter the world of feelings, group process, and facilitation?

As Roger so clearly describes, the early struggle for legitimacy was resolved as the effort of seeking sensitivity evolved into more and more work-focused activities. The loosely structured personal development efforts have now taken the form of team building, culture change, work redesign, total quality, self-management, and reengineering. Seeded by the early sensitivity-group work, managing cultural change has now become conventional and commonplace in most organizations. The popularity of organizational change work now carries its own set of problems, however. After thirty-five years of evolution, the crisis facing organization development is that it has become mainstream.

When a fringe concept becomes conventional wisdom, it inevitably loses its meaning. What began as innovative ideas about managing change, employee involvement, total quality, and empowerment have now become breakfast cereal. Organizations of every stripe boast of their quality improvement and people skills in their advertising. The large consulting and accounting firms, which a few years ago scoffed at the "softness" of organization development, have co-opted change management as a growth business for their practice.

Even though the concept of fundamental organizational change is now highly saleable, the question Roger began with years ago remains virtually unanswered: can the promise of authentic cultural change be delivered?

The acid test for fundamental cultural change is whether the change effort has significantly touched the work lives of frontline employees. Are core workers more in charge of their workplace, able to commit resources without begging, acting as owners of the institution, able to find their own voice without too much flinching? Are defensive, non-value-added activities really being eliminated, or simply bootlegged or outsourced? My own answer to these questions is that, aside from some pockets of real progress, little has fundamentally changed in the way our organizations are managed.

Organizations certainly have changed. They have become flatter, smaller, and more focused on the customer. We control inventories better, have improved quality and shortened cycle time. However, if you look at cultural change—specifically, at the way we govern—the belief system on which we base our management of others in the 1990s is much the same as it was in the 1960s. We maintain a religious belief in control and consistency; we hold executives to be a special and privileged class; and we still think we need higher-paid people to motivate, direct, and be responsible for the emotional well-being of lower-paid people.

The strain between the promise required to sell an idea and the integrity with which it can be delivered is at the heart of Roger's journey. The discrepancy between the mainstream acceptance of cultural change ideas and the obstinacy of genuine transformation is a centerpiece of this book. In describing the history of his consulting efforts, Roger has detailed the struggle of all consultants. He is uniquely willing to look at the dark side of our promises. He examines for each of us the limitations of our profession and of his own practice. He has somehow befriended failure. In fact, I think he may be really happy only when he is describing something that did not work; this is an enormous gift in this era of spin doctoring and talk-show marketing.

What is equally impressive about Roger is that even after thirty-five years of consultation and still no cigar, he has not given up. The more resistant the ailment, the stronger the medicine he chooses. He is commited to bringing love and deeper intuitive knowledge into the workplace, and this is no small undertaking.

The Person in Crisis

In addition to chronicling the maturing of a profession, *Consultant's Journey* follows the development of a person. This is important because in the business of consulting, the person is the product. Our ability to facilitate the learning of others is absolutely dependent on our own consciousness and on our willingness to make our own actions a legitimate subject of inquiry. To pretend that a consultant has a technology that is independent of the person applying it is a form of manipulation.

In our efforts to legitimize organization development, we have tried to emulate science. We talk of organizational diagnosis as if two consultants looking at the same organization would see the same thing. We talk of intervention theory as if our actions were replicable across all clients, or across all consultants. We ask people to use a seven-point scale to report their feelings and we call the results data.

While it comforts us to wear the clothing and conventions of a fact-based profession, the work of managing change requires deep personal reflection. In this effort, Roger offers a fine model. He details for us the intimate connection between his professional relationships with colleagues, his personal relationships with women, and his capacity to have an impact on his clients. Granted, we all have the right to choose our own pathologies; but the process is universal. Roger's personal reflections invite our own. In this way, the book is deeply political. If there is ever to be a genuine redistribution of power, between women and men, between minorities and their colonists, or among members of an institution, it will come from each of us examining our own complicity in creating the suffering around us.

Despite our love of victims and our passion for entitlement, we have each constructed the environment in which we live. Roger's willingness to let the personal become public is a political act in service of genuine institutional transformation. Allowing the personal to become public is the act of responsibility that initiates cultural change and reforms organizations. Our need for privacy and our fear of the personal are primary reasons why organizational change is more rhetoric than reality. Real change comes from our willingness to own our vulnerability, confess our failures, and acknowledge that many of our stories do not have a happy ending.

Roger and Me

The beauty of this book and of Roger as a person is how tightly he has woven together the personal and the organizational. My first contact with Roger was as a member of one of the graduate sensitivity groups at Yale that he describes in the book. He ran a class with no structure, no leadership, and for which everyone got the same grade—a B. We all went crazy, and Roger was right there with us. He was committed to his own learning, open about his mistakes, and willing to be vulnerable. These were, and remain, radical acts for a Yale University professor. He has always identified with the underdog—in this case, the students—and that put him at odds with the university. His instinct for reflection and his passion for taking on what is difficult remain to this day and are the strength of this book.

After being his student, I became his client for several years at Exxon. Every couple of weeks, Roger and Barry Oshry would spend a day propping up Tony Petrella and me as we tried to get a change effort started at Exxon's research and engineering facility. The two of them were midwives for our entry into this field and always took us to the edge. We experimented with such social science interventions as trying to live in the moment by liquefying our food at lunch and holding meetings without any words. We would sit there in silence and every few minutes, when the tension became unbearable, one of us would slap the other on the shoulder. I forget what we were supposed to learn from that, but I will never forget the spirit of discovery and inquiry that Roger carried with him as an aura. We were explorers, and Roger was leaning forward on the bow.

In addition to being personally present, Roger has a unique gift for giving intellectual order to chaotic human affairs. If you like models and love concepts that stick to your ribs, you are going to love this book. He has constructed a tale that makes a fierce demand on each of us to constantly put ourselves on the line, and to see, without blinking, the limitations of being human and how naive we remain about creating organizations that live out our intentions.

Mystic, Connecticut   Peter Block
March 1995

PREFACE

Consultant's Journey: A Dance of Work and Spirit is for people who have an interest in the field of organizational change and in consulting to those who manage change. A professional autobiography, it tells the story of my development as a consultant and my development as a person through my work. I am convinced that we who use the self as an instrument of change and growth, placing ever deeper aspects of ourselves in service to our work, experience similar dilemmas, temptations, triumphs, and failures. For me, the road toward using the self has often been a lonely one. Here I share, as honestly as I know how, how the journey has been for me, and I expect that my readers too will find their own stories reflected within these pages.

They will also find both the light and the shadow sides of my practice over a long career. In my development as a consultant, I have not found professional reading and presentations given at professional conferences very nourishing, because they usually focus only on success. There is a place for success stories and descriptions of methods that work, but in the literature of consulting, these stories and descriptions are insufficiently balanced by explorations of the shadow side of our work: the struggles, the dilemmas, the failures and disappointments, the blind alleys that make up so much of our daily lives. I believe most of us tend to learn more from our difficulties than we do from our successes, but we report our successes in public and ruminate about our failures and disappointments in private. If anything, I have reversed those priorities here, in a determination to let it all hang out!

Each of us, if he or she is thoughtful and self-aware, questions his or her own performance at times. Though I have achieved a measure of success and reputation in my career, I have certainly had my share of self-doubts. In being open about the ups and downs of the spirit that have characterized my learning, I intend to give encouragement to others in those moments when it seems the game may not be worth the candle.

For both those beginning and those well launched on a career in consulting or in the management of change, I have included my reflections on the common choices and dilemmas that we who deal with organizational change face in our work, together with stories and examples from my own practice. How we do what we do has always had fascination for me, and much of my reputation has been built on my writings about the theory of our practice. In my *Collected Papers*, the companion volume to *Consultant's Journey*, most of my written work has been brought together for the first time in one place. In *Consultant's Journey*, I share my current insights and convictions about the practice of organization development, and I offer some guides to the field. Many of these views and beliefs are implicit in my former writings but have not previously been stated fully. Indeed, some of them came to me only as I reflected on the experiences described in this memoir.

Consultant's Journey is also my personal history of the growth of the field of organization development. My career as a management consultant began in 1956, and I have seen the field evolve from its antecedents in the fifties in group dynamics and sensitivity training (T-groups) to its beginnings in the sixties with the invention of such methods as team development and my own role negotiation to its fragmentation in the present day. By fragmentation, I mean the splitting of our focus between, on the one hand, soft approaches such as organization transformation and spirituality in work and whole systems approaches such as future search (Weisbord and others, 1993) and, on the other hand, hard, rational approaches such as organization reengineering. Here, I share my experience of the trends, fads, and fashions that have graced our field during my nearly four decades of practice, along with my convictions about what is fundamental and of enduring value.

At my present stage in life and work, I am experiencing a nearly irresistible urge to *give back* some of the help, hope, and encouragement I have received along my own path. *Consultant's Journey* is intended to be part of that return. It provides a map of the territory, and it points to the pitfalls and promises, the joys and sorrows that are to be found along the way. I have written it to share the excitement and wonder that the field of organization development has brought me in such plentiful measure. It has been a fascinating and deeply rewarding trip so far, and it feels good to stop along the road and look back in awe and reverence before traveling on.

Overview of the Contents

I was born in 1930, so as this book goes to press I shall be sixty-five years old. In Chapter One, I cover my life from my childhood to the age of twenty-six. The events and processes of that time foreshadowed my later passions and predilections as a consultant and as a person, and prepared me for life and work. My intent in this chapter is to identify what has been the grist for my mill, describing the early experiences, inner and outer conflicts, interests, and preoccupations that have entered into my process of learning and development. These elements have laid the foundation for what I have become as a person and as a professional. One of the strongest elements that will become apparent in that foundation is struggle. I have struggled to overcome internal blocks and barriers to my own development, and I have struggled to define myself and take control of my life.

Chapter Two tells of my years as a young professional at Procter & Gamble, my love affair with T-groups, my move to Yale University, and my mission to bring experiential learning into the university classroom. I describe my early consulting experiences, and my growing disillusionment with academic life. At the beginning of this period, I directed my efforts toward learning to contribute and to meet the standards of others, but soon a strong drive for self-definition and self-expression intervened and set me on a different course. This chapter also deals with my development of the tools of the consultant's trade, tools honed while designing and conducting T-group laboratories and experiential classroom learning. I learned about the power and the limitations of openness. I became skilled in observing group and interpersonal processes and intervening in them. I learned to manage the level of confrontation and stress in small-group learning experiences. And I learned that structure and systems are usually more powerful determinants of behavior than motivation.

Chapter Three deals with the transition I went through during the years from 1965 to 1968, when I was finding my own voice as a writer, enjoying the fruits of my efforts to make my classroom a haven for experiential learning, and becoming free at last from the crippling anxiety that had plagued me for a long time. I gave up my academic career and spent a year as a staff member of the National Training Laboratories in Washington, D.C., finding there a close collegial family. But my needs for autonomy propelled me on, and I went on my own as a freelance consultant in 1967. I was disengaging from much that had given my life structure and support and had placed limits on my self-expression.

In Chapter Four, I discuss my sojourn in Europe from 1968 to 1976. It was a time of adventure, excitement, creativity, and professional and financial success. During this period, I also met and married my second wife, Diana, and our daughter, Susan Jane, was born. At first, my work issues centered around establishing myself as a consultant in Europe, learning how to live and work effectively in other cultures, and endeavoring to make a real difference in the lives of the organizations and people with whom I worked. This was the time in which I first experienced to the full my personal autonomy and power. I achieved professional success and monetary rewards, but I was not satisfied with the results of my work in the world. My observation of the cultural differences between U.S. and European T-groups led me to develop the autonomy laboratory, a new form of experiential education. My experiences with this tool taught me a great deal about how people learn and, later, enabled me and my colleagues to design several effective programs for training people in interpersonal skills. In this work, I discovered and brought to full maturity my creative abilities in the design of management training and education.

Chapter Five relates how my interest in personal power, a passion for me for a number of years, took me and a colleague into the development of the Positive Power & Influence Program, which we began using in 1971 and which enjoyed rapid success. In 1976, I returned to the United States with my family to live in California. I was tired of being an alien, and I also wanted to change to a softer and more cooperative and heartful personal style. But as the co-owner of a new business formed to market the Positive Power & Influence Program, I lived in a three-way struggle for five years, pulled in different directions by my drive for autonomy, my need for financial security, and the demands of the business and my partners. A fourth force, still in shadow at that time, was my process of spiritual evolution and my need to bring my work into congruence with my heart and soul. I did good work during this time, but I was increasingly dispirited and unfulfilled. In the end, I brought the whole edifice that I had constructed for my work life crashing down around my ears.

In Chapter Six, I backtrack a bit to describe my search for a way to integrate my personal and spiritual process into my work. Begun in 1976, the search centered on finding a way to work and relate to others that was more from the heart and less from will and intellect. By 1981, I had achieved a new vision of organizational balance and wholeness, and by 1985, I had created a way to talk about it that I could take on the road. However, something was still not right. I felt listless and dispirited a lot of the time, and I kept casting about for a way to nourish my longing for deep meaning in my work.

Chapter Seven deals with my writing, speaking, and consulting work from 1984 to 1990. My search for metaphors and models for talking to managers about releasing love in organizations led me to renew my interest in organization culture. I developed new instrumentation, brought my model of types of organization culture to a higher level of sophistication, and took on two ambitious culture change projects, learning in the process a lot about what does not work and something about what does.

In Chapter Eight, I take up my personal and spiritual development after 1983 and continue the story of my attempt to transform myself through embracing my own shadow, those aspects of self that lie hidden and unacknowledged under our roles and everyday behaviors. As I walked this path of self-discovery, I was increasingly drawn to explore living in community: first through a consulting project with a Zen group, then through a variety of connections with the Findhorn Community in Scotland.

In Chapter Nine, I describe my entry in 1990 into the spiritual community where I resided until just before this book was published. Living in community, with all its light and shadow, has suited me. In this chapter, I explore some blocks and barriers in myself to living comfortably in community and discuss how I have coped with them. I share a new model of organization culture that has emerged from my life in community, and I reflect on the place of surrender in relationships and organizations. This chapter also describes how I have ventured into building more ambitious and prescriptive models for managing change in organizations, and it brings my professional history up-to-date by describing my recent work on organizational learning and healing, processes that are intimately interrelated although seldom mentioned together by others writing on organization learning.

Chapter Ten summarizes what I have learned in more than thirty-five years as a consultant. I share my deeper learnings about the work of organization development and how they have grown out of my practice, giving special attention to the ways in which my intuitive abilities have expanded over the years and how I use intuition in my work. I discuss, from the point of view of my practice, dilemmas that I believe all organization development consultants face frequently or continually. And I end with a look toward what the future may offer, both for myself and for the field of organization development.

Finally, I would point out that *Consultant's Journey* is primarily about my process of evolution and only secondarily about other people and events. Those who are interested in how a consultant may develop personally and professionally, using the interplay between outer and inner work, will find much to ponder. Those who are looking for juicy anecdotes about the people who pioneered in our field will perhaps be disappointed. I have endeavored to be as open as possible about my own process but not to tell secrets that are not mine to tell.

Acknowledgments

This book is dedicated to all those who have participated in my learning and growth, both professional and personal. In the process of reflecting on my life and work, I have been amazed at how many of these people there have been, how deeply they have touched me, and how broadly they have enriched my thought, my feelings, and my spirit. There has been help, seen and unseen, at every twist and turn along my road, and I have been shaped beyond knowing by those who have given so generously to my formation. The list that follows is only the tip of the iceberg, brought to mind through the process of writing this book.

My mother gave me her love of words, ideas, and fantasy; her interest in things English; and a forgiving heart. My father provided settings for me to grow my will, my persistence in the face of obstacles, my love of work, and my fascination with business. The petty tyrants and social arbiters of my school and neighborhood gave me early opportunities to know myself as a being apart at the same time as they sharpened my lifelong desire for deep connection. My brother, Terry, has been a faithful companion, listener, and interlocutor down these many years.

Albert Hastorf, professor of psychology at Dartmouth College, opened for me the delights of inquiry into the human mind. Charles Hedrick, my first boss at Procter & Gamble, had the faith and confidence in me to let me fly solo for the first time. The late Richard Wallen introduced me to the fascinations and arcane pleasures of T-groups. Chris Argyris gave me the opportunity to enter both the academic world and that of group dynamics training. As he has done for many, he stimulated and provoked me to think for myself.

As a young academic, I received sage advice and counsel from the late Donald Taylor, and Howard Perlmutter guided and supported me as I went about ignoring it. Among my many colleagues in the National Training Laboratories network, I want especially to acknowledge Barry Oshry, Jerry Harvey, Edie and Charles Seashore, John and Joyce Weir, and the late Ron Lippitt for their friendship, support, and guidance. I owe a great debt of gratitude to Jacob Levine, a psychoanalyst with a heart. He helped restore much of the trust that I had lost in humankind. My friends and colleagues at the University of Puerto Rico, especially Luz Beytagh, Marya Muñoz, and José Viñas, provided nurturing friendship, love, and laughter with a Latin flavor.

Raymonde Mérialdo welcomed me at the start of my sojourn in Europe and has given me more than a quarter century of friendship and hospitality. David Berlew, friend and colleague, shared with me many of my most creative moments and, together with David Kolb, Irv Rubin, and Fritz Steele of Development Research Associates, gave me a long-term collegial anchor to things American during my eight years as an expatriate. Sir John Harvey Jones, then of Imperial Chemical Industries (ICI), gave me my first opportunities as a freelance consultant in Britain. Philip Gray, Arthur Johnston, and many other colleagues at ICI helped me negotiate the cultural mazes of British business. Jacques Mareschal, then of IBM Belgium, took the risk of joining me in creating my most audacious training venture, the Autonomy Lab, and launching it into the mainstream. Neil Rackham, researcher and training designer extraordinaire, was an endless source of exciting ideas and concepts. Mike Minty, then of Rank Xerox, brought more fun and laughter into the business of training than I had hitherto known, as well as contributing substantially to the refinement of the Positive Power & Influence Program. Dermot Egan of the Allied Irish Banks; Liam Gorman, Ruth Handy, and their colleagues at the Irish Management Institute; and Dave and Oona Walsh, entrepreneurs, have been ever ready to give my newest ideas a trial, and their warm Dublin hospitality will dwell in my heart forever. My Scandinavian colleagues, the late Björn Dahlback and Thore Sandström of Stockholm and Arne Ebeltoft of Oslo, have encouraged, joined, and supported my work in self-managed learning, both concretely and spiritually, as have Ian Mangham, David Megginson, and Mike Pedler in Britain and Hans van Beinum and Pieter Kruijt in the Netherlands. Diana Harrison, former spouse and colleague, enriched my life with love, friendship, and laughter. Our daughter, Susan Jane, brought me the unending joys of parenthood, along with deep spiritual teaching and insights about the cyclical processes of human learning. Hans and Els Zuidema of the Netherlands were ever generous in our business together with the Positive Power & Influence Program and became staunch friends as well. Oscar Ichazo and the staff of the Arica Institute in London launched me on the spiritual quest that I still pursue.

On my return to California, Susan Campbell, Barry McWaters, and other associates at the Institute for Conscious Evolution in San Francisco provided a nursery which nurtured my early efforts to integrate my spirituality and professional practice. Colleagues and friends Margaret Barbee, Kim Barnes, Juanita Brown, Cathy DeForest, and Jim Kouzes made me welcome to the Bay Area and helped me find my heart while engaging in the business of management training. My ventures into New Age thinking were given form and energy by endless discussions and chicken dinners with Juanita Brown, Sharon Lehrer, and Emmett and Sandy Miller. In our many days of dialogue, David Nicoll, friend, counselor, and shadow consultant, has provided a rich stimulus to my creativity and the courage to speak my truth through his rare combination of original thought and deep listening. My first steps to bring love out of the closet and into the arena of work were provided audiences and encouragement through the efforts of Edward Posey of London, Pieter ter Haar of the Netherlands, Roger Benson of the Findhorn Community, and Graham Dawes and Jane Cooper, then of Roffey Park Institute. Jane Cooper and Graham Dawes also joined me in the ambitious effort to craft a model for the practice of organization development, and Graham cajoled me into my present project of publishing my collected papers together with this professional memoir. He gave critical impetus to the project by interviewing me for eight hours about my journey, and providing me with transcriptions of the tapes. Without his faith and support, *Consultant's Journey* might well not have been written.

Celest Powell was a friend and companion on my journey through light and shadow that led to my embracing my feminine side and opening my heart. Virginia Dickson and Carl Peters showed me new paths of healing when I needed them the most. The staff of the Expanding Light in the Ananda Community, founded by J. Donald Walters (Kriyananda), introduced me to the teachings of Paramhansa Yogananda and to the joys of a devotional path.

Sarah Polster, my editor at Jossey-Bass, earned my respect and trust for her wise and restrained counsel. The structure and integration of the book owe much to her skill. My wife, Margaret Harris, encouraged and supported me in the labor of writing and created a healing and nurturing environment which gently warms and stimulates the creative process.

March 1995   Roger Harrison
Clinton, Washington

THE AUTHOR

R oger Harrison is widely acknowledged as a pioneer practitioner in the field of organization development. He has participated in and contributed to nearly every phase of its growth—from survey research and team building to large-systems change and organization transformation. In addition to his successful career as a consultant, he is a leader in identifying emerging issues of theory and practice and crystallizing them in his writings and presentations. He has written numerous articles on learning, organization development, and organization culture, and several of these articles have become classics in the OD field. He was among the first to write about culture in organizations, and he has published (with Herb Stokes, 1986) a widely used instrument for assessing organization culture. His collected papers are soon to be published by Jossey-Bass and McGraw-Hill. He has also designed a number of innovative training programs, including (with David Berlew) the Positive Power & Influence Program.

Harrison received his B.A. degree magna cum laude (1952) from Dartmouth College, and his doctorate in industrial psychology (1956) from the University of California at Berkeley. He began his consulting career with Procter & Gamble, then taught organizational psychology at Yale University until 1966. He was on the staff of the National Training Laboratories before moving to Europe in 1968. He practiced in Europe for eight years as an independent consultant, establishing an international reputation as a consultant and trainer of consultants with such multinational companies as Rank Xerox, Imperial Chemical Industries, Mobil, Esso Europe, Shell International, Norsk Hydro, and Volvo AB.

Harrison returned to the United States in 1976 and continues his consulting practice, now based in Clinton, Washington, on Whidbey Island. He is also a senior consultant with Innovation Associates of Framingham, Massachusetts. During recent years, he has focused on working with leaders to develop humane strategies for large-systems change, to implement learning, and to facilitate healing of the traumas of change. He is currently at work on a book exploring the relationship between healing and learning in organizations. He is also engaged in the practice and development of large-group methods for working with whole systems and in applications of dialogue to organizations.

Roger Harrison can be reached at:
3646 East Redtail Lane
Clinton, WA 98236
Phone: (360) 579–1805
Fax: (360) 579–1798

CONSULTANT'S JOURNEY

INTRODUCTION

I began to practice as a consultant before the term *organization development* (OD) was invented, and I have involved myself in most of the activities now included under that label. The idea of writing the story of my own development as a consultant and person arose originally out of the impending publication of my collected papers and my desire to put each of the papers in context. I wanted to give each a setting of time and circumstance and a place in the short history of the development of the OD field.

As I worked on this task, I saw how the articles reflected my process of learning and development as a consultant and as a human being. I have never separated my work and my personal life. Instead, I have sought for ways to work on my own developmental issues through my professional life. Such a practice can be self-indulgent, even unethical, when not kept within bounds. It can also bring unusual levels of energy, passion, creativity, and commitment to one's work. For myself and many OD practitioners, the practice of our profession is an important aspect of the crafting of a life. As an art, OD requires us to involve our whole persons. When we participate fully, professional dilemmas become personal ones, and triumphs and failures become opportunities for self-confrontation and learning at ever greater depths. When we do not participate fully, our performance becomes at worst mechanical or manipulative and at best playacting or cold and clinical activity.

My *Collected Papers* (Harrison, 1995) reflect both a work in progress and a life in process. As I reviewed them, I came to feel that the story of my own development could have relevance for others. However, writing one's own story is not a modest thing to do, and I have had to overcome self-doubts along the way.

1

There have been long periods when the work lay untouched. Without the encouragement of colleagues and friends, in particular, Graham Dawes and Mike Pedler, I could not have completed it. Now, I believe the effort has been worthwhile. There is much congruence between my story and that of my colleagues, and this volume provides a way for me to share what I have learned along my journey. Only partly about the practice of consulting, it is mostly about how to learn and grow.

My most fundamental insight is about the dance between work and spirit. My creativity flourishes and my work thrives when the work I do with my clients draws energy from my striving to overcome inner blocks and barriers and to live in the light of truth and love. When what I do is motivated primarily by security motives such as having enough money, not losing a client, or having enough work, then I find myself on a plateau. Then I am neither very creative nor personally fulfilled in my work.

Until recently, my pattern has been to explore some aspect of learning and practice until it did not feel creative anymore. Then I would finish that phase by writing about it, to share with others anything of general interest that I had learned. Each article marked the end of a phase in my personal or professional development. By the time the article was published, I was usually interested in something else. I have felt at times like a kind of professional butterfly, sipping the nectar first from one flower and then another, without a backward look.

Now, when I look back on that seemingly random, zigzag path, I see enduring themes that have animated my efforts. One theme has been empowering the individual and fostering the growth of the human spirit in organizations. Another has been making organizations more nurturing and more compassionate and humane places in which to work. Still a third has been fostering a climate of openness. Put succinctly, my task has been to release energy, love, and truth in organizations.

As I look at the story of my own development, it is a striking parallel to an evolutionary process I see in organizations. Organizations are arenas in which people play out their own personal development toward higher (or lower) levels of consciousness. I have moved on the dimensions shown in the table on page three, and I believe this movement is traced out in my written work when it is looked at chronologically.

As I have experienced my own growth, it has not been possible for me to go from stage 1 directly to stage 3 without going through the central, self-oriented stage 2. I have had to work on becoming free before I can work on being enlightened—or even being good! I have never completed the work of one stage before beginning another, but the earlier stage needs to be well on its way, in both thought and action, before I can begin the next.

As I reflect on my experiences with organizations, they, too, seem to have to work each issue in turn. Of course, some organizations are born at a higher level

MY PERSONAL JOURNEY.

Stage 1 Transactional (Central from birth through 1966; age 36)	Stage 2 Self-Expression (Began in adolescence; central from 1966 through 1977; age 47)	Stage 3 Alignment (Began in 1950; central from 1960 through 1974; cyclical thereafter)	Stage 4 Mutuality (Began in 1958; central from 1978 through the present; age 64)
Being driven by events and forces outside myself	Striving to control events and forces and bend them to my will—proactive	Feeling motivated by vision and purpose; concentrating my efforts on achievement of ideals	Being drawn to a vision of the highest good for myself and others—interdependent, mutual
Learning from others; being taught, shaped, and molded by requirements and incentives; experiencing events and forces in life as pressures to change	Learning from experience and experiment; undertaking my own self-development projects; experiencing events and forces in life as successes and failures	Learning from experience and experiment, guided by intuition; experiencing successes and setbacks as learning events in the progress toward a goal	Learning from intuition, observation, and reflection; experiencing events and forces in my life as teachers in a journey toward the light
Being weak, dependent upon others; acting according to their will	Being strong and self-reliant; acting for myself	Making common cause with others who are committed to the same purpose as myself	Being interconnected with all humankind; acting for the good of the whole
Following the rules out of fear	Making my own rules	Justifying my actions by the nobility of the purpose	Doing right because it feels right
Experiencing scarcity consciousness: feeling there will never be enough for me	Experiencing competition consciousness: believing there is enough for me if I am strong enough	Experiencing creation consciousness: believing we can create what we can imagine and intend	Experiencing holographic consciousness: sharing and giving; believing in the unity of all beings
Being preoccupied with survival, material gain, and meeting others' expectations	Being preoccupied with power, success, creativity, energy	Being preoccupied with overcoming obstacles and achieving my ideals at any cost	Being preoccupied with being loving, moving toward truth and light

of development than others because their founders imbue them to a degree with the founders' own consciousness. And retrogression occurs in organizations, just as it does in individuals. But most organizations I have worked with have started at stage 1 and have worked on becoming energized and potent before they could work on becoming interdependent and cooperative.

I believe one reason for the phased growth I have observed in myself and in organizations is that there can be no grounding of love and goodness without power (strength). Love that is not founded on inner strength is easily destroyed by power. Caring that is based only on the wish to be nice and to be comfortable in one's relationships blows away as soon as the wolf is at the door. This is true in people's personal lives, and it is paralleled in organizations.

CHAPTER ONE

A CALL TO SERVE

My personal theory of developmental psychology has been strongly influenced by Eastern ideas of reincarnation and karma. I look at life on earth as a school to which we come with learning assignments. In trying to understand my own or another's life, I look for a few central learning issues that have been worked over repeatedly until they have been resolved and internalized. I believe I came into life with the intent and capacity to love, indiscriminately and unconditionally, and to be of service. I was also given a package of resources for my life's journey, including strong intellectual and intuitive capacities, a high degree of sensitivity and emotional responsiveness, a healthy body, a strong will, plenty of vitality, and a passion for truth and learning. I also brought with me a number of contrary tendencies: blocks and barriers. I was then given experiences and training that required me to work intensively to change my own tendencies. I have also had to work against the influences of this time in history and this society on my way to realizing my intent. My blocks and barriers have included an obsession with scarcity, security, and wealth; a warrior mentality; an excessive reliance on reason; a distrust of others' motives; a disposition to be manipulative, deceitful, and sometimes larcenous; and a belief that I am unworthy of love.

The interactions among all these personal elements, together with the circumstances and events of my life, have produced the person, public and private, that I am today.

Note: Articles cited in the text that are reprinted in Roger Harrison's *Collected Papers* are indicated by [†] following the citation on its first appearance in a chapter. If the title given to the article in the *Collected Papers* differs from the original title, the revised title follows the [†].

Foreshadowings of the Future

In my experience, many of those in the helping professions have had childhoods that they regard as unhappy. They have experienced psychological pain and inner conflict severe enough to propel them into psychotherapy or some other form of inner work. I include myself in their number. On balance, I have benefited as a person and a professional from the process of overcoming my handicaps and difficulties, although I would certainly rather have come to my present state of mental and physical health and professional acumen by some less rocky route. I am glad to have my early road behind me. I emphatically do not believe in the maxim, "No pain, no gain," because it supports such a variety of addictive patterns. However, my own pain has led me to a depth of empathy, compassion, and intuitive understanding of complex social and psychological processes that I might otherwise not have achieved. I am not grateful for the pain, but I am grateful for the grace that brought me its fruits.

During part of my adulthood, I found it soothing to blame my parents for my inner conflicts and difficulties. In fact, however, my parents were decent, caring persons who worked hard and made sacrifices to give me all the advantages of a good education, family values, and high-minded aspirations. Yet I always felt there was something missing. There was a time when I felt that I was somewhat abused, that I was not loved enough and that too much was expected of me. I have learned to know, from having known others who *were* abused as children, that what I suffered was not abuse but something more like misunderstanding. For a long time, I felt like a stranger in most areas of my life. As a child, I was mentally quick and socially slow. I found it difficult to relate to my parents and to my classmates, and I felt myself to be an outsider at home and at school. Longing for friendship, I was too shy to reach out to connect with others at a deeper level. Although I am agile and well coordinated, I early learned to see myself as incompetent at sports, and I was often the last to be chosen for teams. I developed into a physical coward, avoiding fights with other children except for my younger brother, Terry, with whom I fought regularly. As soon as I learned to read, I turned to the make-believe world of fiction as an escape from a world in which I felt a misfit. I was also subject to minor illnesses, which I exploited as a welcome relief from the rigors of the classroom and playground. Overall, I had quite low self-esteem except in matters dealing with verbal and numerical intelligence, in which I nurtured a covert arrogance.

A Passion for the Ideal

There were signs and signals in my early life of the kind of professional I was to become. I came from a family of scientists and engineers and had inherited a lively curiosity about how things work and a love of tinkering and making things. My father could turn his hand to making, fixing, or growing anything. He was an artist in working with the material world, and he taught me to love the world of science and craftsmanship and to value work as one's major focus in life. My interests also tended to be in solitary activities such as how to spin a rope and make model airplanes. At about twelve, I became interested in electronics and spent most of my free time reading technical books or assembling radios at a workbench. I learned early to set myself very high standards of performance and was seldom happy with the things I made. The airplane models looked crude and clumsy to me compared to the glossy pictures on the box, and often the radios did not work. That, too, foreshadowed my professional life. My visions of what is possible have always had a luminous quality, and the reality of what I have been able to help bring into being has often seemed gross and incomplete by comparison. I have sometimes said (not really joking) that, for me, ideas are more real than reality. My strengths as a consultant are greatest in seeing patterns, understanding complex systems, designing products and programs, and writing about the theory and practice of organization development.

My mother was, and is, very accomplished with words, and through her, I learned to appreciate good writing and to love the world of fantasy and imagination. From her, I received my idealism, my wish to do something to make the world a better place to live. Neither of my parents was religious, but they both loved nature. They taught me reverence for the earth, for its beauties, and for the mystery of life.

We lived in Berkeley, California, in a big old house full of nooks and crannies which I loved to explore in search of lost or hidden treasures. There was even a hidden compartment in which valuables were sometimes kept, and I spent many fruitless hours hunting for it. Although I was afraid of the dark and enclosed spaces made me nervous, I was drawn to explore them as I have always been drawn to activities I fear.

My grandparents and sometimes my aunt lived with us when I was a child, and there seemed always to be many grown-up activities in which my brother and I were not included. I frequently felt that the adults around me were hiding secrets, and I developed a passion for smoking out the truth. I was always asking questions, and if I sensed that people did not want to answer them, that doubled my passion for asking. As an adult, too, I have had a fascination for how the hidden, unspoken darker side shapes and affects that which is manifest and in the light. I have relentlessly sought the whole truth in the organizations with which I worked.

My parents imposed rather strict rules on us children, and my father in particular had a will of iron, so I was usually outwardly obedient, finding subtler ways of asserting myself than outright confrontation. My family espoused rationality and honesty as among the highest virtues, and I put much energy into finding and exposing inconsistencies in my parents' rules and their application of them. I early developed a taste for argument and disputation, but I could never get my father to admit that he was wrong. I had to content myself with the satisfaction of forcing him to resort to his authority when I exposed a logical inconsistency in my parents' rules or discipline.

Although I was far from happy as a child, I had a stubborn hope that things would become better. For the most part, I hid my feelings, even from myself, because I was ashamed of them. My father had grown up in a poor but stable family and had made great sacrifices to put himself through college. He then had not only to support my mother and us children but also his parents, and sometimes other family members. I grew up during the Depression years, and that I did not feel grateful for having plenty to eat and everything I needed to keep me healthy and get me an education was a source of considerable shame to me.

I believe that as a child I was probably depressed some of the time, but I always had a sense of forward movement, actual or potential. Looking back, it seems to me that I never quite gave up on anything. I kept trying to win arguments with my father; I persevered in trying to become more socially adept. There was always something I wanted to learn or achieve, and I kept on dreaming of success. Although I did not feel a great deal of support for who I was at any given moment, I had much feedback on my *potential* to do better. At home, I was continually told, "You can do anything you want to do," and while I did not believe that consciously, my subconscious was thoroughly programmed by the repetition of that phrase.

Adolescent Adventures

My life took a turn for the better when I became an adolescent and began to establish relationships with girls. Finally, I could receive the validation and emotional support that was missing in the rest of my life. Because I was shy and it took much courage to make overtures to girls, I tended to cling to each one with whom I established a relationship. I went steady with one girl during most of junior high and high school, behavior that made my parents nervous to the point of requiring that I "play the field." I was not about to do that but could not bring myself openly to defy my parents. So, although I had previously been quite truthful, I learned to lie about my whereabouts and activities. I thus discovered a part of myself that enjoyed deception, a part that later led me into dark and difficult paths in relationships.

My self-esteem improved a lot during my high school years, partly as a reflection of the satisfactions I was receiving from the relationship with my girlfriend and partly as a result of doing well in my summer jobs. I became active in a church youth group (the only real connection I ever maintained with a Christian church) and made more friends of both sexes. Among these friends, I found myself listened to with respect in our discussions. I began to feel that I was emerging from my isolation and loneliness.

When I was sixteen, I stole a car early one morning for no reason that I can clearly articulate. It was the beginning of summer vacation; my girlfriend was away at camp; I was missing her and feeling frustrated. Unable to sleep, I went out early for a walk and then found myself looking for an unlocked car in which I might listen to the radio for the scores to the previous night's baseball game. I had walked up into the Berkeley hills and, as I sat in the car I had entered, it occurred to me I could get quite a long ride without starting the engine just by releasing the brake and rolling downhill. This was so exhilarating that after I rolled to a stop I endeavored to bypass the ignition switch. I was unsuccessful in this, so I went along the street, looking into other parked cars in hopes of finding one with the keys in it. Engrossed in this activity, I was surprised when a police car stopped and the officer asked me to explain what I was doing. I made up some story about my great interest in the interior configuration of automobiles, and the officer let me go after taking my name and address. I continued home, in great anxiety that when the car I had taken was reported stolen, I would be arrested and brought in for questioning.

My parents, especially my mother, were always very forgiving of my transgressions. I learned early in life that if I confessed with appropriate contrition, I could usually avoid punishment and, more importantly, be forgiven. So it was natural that when I thought I would be found out, I called the police and said I wanted to report a stolen car, giving the particulars. When the officer said the car had already been reported stolen, I said, with a sense of high drama, "I know— I stole it!" My parents were mortified of course. The police were so far from forgiving that they questioned me for hours. They tried to extract a confession that I was the perpetrator of several similar events that had recently occurred in my neighborhood.

Unfortunately for my learning about truth and consequences but fortunately for the development of my self-esteem, this particular act of rebellion was rewarded in two ways. The first was that my father agreed to give me driving lessons. At that time, getting a driver's license was a major step toward manhood. In addition, to keep me out of trouble, he gave me a summer job in the small adhesive manufacturing plant of which he was manager and part owner. I had previously begged in vain to be allowed to work in the summers, but my father wanted me to have the vacations he had missed as a boy. My subsequent belief in the reliability of forgiveness following confession was to bring me pain as an adult. I repeatedly tested the boundaries of relationships, believing that sincere apologies would make everything all right!

I worked at Adhesive Products every summer from age sixteen to twenty-three. At first, I did jobs that required muscle and no brain; later, I worked in shipping and adhesive making, which required both. While studying chemistry in college, I worked in the laboratory of Adhesive Products. I found I liked physically demanding, even exhausting work, although I hated repetitive routine. Doing hard work for a man's pay made me feel manly and strong. I found great satisfaction in doing my work well and in building relationships with my co-workers. These experiences established a pattern, and from then until my middle years, work was always at the center of my life, and my achievements and work relationships were my chief sources of self-esteem.

Of course, I was the boss's son, and so the people I worked with treated me from the outset with extra consideration. They showed me how to work in the easiest way. When they saw that I really wanted to be one of the group, they befriended me in a way that, for the most part, felt genuine. I asked them many questions about the work and listened with respect to their answers. I would have liked to ask more personal questions, but I was too shy. When information was volunteered, I responded with interest and empathy.

As time went on, workers began to share with me their thoughts and feelings about how the work was organized and managed. Because I, too, saw things from the bottom, I took in many of their feelings and attitudes. I would often share these with my father, without identifying the source, and he would then set me straight from his perspective. He was greatly respected, indeed loved by his workers, but they also feared to cross him. It took a strong personality to stand up against my father's sense that his own judgment was invariably right. He was thoroughly paternalistic in his values and attitudes and took good care of his employees in much the same way he took care of my brother and me.

As I talked with workers and then discussed their issues with my father, it became clear to me that he did not inhabit the same organization as the workers did. Seeing the issues from both sides was my first experience of the in-between quality of a consultant's work. It excited me to think of myself as a bridge between the perceptual worlds of different parts of an organization. It was fascinating to me how my father and his employees could share the same small organization and yet have such different perceptions of it. I thought the workers had many good ideas. Later, when I studied psychology, I was drawn to explore questions of how to bring people into better communication in organizations. My experience at Adhesive Products had taught me that workers could contribute to improving the work processes, and I wanted to make that contribution possible.

My Pilgrimage to the East

My father had wanted to pursue his studies in chemistry at the graduate level but had abandoned them to give financial support to his own parents. He was eager that Terry and I have the best educations available, and he encouraged me to apply to such schools as the Massachusetts Institute of Technology, Princeton, Amherst, and Dartmouth. I believe he was more than a little motivated by the desire to separate me from my girlfriend as well. I would have preferred to join her at the University of California at Berkeley, but I was unable to assert my social priorities over the academic ones. It was not only that I found it hard to cross my father. I genuinely believed that one should make sacrifices to get ahead and that I was being given an opportunity that would make a difference for the rest of my life. I was accepted at both Dartmouth and Amherst. I liked what I learned of Amherst; however, my father had a dear friend who had been to Dartmouth, and I found it impossible to resist my father's insistence that I go there, too. I did not know enough about either institution to put up a good argument, and after all, he was paying the bill.

My four years at Dartmouth College were academically quite successful, but they were probably the most unhappy of my life. Berkeley was very provincial in 1948, having little or none of the trendy leading-edge image it later acquired. Dartmouth, in contrast, then an all-male college, seemed to me to be dominated by well-to-do, sophisticated young men from Eastern prep schools beside whom I felt socially awkward and ignorant. They drank, swore, and spoke knowingly about their sexual experiences, real or fantasied. They often traveled the 150 miles to such women's colleges as Smith and Holyoke where they partied all weekend long, returning with exciting stories about drink and sex. My shyness and tight budget combined to curtail my social life to a painful degree. In addition, I found it uncomfortable to share a room with others and ended up living by myself for three of the four years, much of that time very lonely and rather lost. It was a great deprivation to me to be at an all-male college. Dartmouth's culture was extroverted, self-consciously macho, occasionally brutal. Even close friendships tended to be characterized by continuous wisecracking and competitive one-upmanship. I learned to play such games—indeed, that pattern was not unknown in my family, but it has never warmed my heart or nurtured me. It was only in my thirties that I began to learn to create intimate one-on-one relationships with men that did not send one of us into a homophobic reaction.

Most of Dartmouth's social life centered on fraternity parties. When the fraternity rush season arrived, I went the rounds, hoping to be invited to join. I was so desperately needy that I found myself with nothing much to say and made no impression on any fraternity selection committee. The fraternities were ranked by social standing, so when some friends later asked me to join one of the lowest ranked fraternities, I declined. I believed that people were judged according to the company they kept, and I told myself that I preferred loneliness to the company of those regarded as socially inferior. I knew my decision was stupid and self-defeating, but I felt compelled to make it. I sometimes followed that pattern later in life, giving up activities that I enjoyed, such as tennis and sports car racing, because I could not excel at them.

Nevertheless, had I not attended a liberal arts college like Dartmouth, it might have taken me decades to find my calling as a professional. Until I was about nineteen, it had never occurred to me that I would become anything but a scientist or engineer. Every man I looked up to in my extended family was one or the other, and I had developed a passion for electronics. It felt natural to me when I entered college to pursue undergraduate studies in the physical sciences. At Berkeley, I would have specialized in science or engineering from the outset. But at Dartmouth, we were required to diversify our studies for the first two years among the arts, the humanities, and the sciences. I had to choose among courses that, left to myself, I would never have considered. I found I had a taste for sociology, psychology, and philosophy. I began to debate social, religious, and political issues with other students. There was usually a lively discussion going on in the room across the hall from my single room, and none of the residents of that room were in the sciences. I listened to music; I developed an interest in modern art. I began to question the middle-class conservative values, beliefs, and attitudes I had taken on from my family and my narrow world.

Starting to Think for Myself

I entered college in 1948, when the world was putting itself back together economically after World War II but failing to find to find any formula for securing peace. I feared atomic war almost to the point of a brooding obsession, and I came to believe that developments in the hard sciences had brought us to the brink of self-destruction. War seemed incomprehensible to me, while science seemed completely inadequate to tell us how to live in peace. As a child, I had been horrified by the picture histories of World War I that I found in our basement, nor could I understand or accept what I learned of the cruelty and suffering of World War II. Ensuring world peace seemed such an urgent cause to me that I could not understand why we gave anything else a higher priority. Science seemed to me amoral or worse in its unwillingness to accept responsibility for the consequences of its inventions.

I had never found religion helpful with any of my fears or questions—it felt long on rules and short on explanations. So I turned to philosophy and the social sciences in my search for answers to the basic questions of life: Who are we? What are we here to do? Why do we cause so much suffering for one another? What does it all mean, anyway? My explorations eventually led me, during my third year at Dartmouth, to a course called The Philosophy of Mind, taught by a dynamic and popular professor, one Francis Gramlich. To my surprise, the course turned out to be an introduction to Freud's work, ideas which had not yet become ideas in good currency in any circles in which I moved. Gramlich himself was following a *didactic analysis* at the Boston Institute of Psychoanalysis, and he was a passionate and convincing lecturer. At first, I was intrigued, then fascinated, then horrified as I began to apply the ideas to myself. I became obsessed by the questions and fantasies raised by Freud's work on dreams, the Oedipal complex, oral and anal fixations, and the like. I began to fear that beneath the shyness and conventionality I had believed to be my real personality, there might be a beast craving all sorts of perverse and forbidden pleasures. There was no one I could talk to about any of this, isolated and ashamed as I was. The pressure just built, lecture by lecture, chapter by chapter.

Moving Out—The Hard Way

As it got closer to Christmas vacation that year, I began to dread going home. For one thing, I was close to deciding that I wanted to drop my studies in chemistry, but I was not sure what I wanted to study instead. I knew there was a program in the Philosophy Department for those who did not know what they wanted to specialize in. In it, I could combine courses in science and philosophy with some of the social sciences and humanities. I also knew that my parents would be upset at my abandoning a solid career path for such a wishy-washy course of study. My father in particular had been pleased when I decided to specialize in chemistry and had had visions of my taking over his work in the future. He would be very upset at the change in my plans.

Another fear added to that one. It was one thing to deal with my obsessive thoughts and fantasies while 2,500 miles away from home, quite another to be face-to-face with those who figured in those thoughts. One night, I woke in a state of utter panic. I was so afraid that I believed if I did not find some relief right away I might have to kill myself to escape the unbearable anxiety. The worst of it was that I had no knowledge of what I feared, so there was no action I could take to resolve the fear. I knew it was in some way connected with Gramlich's course, but I could find no conscious connections. At last, not knowing what else to do, I got up at about 2:00 A.M., telephoned Professor Gramlich, and trembling with shame and fear, told him what was happening to me. I said I thought it had been brought on by the subject matter of his course. It was clear he did not want to hear anything about my inner life right then (or ever, as it turned out, he being rather longer on theory than on praxis). He suggested I go to the college infirmary, which I did. There, the resident on duty inadvertently added to my humiliation and shame by asking the standard questions for testing a patient's degree of disorientation: "What's your name?" "What day is it?" "How many fingers am I holding up?" and other such posers. He then gave me a sedative and put me to bed where I stayed for the next three or four days. I had several sessions with a psychiatrist during the next several weeks and then went home for Christmas with a bottle of phenobarbital and a fearful heart.

Somehow, I got through a confrontation with my parents over my decision to give up my chemistry major and graduate in philosophy. They were disappointed and baffled by my decision and by my anxiety. They had, perhaps, some shame over the latter—certainly, I felt shame over what seemed to me weakness and inadequacy.

My anxiety went everywhere with me during the next sixteen years. I had a succession of therapists, beginning with a rather rigid Rogerian counselor at Dartmouth whose idea of a good session seemed to be one in which he successfully evaded any temptation to react to anything I said other than with encouragement to keep talking. I was desperate for some sense of direction and support, so although I finally figured out the rules, I did not get much out of the sessions. He was the only person I could talk to about my feelings, however, and I figured he would probably call for assistance if I got really crazy, and that gave me some feeling of safety.

I did not have very good luck with therapists initially. I felt as little understood by them as by anyone, and it was far from clear to me that they knew what they were doing. I knew I was in a classic bind: "I am the sick one here, so I can't trust my own judgment about the competence of my therapist. I could only make an accurate judgment if I didn't need the therapy." My breakthrough came only after I had turned thirty and was teaching at Yale University. Then, for the first time, I fired a psychoanalyst for being cold and uncaring and found another with whom I felt some real rapport.

In Search of a Path of Service

In my crisis of meaning, I abandoned my scientific aspirations, took some more humanistic courses, and graduated in philosophy. I then returned to Berkeley to take my doctorate in psychology at the University of California. I chose psychology partly because the transitions I was undergoing had triggered a great deal of anxiety and confusion in me. The study of psychology put me in a setting where I did not feel quite so much like a pariah for being in psychotherapy and where I could study myself. I suppose I have been studying myself ever since. A wonderful teacher of psychology at Dartmouth, Albert Hastorf, had also inspired me to study psychology. He made psychology come alive beyond the hackneyed and boring textbooks of the day. Although I and my classmates were undergraduates, he talked with us about the unsolved issues in research. He exposed for us the debates currently going on in the academic world about learning, perception, motivation, and the like. He showed us how cleverly designed experiments could tease out the patterns and laws of behavior. It all appealed to the scientist in me, and it gave me hope that the mind could someday be known as well as the physical world.

I had started agonizing over what I would do with my life when I left the study of chemistry, and I did not settle down until midway through graduate school. I was drawn by clinical psychology; however, I feared the work might be upsetting for me, unstable as I felt myself to be. I found everything about groups and interpersonal interaction fascinating, I liked the idea of applying what I was learning to business, and in the end, I settled for industrial psychology although there was almost nothing about organizations in that specialty then. As I remember, it was all tests and measurements, motivation and productivity. At one point, I was tempted by an opportunity to take an applied research position with the U.S. Army, studying leadership in combat teams, and I almost left graduate school halfway through.

I was eager to get out where I could study real people in their natural settings. Although I did well in my studies, I never liked school: not grammar or high school, not college, and not graduate school. Although I was a voracious reader of fiction, it was always distasteful to me to follow assignments and to have to study things in books. I enjoyed laboratory work, and I learned most from dialogue with professors and other students. I also liked observing people interacting. I liked trying to understand what was happening and then talking to other people about their observations. Yet the educational institutions I attended did not greatly value such active learning.

It was not until I left graduate school and got my first job at Procter & Gamble Company that I realized learning could be exciting and fun. Yet I had always expected I would become an academic of some kind. My professors in graduate school agreed, and one tried to dissuade me from going off to industry. However, I felt it was inappropriate for someone without experience of business or industry to teach others about it. My experiences at Adhesive Products had made me interested in empowering individuals at all levels to contribute and communicate freely. My education as a psychologist had not addressed these issues at all well. I believed that my real education would come from being in the field where I could work with people who produced goods and services. I certainly did not feel prepared to teach anyone anything about the psychology of work or organizations. I now believe I have used my experience at Procter & Gamble well, and it continues to serve as an important grounding and reference framework for me.

I also still feel that there is something not quite right about teaching that which one has not experienced. For example, I know that it has taken me many years and all the empathic ability I possess to be able to feel my way into the inner life of people who have great authority, power, and responsibility. I have had to overcome much prejudice and many projections derived from my early experiences with my father and other authority figures. Through my inner work and my many encounters with tough and powerful people, I have come to appreciate the humanity that is behind their presentation of self. I believe the healing that took place between my father and me during his last years and final illness has been an essential part of my development of compassion for the strong and powerful. As he weakened and softened I saw under his stern exterior the child who longed for love and nurturing. Even so, I am often painfully aware of how much I do not know that would be helpful in connecting with leaders and managers. I have not been one myself except for a year as a foreman at Procter & Gamble, but that one year has stood me in good stead. I do have something of a gift for connecting a few data points and making a fuzzy hologram from them.

First Travels

I met Barbara DeBorba on a skiing trip my first year in graduate school and married her in 1954. She supported me during my final two years of graduate school by teaching, and we also saved enough to take six weeks in Europe prior to my reporting for work at Procter & Gamble (P&G). In June of 1956, Barbara and I drove to Cincinnati, Ohio, and stored our car and our few belongings to be reclaimed on our return. Then, we took the train for Quebec, from whence we sailed to Le Havre, France.

My first adventure abroad was a mixed experience. Neither of us had done anything like this before, and it was exciting to be off on our own with every day an adventure. It was a real thrill, too, to find that my high school French was good enough for us to get around Paris if not to have much of a conversation with anyone. I was a nervous traveler, always uncertain about how much to tip waiters and taxi drivers, anxious to do the right thing and not be seen as unsophisticated. I worried about how much everything cost. I was on my guard lest I be taken advantage of over money. I need not have worried, but I always did. When I gave a trolley conductor in Paris a large bill and moved off without waiting for my change, he called me back. He counted out my change and shook his finger at me in a friendly way, saying, "*Faites attention, faites attention!*" After a few moments, I figured out that he was telling me to "pay attention," and I thanked him shamefacedly, and we moved to take our seats. I cannot remember that anyone tried to cheat us during the entire trip.

It was a time when the dollar was king, and North Americans were almost the only ones who could afford to travel. Everyone else was busy putting lives and cities back together after the war. Our room on the Left Bank in Paris cost us around two dollars a night, and the rest of the prices were commensurate. We did our version of the grand tour: from Paris by sleeper to the Italian Riviera, then on to Rome, Florence, Venice, Switzerland, the Rhine, Amsterdam, London, the Lake District, and Northern Ireland. We returned by plane to New York on Labor Day, and thence back to Cincinnati to start our new jobs: me at P&G, Barbara in the classroom.

It was a specific moment on our trip that triggered the process that would eventually bring me back to Europe to live and work for eight years. On a sightseeing tour outside London, the tour conductor pointed out how the Christians had used some Roman bricks in the walls of the ancient church we were visiting. As I looked at the row of narrow flat red bricks, a tremendous shiver went all the way up my spine. I had a deep bodily sensation of connection with a long line of English forebears, perhaps stretching back to the people who cast those bricks or who salvaged them for their church. I suddenly felt at home, and feeling at home was not an experience I had very often.

I returned to the United States determined to return to Europe, but I knew

I did not want to go back as a tourist. I had not enjoyed the sense of being on the outside looking in, experiencing all the surface sights, sounds, smells, and tastes and understanding nothing in depth. I wanted to participate or not to be there at all. I promised myself I would find some way to return to do some kind of professional work. It took me twelve years, but when I came again, I had enough participation to satisfy my dreams and fantasies.

In some ways, it seems strange to me that I chose to be a consultant and that it has suited me so well. I have a passion for participation and active involvement. I am uninterested in spectator sports, live or on television. I was avid to race sports cars when I first lived in Cincinnati. Eventually, though, I gave it up because I cared more about my own safety and that of my car to do well at it. After that, I never went to see others race. When I sit in client meetings, it requires all my patience and discipline to keep from butting in and giving my opinion, and I do not always succeed! Yet there is a part of me that passionately cares about others' empowerment. I do not want my clients' jobs. I have never wanted to be in authority over others—I have thoroughly disliked having formal authority when it has been thrust on me, as in the university classroom. I have wanted to be heard, to be included, to be influential, to speak my truth. Even if I cannot persuade others, I have never wanted to be able to compel compliance. That trait has shown up most strongly in my work as an educator, where I devoted all my understanding and skill to creating processes that gave control and autonomy to the learner.

I do not enjoy learning about things secondhand either. Although I love fiction, I am not a great reader of professional literature. I would rather write than read, preferring to do my learning through experience and through dialogue with others. I will turn to books when I am in the middle of an experience and want to get another perspective. I will read for information I can use to solve a problem. But I never approach a new subject by reading about it. Instead, I will go to a workshop or training, or I will question others about what they know, and then, when I have a little knowledge, I will strike off on my own.

CHAPTER TWO

ENTERING THE WORLD OF AFFAIRS

It has always been difficult for me to authorize myself to go counter to accepted standards and to strike out into new territory. I easily become frightened that I will be alone, beyond the pale, without support, and with inadequate resources to manage on my own. Until recently, I never had much confidence in my ability to look after myself unless I had the emotional support of others. Yet I have lived most of my professional life as an independent contributor, a loner, and an outsider by choice, placing myself repeatedly in situations that evoked uncertainty and fear.

I went to Procter & Gamble (P&G) in 1956. Most people who do well in their work can look back on a few teachers or mentors who opened up new opportunities for growth for them. I had such an opportunity at P&G when my new boss, Charles Hedrick, gave me carte blanche to define my job. In effect, he said, "Why don't you just take some time to look around the company and see what needs doing? I will support any reasonable proposal you make."

That was the real beginning of my development as a self-motivated, self-directed learner, and it was very threatening. I had never been told to define my own job, and neither had anyone else I knew. I spent several weeks in a state of high anxiety. The ideas I came up with seemed trivial and inadequate. I was also shy and in awe of authority. To move any of my ideas ahead, I needed to initiate contacts with people at higher levels who could sponsor my work. I spent a lot of time looking out of my office window or walking around the grounds, feeling scared.

However, I also did some reading and became interested in something new that was happening at the University of Michigan and at AT&T. It was called *survey feed-*

back, and I liked the idea of using attitude survey data to improve understanding between management and workers. It connected with the interests that had originally brought me into industrial psychology. So, I eagerly turned to the task of building a more participative approach, first in one P&G plant and then another.

Like many of my professional dreams, this one proved quite difficult to achieve. At the time (the late fifties), U.S. management saw no compelling need to change. Everybody was making money; the United States was the dominant world economic power. While managers were tolerant and occasionally even welcoming toward experiments in human relations, there was no real will to do anything radically different. Moreover, each survey I conducted awakened some expectation of change among employees. But when I set up a couple of rounds of meetings between managers and workers, both groups felt awkward and uncomfortable, not knowing quite how to go on nor even what they really wanted. In the end, nothing much happened. With each experience, the cynicism of the rank and file about the intentions of management deepened. (I have since seen that pattern dominate U.S. and British business. Until the eighties, when foreign competition created strong external forces for change, there were many experiments, some successes on a limited scale, but few fundamental changes.)

It turned out to be easy to obtain good information about what was not working at P&G, but very hard to use that information to change the situation. So, this early work gave me a strong bias toward action research. I believed then and I still believe that there is no point in collecting information if the will does not exist to use it to make things better. I now advise clients, "Don't ask any questions you don't really want the answers to." Every time we consultants ask how people would like to see things change, we create an implicit understanding that we intend to take action. Too often, management is just fishing to see what is down there beneath the glassy surface of employee attitudes, a surface that in normal day-to-day interaction reflects only the comforting image of the manager's own face. Faced with the deeper reality of employee attitudes, many managements turn and run—understandably. They are unprepared, emotionally and by experience, to see the process through.

At Procter & Gamble, I found out that managers have hearts, a discovery that has been gratifying to me as well as useful. Then as now, there were many questions raised about the bottom-line benefits of organizational improvement efforts (in this case, attitude surveys), and I discovered that managers were often quite eager to be convinced of the business advantages of the work I did. In their hearts, it felt to them like the right thing to do, and I formed the belief that managers often really want to make the workplace more humane, even more participative. However, the business ethic is a strange master, requiring that before people can do what they feel is right, they need either a legal or an economic justification. What I learned was that the justification needs to be persuasive but not very tight, so long as the project at hand is heartful and not too threatening to managerial power. The latter is the real rub!

A Vision of the Possible in Human Relationships

There have been moments in my life when a door opened through which I glimpsed a vision of a level of being that was higher and finer than anything I knew. One of these moments occurred in 1958, when I attended my first sensitivity training group (T-group). That experience changed my life by opening up possibilities of hitherto unimagined levels of openness and intimacy between strangers. This vision was naïve, but it was very powerful. I was enthralled by the idea that by meeting with no agenda other than to understand what was happening in our group, I and the others in the group could come at the end of five days to respect and appreciate each one of the strangers we started out with. We felt love for one another, though not necessarily liking!

That T-group was personally very gratifying to me. I often understood and could communicate to others what was "really" happening in the group. I got positive feedback for my contributions, something that was almost totally lacking in my job. There I had much permission but few strokes. At the end of the T-group lab, I rushed up eagerly but shyly to Dick Wallen, who had so masterfully guided our group. In fear and hope, I asked him whether he thought I had the potential to become a T-group trainer. When he encouraged me, I was in seventh heaven. From that day forward, I had a passionately held goal for my professional and personal development, but I soon learned that it would be difficult to pursue my passion while I was working for P&G. Shortly after that, I began looking for the academic position to which I had always meant to go after I had gained some practical experience.

I got my next job, an associate professorship at Yale, by writing Chris Argyris a fan letter about his first book. He invited me to visit him, and on our first meeting, we had one of those instant connections that have so often heralded major changes in my life. Chris did not stop at offering me a job. To my utter delight, he was able to arrange my attendance at the first Behavioral Science Intern Program of the National Training Laboratories (NTL) at Bethel, Maine. Thus it happened that during the summer of 1960 I spent ten weeks in T-groups, a real total immersion experience. I drank deeply of the heady emotional and optimistic atmosphere that surrounded the development of this new technology. It was a wonderful meal of intimacy, intensity, and self-disclosure, but it did not sate my appetite.

One story stands out from the many, an event which occurred in the interns' T-group, led by Warren Bennis. Warren's skill in intervening to drive dialogue to a deeper level was formidable, and he had just made an intervention that seemed to strip away one of Barry Oshry's more cherished defenses, making him look rather naked and vulnerable. Barry said, "Warren, when you use that scalpel, I don't feel a thing at first—but when I look down, there are my guts, spilled all over the table." Warren, in total earnestness and genuine concern, asked, "But, Barry, didn't the warmth come through?" The rest of us in the group howled as though it was the funniest thing we had ever heard. Yet the exchange did epitomize T-group norms, according to which individuals were expected to receive tough criticism in the service of learning. As I had occasion to learn, the line between compassionate surgery and controlled sadism was hard to define. For years thereafter, whenever one of my NTL colleagues looked as though a bit of feedback had come too close to the bone, another would say, "What's the matter; didn't the warmth come through?"

Looking back, I see that internship as a summer idyll of innocent love, learning, and laughter, in which we had abundant time for one another's emotional needs. I came to Yale after that experience with stars in my eyes. My feet were about a yard off the ground. I was so proud to be a T-group trainer, and it was all I really wanted to be. I had learned that I had a real gift for working with groups, and during the summer, I had gone from an awed reverence for the more experienced trainers to a cocky brashness. I became rather a pest in staff meetings. I had also learned that I was afraid of giving lectures, even the short ones trainers gave in T-group laboratories. Whenever I got in front of a group, my mouth dried up, my knees began to tremble, and my mind went rigid. It was to be decades before I acquired the ease I now feel in presenting to groups.

My Struggle to Ground the T-Group in Traditional Education

At Yale, my passion for experience-based education led me to try to convert my classroom into a T-group, and I immediately experienced disastrous results. That first semester, I shared an introductory course, The Psychology of Administration, with Donald Taylor, a senior professor. He gave the lectures, and I mismanaged the case study sections.

When, in classic T-group style, I asked the students what they wanted to talk about, they were first nonplused then resistant. To them, my asking them to set the agenda meant either that I did not know my subject or that I was playing games with them. I backed off and adapted to a degree but continued to press them to take more responsibility for their own learning than they were ready for. That semester was unhappy on both sides although it was probably worst for me— I felt so incompetent and confused! What had worked so brilliantly at Bethel provoked confusion and anger at Yale. It was the first time I had even come close to failure in anything to do with my schooling or work, and I vowed to overcome it. Eventually, I succeeded mightily, but it seemed a very long road while I was traveling it.

While at Procter & Gamble, I had heard a very insightful paper at a meeting of the American Psychological Association. I shall be forever grateful to the author, even though I confess I no longer remember his name. He had conducted an experimental study of deviancy in groups, and as I remember it, he had given several groups a difficult problem to solve. A stooge planted in each group was given the right answer but instructed not to reveal the source of his or her information. In some of the groups, the stooge conformed to the norms that developed in the group; in others, the stooges violated those norms. After several sessions, each stooge offered the group the correct answer to the problem. To no one's surprise, the conforming stooges more frequently convinced their groups than did the nonconforming ones. There was also additional research, and what I remember from it is that the people who established a reputation for competence and then later began to transgress group norms actually enhanced their reputation. In other words, once a foundation of respect has been laid, credibility is increased by deviant behavior. One gets "credibility credits" for conformity, and they can be invested in deviancy with a return.

My work with clients has been affected by that research. In early meetings, I conform to the dress code of my clients, I mind my manners, and I listen more than I speak. Eventually, there comes a time when I feel that more deviant, confronting behavior will enhance my charisma. I did not apply these principles in my early interactions with Yale students. Instead, I cheerfully violated their norms and expectations immediately, believing that I had the "right answer" to the problem of learning about human behavior in business. They responded just the way the study predicted; they rejected both me and my right answer! Except for Chris Argyris, my senior colleagues viewed my passion for experiential learning as a distraction from my real purpose as an academic. Donald Taylor, who tried hard to help me, made it clear that as long as students did not actively complain about my teaching, it did not much matter what I did in my classroom. He recommended that I learn to give sound lectures and that I apply my creativity to my research, not my teaching.

In those days and for a long time thereafter, I displayed a regrettable tendency toward counterdependency, and at Yale, I guess I bit just about every hand that tried to feed me. In short, I had a substantial "authority problem," which later led to my departure from academic life and my eventual choice of freelance consulting as an occupation. So, I ignored the advice of my betters. During my years at Yale, I struggled to create an experiential, student-centered classroom in the midst of a strongly traditional, authoritarian, teacher-centered culture. It was just the kind of tilting at windmills that my quixotic spirit needed, and it gave me much quiet satisfaction when I eventually succeeded, about four years down the road. After I left Yale, I wrote a long paper, "Classroom Innovation: A Design Primer" (Harrison, 1969 [†]), in which I included everything I had learned about experiential classroom learning.

While I was still teaching, I frequently traveled to other colleges and universities as a staff member of an NTL program for developing student leaders. My experiences with students on other campuses kept me going during my early discouragements when my own classroom was not working. These weekend T-groups were energetic, enthusiastic, heartwarming experiences in which staff and students quickly developed cooperation and trust in the service of learning. After such an experience, I would return to Yale and confront the bored, sullen faces in my classroom. Surely these youngsters were essentially the same as the ones I had had the love-in with during the weekend! What did I have to do to reach them, to turn them on to learning?

Becoming a Social Architect

In my second year at Yale, Howard Perlmutter befriended me greatly. I believe Howard's was the only hand I did not bite at Yale, and that was partly because as a visiting professor he was not part of the establishment. He was kind to me in my earnest efforts to learn and generous with his time.

Howard was working with a concept he called *social architecture,* and it gave me the conceptual support I needed for my experiments in the classroom. Howard proposed that all the parts or aspects of a social system had to support one another, or there would be pain and malfunction in part or all of the system. To me, it was a brilliant insight. I saw immediately that I was endeavoring to construct a room in the larger building that was Yale. That room, however, was not supported by the usual girders of authority and structure. I was trying to support it on my own charisma! I was divesting myself of the power to control access to graduate school through grades. I was violating the shared assumption that the student was an empty vessel who needed to be filled up by the professor. When I gave students freedom to choose what they learned and how they learned it, they did not know what to do to acquire the high marks that were their goal—but not mine. That made them anxious and angry. It was bad social architecture. A few students did value the opportunity to enhance their abilities to learn on their own, but most did not. Because lectures were not my strongest suit, it looked to most of my students as though I did not know much about my subject and was not really qualified to teach it. Moreover, when I relaxed my grading standards to give students more freedom to experiment and take risks, energy leaked out of my classroom. Students devoted their time to meeting the standards of more exacting teachers. That, too, was bad social architecture. I thought of myself as egalitarian. I hated to use grades as a carrot and stick. But under Howard's patient counseling, I began to see I had to use grades to build an *authority fence* to keep the students' energies and activities in my classroom. Once I had built a kind of corral around my class, I could give students a lot of freedom within that space. This is a lesson every participative leader has to learn as his or her organization evolves away from a traditional organization based on rewards and punishments administered from the top. I am lucky I had to master it so early in my career.

I have always believed that accurate understanding (diagnosis) of the system one is working in is the key to success in organization development. A good diagnosis is worth a thousand trial-and-error interventions. It permits people to achieve positive results with minimum effort, and it prevents the harm that normally occurs as a result of change efforts which are not grounded. Once we understand the essence of the problem, an elegant solution may soon present itself, and that is what happened in my teaching. In my classroom, I wanted to provide my students, many of whom had never worked in a business, with a simulation of the organizational world that they would soon be entering. I wanted them to learn about working in groups because in business most productivity occurs through cooperative effort. I also now knew I had to use the grading system to get students to take group work seriously or to engage in it at all. Their cooperative skills were undeveloped, and their authoritarian bias meant they would not willingly see other students as useful sources of learning. They were used to a system in which cooperation on learning tasks was defined as cheating!

The innovation I came up with was to assign students to do small research projects or to write papers on the lectures and readings in four-man groups. I assigned a number grade to the group product, and each student then divided three times the number of points I had given his group's product among the other members of the group, rewarding each according to his perception of their relative contribution to the task. For his final grade on the group product, each student then received the average of the grades assigned to him by the other group members.

It worked like a charm! Product quality went up. It was seldom necessary to assign a low grade to any project. Students were lively and attentive in class (by this time, I was becoming accustomed to giving lectures although they still were not my favorite thing). My finest hour came when a couple of students came up to complain that they were spending too much time on my course because they did not want to let their group down!

During these years in the early sixties, I developed a passion for reforming the process of higher education. My experiments in the classroom were exciting and gratifying. I imagined the possibility of making the university classroom a place in which students could learn and grow, and it was frustrating to me that beyond my own classroom there was virtually nothing I could do to affect the teaching and learning process at Yale. If I had been as deviant at Procter & Gamble as I was at Yale, either I would have had to be brought into line or the system would have had to change. I did not then have the concept of loosely coupled systems to explain the situation I experienced at Yale. Nevertheless, it became obvious to me that in universities the individual parts can vary greatly without strongly affecting the overall output. The university system is very resistant to change in overall direction. It tolerates and absorbs a high degree of variation and even eccentricity in its members, with little or no overall effect.

My First Steps in Consulting

I began consulting and training for business organizations as soon after arriving at Yale as I could, and I did as much as I could. My ideal was to combine consulting and research, as did my mentor, Chris Argyris. Chris gave me my first such combination assignment, helping him with the action research for his influential book *Interpersonal Competence and Organizational Effectiveness* (Argyris, 1962) and I wrote a chapter for that book on my findings (Harrison, 1962). Most of my consulting work came through my association with National Training Laboratories. For several years, Barry Oshry and I worked closely together in a General Electric plant in what was meant to be a groundbreaking study of the application of T-groups in business. My first publications grew out of that work and out of studies I did of what people learned in T-groups at the NTL summer laboratories in Bethel, Maine.

In 1963 or thereabouts, I found an opportunity to innovate in teaching and learning in the Peace Corps. That organization was struggling with how to prepare young adults for the rigors of life and work in Third-World countries. Most of the training was contracted to universities and colleges and was classroom based—inappropriately so, I thought. The results were generally indifferent. I believed, as usual, that I knew how to do it better. I interviewed with the Peace Corps for the position of director of training for Latin America, but then turned that position down in favor of an opportunity to work with the Peace Corps as a consultant. Soon, I was working with an idealistic and innovative client, Richard Hopkins, then the director of the Peace Corps Training Center in Puerto Rico. Dick was an academic, but he was an ideal client for me: bright, iconoclastic, charismatic, and a risk taker. Our task was to convince the returned Peace Corps volunteers who were responsible for implementing the training at the center that they had the capacity to design and conduct high-quality experience-based cross-cultural education.

This was no easy task. The returned volunteers were little older than their students and tended to identify with them. They did not easily see themselves as trainers. Also, as Dick and I discovered, they did not know what they had learned in their sojourn abroad. I say that they did not know, rather than that they could not communicate, because they all had war stories, and they told these stories often to convey a sense of what it was like to live and work "in-country." But when it came to generalizing from their experience to other situations, they tended to become vague and inarticulate.

This was the first time I had come across the problem of articulating and transmitting the meaning of experiences that have few anchors in present reality. I came to see the problem as similar to that faced by a person who has had a psychotic break followed by remission. Although the experience is powerful, perhaps transformative, it is very difficult for the individual to verbalize what he or she has learned in terms that convey a new vision of truth to others. When the former patient returns to "normal" reality, the memory of the "unreal" events may still be vivid, but the concepts to communicate the underlying patterns and insights are missing. Similarly, individuals who have not been in-country lack the experiential reference that would help them understand and apply what they had learned from the returned Peace Corps volunteers' war stories. Later, through my own experience, I came to see that similar problems are experienced by those who have had a powerful spiritual awakening.

Creating a High-Commitment Organization

At this time, I was devoid of spiritual interests, and such wonderings were far from my mind. I addressed the Peace Corps problem in a straightforward fashion. I reasoned that strange and wonderful things happened in T-groups and that participants came to understand these things by sharing perceptions and trying to build theories that would explain them. (This idea of the T-group derived from Kurt Lewin's ideas of action research. It antedated encounter groups, in which experience tended to be valued for its own sake.)

I conducted a number of team development sessions for the training center staff in which these and other, more personal issues were raised and occasionally resolved. The aim was to build their trust and confidence in themselves and one another and to develop consensus around using an experiential approach to cross-cultural training. The groups had much the look and feel of T-groups but with an action focus. They were quite intense. The training center was isolated in the Puerto Rican jungle, and when the staff addressed their relationships with each other, there was not any place to hide. So, I was less confrontive than usual and tried to be protective of people's egos when that was needed.

In due course, the staff designed cross-cultural simulations for the trainees with my help. The trainees were sent, alone, into hamlets in the surrounding countryside where they lived for a week or so with villagers and had to use their rudimentary Spanish to communicate with their hosts and with the neighbors. On their return from their sojourns, they would meet in groups with other returned volunteers who were on the staff, who led discussions intended to enhance self-understanding. The discussions dealt with such questions as, "How do I, the trainee, tend to act and feel under the stress of a cross-cultural experience?" "What constitutes effective behavior in such situations?" and, "What do I need to know and be able to do to be effective in such situations?"

I believe the training was good although I had no way of knowing how good. I am quite sure it was better than the academic model it replaced. My clients and I created the first high-commitment organization I had ever experienced outside of the temporary systems that develop when the staff of a T-group lab get together and thrash out a design. Such systems provide wonderful experiences in cooperative teamwork. The evolving confidence and cooperation among staff members are exciting and fulfilling. Such experiences have helped me keep alive the dream I have carried so long that work can be exciting, loving, creative, and productive all at once. I do not always believe the dream that we can "have it all" without any trade-offs, but I always carry it in my heart.

Up to the time of my assignment in Puerto Rico, I had no good reason to believe that consultants could create and stabilize such a high-commitment system.

The experience in Puerto Rico gave me reason to hope greatly. (I have always said to OD consultants in training that if you cannot live on hope, you should go and learn another trade.) However, there is a dark side to everything in earthly life, and this situation was no exception, as will be seen.

Choosing to Live Free or Die!

Just about the time the training center was humming along, Dick Hopkins left to do something else, and a conventional academic replaced him. This person insisted that the curriculum be returned to something more closely resembling traditional higher education. I was not present during his short reign, but he soon left in what appeared to be disgrace. Later, the next director invited me to visit. I learned that the traditionalist director had provoked many of the staff into open revolt in defense of their experiential model. The director fired some of them, but conflict continued. Morale continued to fall, and eventually, he was replaced.

Reviewing the experience, neither I nor the staff members believed that staff would have been rebellious toward the new director previous to our work together. We had created an organism with a life and will of its own. It was willing to sacrifice that life in resistance to oppression and in the service of its principles and ideals. The experience caused me to ponder the ethical issues involved in giving people freedom and power that may later be taken away from them capriciously. OD consultants' most open, participative clients are more frequently than not replaced by more authoritarian managers. The consultants have participated, then, in setting up the subordinates for betrayal, raising hopes that they know will probably be dashed in time. What I know from my own life is that learning to suffer and forgive betrayal has been part of learning to be able to trust, but I am not sure that is true for everyone. The dilemma remains unresolved for me.

The Peace Corps experience gave me a great respect for the power of human bonding. I recalled it later when puzzling over the reluctance of leaders to implement production methods based on self-managing work groups. Leaders resist these new arrangements in spite of their proven economic superiority. Perhaps they know, not wholly consciously, that such systems will develop lives of their own. Then, they will self-destruct rather than submit to the capricious use of authority.

Many years later, discussions with the managers and workers at one of the earliest and most successful of the new plants based on self-managing work teams, Procter & Gamble's Lima, Ohio, facility, confirmed these musings to my own satisfaction. I am not fond of conspiracy theories. However, I do believe that persons in high places collude, consciously or unconsciously, to maintain their power and prerogatives at the expense of the economic performance of their organizations. I have, in the recent past, heard a manager assert that he would rather give up his job than his assigned parking place. Though he made that comment without thinking and in the heat of a passionate moment, it reflects a state of mind that is not uncommon at or near the top of traditional organizations. The drive to maintain personal power strangles rather than releases human energy in the organization. It seems likely in time to cause the demise of some business firms that are now household words.

A Door to the Counterculture

My experiences in Puerto Rico led me in unexpected directions and to some recognition that pleased me. Together with Dick Hopkins, I wrote an article based on our experience and titled "The Design of Cross-Cultural Training: An Alternative to the University Model" (Harrison and Hopkins, 1967 [†]). The article won the Douglas MacGregor award, which was nice because I was only then beginning to find my voice as a writer and needed any boost to my confidence I could get. More important to me, though, was that in some radical student circles the article was seen as a stirring indictment of the traditional university system.

Our ideas appealed to the radical students and faculty who were engaged in struggle and experiment to make higher education more relevant to life and more responsive to students' needs. To my delight, the article opened a door to that world for me. I was invited to Dartmouth College to participate in a conference of students and faculty on the reform of higher education. There I met for the first time some of the pioneers in the movement. I remember a long evening's discussion when among those present were Michael Rossman, a leader of the Free Speech Movement at Berkeley; Cynthia and Jim Nixon, who had pioneered the Experimental University at San Francisco State; and radical students from other universities. I had my first experience of marijuana that night, and I tasted the sweetness of being trusted by these leaders of a revolution, even though I was over thirty! It meant more to me, then and now, than academic recognition, and that was not just sour grapes. I felt that evening that I was home with the people with whom I belonged.

As I cast back over my life in preparation for writing this book, I experienced anew, for the first time in decades, my deep sadness and disappointment at the collapse of that reform movement. We, the faculty and students in the movement, learned so much about the empowerment of the learner in higher education, but in the ensuing years, it seemed to come to very little change. The conference at Dartmouth in 1967 or thereabouts was close to the high-water mark of student agitation for educational reform. Shortly thereafter, that energy was diverted into the antiwar movement. As students became more oriented to the politics of war and peace, the forces of tradition within the universities quietly reestablished their hegemony. After the war ended, the next generations of students took more interest in what they could get from their universities than in changing them. A window for change had opened then closed again, leaving some freedom fighters bitter and disillusioned, and leaving me with broken dreams of true partnership among teachers and learners in the classroom.

Research on T-Group Learning Processes

There were three sides to my professional life at Yale. One was the struggle I have described to incorporate experiential learning into my classroom. The second was my outside work as a consultant, including my work for the Peace Corps and my continuing involvement in T-groups. The third was my attempt to achieve promotion through my research and writing.

It was natural that I wanted to conduct research on what I had most passion for—T-groups—and I came up with a new approach to the problem of assessing the changes that take place as a result of the T-group experience. While T-group participants and trainers alike were convinced that personal changes occurred, these changes were hard to demonstrate. On the one hand, most of the studies of change had unsuccessfully sought to measure shifts in behavior on the job. However, such change was usually inhibited by the hierarchical and bureaucratic nature of relationships in most organizations. On the other hand, it was fairly easy to demonstrate attitudinal shifts, even though it was questionable whether these changes lasted much longer than it took for the back-home environment to teach laboratory participants that more open, egalitarian behavior was not rewarded or wanted.

I believed there might well be enduring changes in how participants perceived themselves and others, even when the work environment was so rigid that important shifts in interpersonal behavior did not take place. My observation in T-groups was that participants expanded their mental models about groups and about interpersonal relationships. They were able to discriminate differences and see patterns that had previously gone unnoticed. They began to tune in to a range of phenomena that were new to them and for which they had to develop new language, terms such as *feedback, consensus, authority issues,* and the like. They seemed to leave the group with a richer and more complex cognitive map of the world of interpersonal behavior and group dynamics. I believed they had acquired a new set of categories for describing themselves and one another.

Kelly's Role Repertory Test (Kelly, 1955) elicits the dimensions respondents use to describe others. I hoped I could use it to investigate shifts in the cognitive maps T-group participants use and to measure how stable these shifts were. I expected participants to move from more concrete, external dimensions (fat versus thin, rich versus poor, educated versus uneducated, and so on) to more abstract and interpersonally oriented dimensions (sensitive versus insensitive, open versus closed, flexible versus rigid, and so forth).

In the summer of 1961 at Bethel, I developed and administered a role repertory test to participants in a number of T-groups. I followed up with a retest right after the training and again six weeks later. I applied for and got a small grant from the National Institute of Mental Health to process the data. To my excitement, participants' concepts before the lab did change significantly in the predicted direction after the lab. More importantly, participants continued to shift in the predicted direction, so that the differences at six weeks were even greater than they were immediately after the T-group. Even more important was a correlation between the amount of cognitive change and the ratings by participants of how active each individual had been during the T-group. It appeared that active involvement in the learning process was a key to change (see Harrison, 1966).

The Struggle to Write

I took pride in these results, and I was eager to present them to the world, but that was not so easy. Before coming to Yale, I had had great difficulty in writing and publishing an article derived from my doctoral thesis (Harrison, 1959). My difficulties now assumed the form and magnitude of a writing block, which became an extremely painful part of my life at Yale and contributed significantly to the demise of my academic career.

I never completely understood my block. Certainly, it did not yield to the psychoanalysis in which I was engaged from 1960 to 1966. The block seemed at the time a very destructive force in my life. I knew that publication was the route to promotion and tenure, and I believed I was highly motivated to succeed. But when I sat down and began the first page, a panel of internalized professors would begin to evaluate my work. "Silly and trivial," one would say. "He hasn't proved his point," another would point out. "Awkwardly written," a third would chime in. "Doesn't know the literature," a fourth would say. Daunted, I would tear the sheet from the typewriter and begin again, to yet another chorus of negative self-talk. At about this point, I might go to the refrigerator and comfort myself with food. As the problem grew into a pattern, I often found myself taking hours to prepare innovative dishes for Barbara and myself, thus partially satisfying my need to be creative and productive. I wrote little, but we ate well!

I suffered from a severe fear of failure, and it was heightened to the point of panic by my knowledge that success in my career hinged on my publishing competently designed and executed empirical studies. But underneath the fear, anger smoldered. That anger had started in graduate school when I first learned that there were researchable and nonresearchable topics. I was fascinated by extrasensory perception (ESP), especially telepathy, and I wanted to do a thesis in that area. Talking to other students, however, I learned that if you did not take a "safe" topic, you were likely to run into severe difficulties getting your thesis accepted. As a thesis topic, ESP was off the high end of the riskiness scale. I came to feel that psychological research was a pseudo-scientific ritual. If a subject did not lend itself to that dance, then it could not be studied respectably. Such biases seemed neither scientific nor empirical to me.

To me, the essence of the scientific method was that you have a theory, you do things that will test that theory, and you observe whether what the theory predicts actually happens. Or else, you do things first, observe the results carefully, and then come up with a possible explanation of what you see. As long as others can verify your observations under the same conditions, you can assume you are on the trail of truth. I also believed that I and others in my field ought to make room in our science for everything that happened, whether we could explain it or not. For example, in the area of ESP, if there are even a few well-authenticated instances of individuals' knowing at a distance that a loved one is in danger, then we ought to look for more such instances and try to make a place for them in our models. We should not try to discredit or dismiss them or explain them away. My attitude toward the established canons by which my research would be judged was both disrespectful and fearful. That can be a fatal combination.

There was another canon that I did not observe, and I have not met it well since graduate school. That canon was being well read in the professional literature. When I was experiencing my writing block, I was in a frame of mind in which I felt tremendously intimidated by my senior colleagues' ability to quote the appropriate professional literature on almost any point they made. I had spent my four years at Procter & Gamble doing applied work, not reading. I was behind when I came to Yale, and it seemed I could not catch up. My natural tendency is to read very few things and to work on these few deeply until I extract a kernel of truth that I can use. I came to feel inadequate because I did not seem to be able to read as much professional literature as my colleagues did. The more inadequate I felt, the less I was moved to read.

For years, this was to be for me a guilty secret—I wrote, but I did not read. I believed that if others knew I was just getting my ideas from my own head, they would think less of them. Yet I sensed, dimly, that when I read too much it interfered with my own creative process. It stopped me listening to my inner voice, and then I became confused. Until my own ideas are well established, I tend to accept everything anyone tells me as valid, or at least plausible, and to admire others' ideas more than my own. It is difficult to hear my inner voice when I am listening to others, and my inner voice is my best guide for making judgments about what is valid and what is not.

What works best for me is to engage in active face-to-face dialogue with others when I am trying to understand something, and then to withdraw, think, and afterwards to write. Next, I send the writing out and wait for feedback. I attend to the feedback, and if I get none, I attend to that, too. A lack of feedback means to me that my timing is off, that I have said nothing that releases others' energy and interest. When that happens, I usually put my work aside for a time and come back to it later. Or I may repackage it in another form.

Except for my writing block, I really enjoyed my research. I like number crunching, and it was always exciting to conduct statistical tests of significance on the values I had spent months collecting and processing. Each time I undertook a study, it was as if I were betting a piece of my career on the turn of the dice. I could win big or come away with nothing. However, if as a junior faculty member I came away with nothing several times in a row, then I knew I would be asked to leave the casino.

Eventually, I pushed through my writing block enough to publish my study of cognitive change in T-groups (Harrison, 1966). I was proud of what I had been able to learn and demonstrate by following the rules I learned in graduate school. The trouble was, I could not figure out what use that demonstration was. At best, if it interested others, it might stimulate a new line of research (it did not). Ultimately, the research might result in more or less use of T-groups, depending on how it came out. However, I suspected that the fate of the T-group movement would be decided independently of research findings (it was). I wanted to change the world, and I believed that in the classroom and in the T-groups I was running, I could sow the seeds of a better, more enlightened world in the hearts and minds of the people I worked with. I could not see how my research was going to contribute to that. But I had my heart set on an academic career, and I knew I had to play by the rules or abandon that career.

I believe now that there were other powers shaping my career. Certainly, there were powerful parts of myself of which I had only the faintest inkling. They decided against my academic career long before the outcome was clear to me. Meanwhile, I struggled to find a voice, any voice, and to find a way of being productive academically that had inner integrity for me.

Coercive Aspects of T-Groups

My first breakthrough was a little article called "Defenses and the Need to Know" (Harrison, 1963 [†]). I originally prepared it as a theory session in a laboratory for spouses of members of the Young Presidents Organization. It was probably the first paper I published at Yale, and it had most of the earmarks of my later work. It conceptualized and endeavored to resolve a real-life dilemma I had observed or participated in (in this specific instance, the issue of maintaining safety versus pushing for learning in T-groups). It arose as an unpremeditated inner push to share with others something I had learned. It was not quantitative. And wherever the initial thoughts came from that I eventually put to paper, they did not come from my rational mind.

During the mid sixties, I was finding working in T-group laboratories the most exciting and fulfilling activity I could imagine. However, there were times when I was deeply troubled about the propriety of what we were doing. People got pushed hard in the groups, and it was not always in their best interests. I was not even sure it was effective. People would sometimes go through conversion experiences in which they caved in completely to the will of the group. I mistrusted the permanence of those conversions, and my suspicions were confirmed by what I had heard of the research on U.S. prisoners of war brainwashed by the Chinese. With few exceptions, brainwashed prisoners regained their original attitudes and beliefs as soon as their environment no longer supported those "implanted" by their captors (Schein with Scheier and Barker, 1961).

People resist learning emotionally loaded material—for example, confronting information about their interpersonal style—unless they have both a "castle" and a "battlefield" (Harrison, 1963 [†]). Each term refers to a process, not a place. The battlefield is where people disagree, where one's expectations are disconfirmed, and where authority figures behave in unpredictable ways. The castle is the experience of having allies and receiving support and confirmation of the rightness or reasonableness of one's ideas and expectations. The castle is where people are allowed to have their defenses, hang on to their old ideas, and resist change. I came to believe that a good learning situation should provide both castle and battlefield. I tried to manage my T-groups to provide that combination of unconditional support and confrontation.

The battlefield-and-castle principle has traveled better than the T-group setting in which I discovered it. Toward the end of this book, I describe my recent involvement in healing organizations. The metaphor of battlefield and castle applies precisely to the violation of the implicit social contract that is going on in business organizations now. It points the way to healing the trauma of change and loss to which people are so vulnerable in today's organizations. I also believe that this idea about the tension between the need for defenses and the need to take risks in order to learn is very deeply rooted in my own character. I am a deeply passionate person, and when I go for a goal, it is often difficult for me to respect others' boundaries. So, I must remind myself that others need to move at their own pace and direction.

The Dark Side of T-Groups

I developed the battlefield-and-castle model during a time when I was undergoing psychoanalysis, and I often felt anxious and vulnerable. That feeling helped me to be aware of others' needs for protection. I came to feel that T-group trainers were dealing with a very powerful, covertly coercive technology, and that we needed to have our wits about us, and also our compassionate prudence, to guide people safely through the traps and pitfalls of the group.

Sometimes, groups will brutally scapegoat a member. My first wife, Barbara, for example, had a very nasty experience during her first and only experience in a T-group. She was badly hurt by hostile treatment she received at the group's hands, and when I saw in subsequent months how deeply wounded she had been and how long it took for the wounds to scar over, I felt the trainers had been negligent in their handling of the situation.

Sometimes, people had psychotic breaks in T-groups. It did not happen often, but having experienced such an occurrence in one of the first groups I conducted as a trainer at Bethel, I felt once was too often. A participant flipped out during the first session of the group, with no apparent provocation. I lay awake most of that night, overcome with anxiety, and struggling with my feelings of responsibility. It was all right with me if people experienced pain in the group, even quite a lot of pain, but it was unacceptable to me to be responsible for someone's being damaged, hurt to the extent that he or she became less able than before to deal effectively with his or her life.

I felt that I held the ultimate responsibility for making the group safe for learning. I was the one person there who (most of the time) had a reasonably clear idea of what was going on. We trainers could say all we liked about how we were not there to control the group but just to help people learn from whatever they did there. That was a bit facile and disingenuous. For me, being a professional meant knowing when a group was on thin ice or going too far, and setting some boundaries. It was in part my concern for safety and boundaries that led me not to involve myself in the wilder aspects of the encounter movement, which blossomed out of the T-group in the late sixties and seventies.

"Defenses and the Need to Know" (Harrison, 1963) reflected my wish for moderation and balance. Although I believe that it is human nature to gravitate toward the light, in my heart, I have always believed in evil because I have seen it in myself. I see it also in individuals and in groups. I cannot dismiss it as simply error or as reaction to having been treated badly by others—much evil seems choiceful to me. This view has always set me apart from the prophets of the goodness of mankind, such as Carl Rogers, and more recently, from the apostles of the New Age. I cherish the same dreams as they, but I do not see the same reality. All my life, it has been my burden and my gift to see the dark side of what I have loved and hoped for the most.

My track record has been mixed in managing the balance for myself and others between confrontation and support. I have been incautious and impulsive in making myself vulnerable to hurt. I am sure I have hurt others through aggressive truth telling. However, I have always held, if not always lived out, a value of compassion for resistance and defensiveness and a wish to work with those elements rather than to make them my enemy by trying to overcome them. The quality I most value about my style as a consultant and educator today is my ability to deal with the energy of resistance, disagreement, and even personal attacks. I have found a way that moves *with* the energy of the questioner or attacker rather than setting up a win-lose confrontation.

Trust, Openness, and the T-Group

My view of the history of organization development has OD growing out of OD consultants' failed attempts to bring openness and truth telling into organizations through the use of T-groups. There was a time in the sixties when our efforts as consultants were pretty much limited to finding ways to get people in organizations to tell one another the truth. The T-group method proved more powerful than reliable. We left behind too many bruised and damaged persons and work relationships. By the mid seventies, T-groups had such a negative reputation as organizational interventions that many of us took them off our résumés!

We began to develop safer technologies that limited and channeled the expression of feelings, methods such as process consultation and task-oriented team development and my own role negotiation. These interventions were still mostly in the service of fostering openness and truth telling. Over time, our interest expanded into working with organization culture, systems redesign, and the like, but in my experience, most of our work is still limited by the level of trust and truth telling in the organization.

At the time, it seemed that a free flow of information would be the great leveler. When workers could with impunity speak openly to people in authority, and those in authority were open and honest in turn, then authority would become more responsive, and the people would be correspondingly empowered. I think most of us believed at that time that a major standard for the OD professional was his or her ability and willingness to speak the truth to authority and willingness to risk his or her project or position in the service of the truth. Everything I have learned about how to tell the truth without becoming a social outcast was learned through trying to live up to that ideal, and I have the scars to prove it!

In our team development and training situations, we consultants could establish, and participants could learn, a consistent culture of trust and cooperation. But at the end of our work, the participants stepped back into a culture where the shared rules and assumptions were different. Relationships went back to pretty much the way they were before. Even the leaders had to bow to the power of culture. They could change structures and rules, and they could create some light around their persons, but unless they learned to work with the forces in the culture and did so over a long period, their impact was quite limited. The most frustrated clients I have worked with are of two sorts: those who are subject to the oppressive power of others and those who are endeavoring to liberate and empower their subordinates.

Why did we bother? Why do so many of us continue to bother, in a climate of increased competition and self-orientation, where it often seems that organizations are jungles in which each person's hand is raised against every other person? My answer to that question is my own, but I believe it holds for others. My process has been similar to that which, down through the centuries, has inspired missionaries of all faiths to move out into the world and share their light with others, against all the odds. Having experienced the joys of trust, intimacy, and openness in my first T-group in 1958 and many times subsequently, I wanted all my relationships to be like that. I had a vision of heaven on earth that was rekindled again and again even though it was nearly as often frustrated. I believed then, and I know now, that trust, truth, cooperation, love, and intimacy *can* be created in both work and interpersonal relationships. It is possible; it just is not easy. Along my way, I have striven for knowledge, for power, and for money, and I have had some success with each. Each has its own excitement, its own rhythm, its own dance, and each brings satisfaction. Nevertheless, for me, there is no music and no dance that compares with the flow and rhythm of teamwork, no excitement like that of risking oneself in vulnerability and openness, no satisfaction like the expansion, spontaneity, and love that accompany the establishment of trust. It is far from the only game in town, and it may well be the hardest, but it is the one game that is always worth the candle.

Being in T-groups transformed my way of relating to others at the level of style. I came to value openness highly, and I put a lot of energy into it in groups and relationships. I also learned to listen a lot more, to look for creative solutions to conflict, to try something different if what I was doing did not work. I became more flexible but also more manipulative. My first wife, Barbara, commenting on the changes she had seen in me during this time, said, "It's not that you do different things, but you're a lot smoother and more clever in the way you do them." There was justice in her evaluation. At first, my listening and flexibility were more in service to my needs for power and influence than to my heart.

T-groups worked for me, and they worked for those of my colleagues who used their experiences in labs to change themselves. We used T-groups to experiment with new behavior in a safe situation, and then we would try out the behavior in the world, moving back and forth from laboratory to application and learning as we went. I did six years of psychoanalysis from 1960 to 1966 with a compassionate analyst. T-groups and my working relationships with other staff members in labs provided a practice field, where, without too much risk, I could try out ideas that came up in my analysis. I consider my analysis to have been very successful although others I know have found Freudian psychoanalysis disappointing. Long after my analysis was over, my analyst, a wonderfully wise and caring man named Jacob Levine, told me that I had provided one of his more successful cases. I attribute that in large part to having had a place to practice. I still experiment a lot with new behavior, but now, I can practice anywhere. At that time, the world seemed a dangerous place, and I felt each practice, each risk, was fraught with the possibility of disaster. The two settings, T-group and analyst's couch, fed and supplemented one another beautifully.

Beyond Academic Standards—Finding My Own Voice

The reprinting of "Defenses and the Need to Know" in the Harvard Business School case book (Harrison, 1965b) a couple of years after I wrote it was a source of satisfaction to me. It was my first intimation that I might have something to say in print that could be useful to others. It set a pattern for my writing that I have followed until recently, and I became a kind of miniaturist. Until recently, I had never written a book but had expressed myself through a series of articles. Each was intended to communicate the essence of something I had learned and to be complete in itself. When those articles are reprinted, it is immensely gratifying and validating to me, but I have wondered why I never had enough to say on any topic to make a book of it!

After my research into what people learned in T-groups, I continued to probe the conditions and correlates of personal learning in groups. I conducted additional empirical research in the T-groups that Barry Oshry and I were running in a General Electric plant, collecting a mass of rather indigestible data that took me three years to analyze, and I produced findings that were tantalizing but mostly inconclusive. I had hoped for much from that study, but the main thing of value that came from it was the Organization Behavior Description Survey, a neat little instrument for assessing styles of leadership and interpersonal behavior (Harrison and Oshry, 1972).

There was one important finding from that study that has attracted no notice, so I shall just flag it here (again!) in the hope that it may yet be helpful to others. The Organization Behavior Description Survey was constructed to test a prevailing notion among T-group trainers that more or less equated openness with interpersonal competence. This notion was based in part on Chris Argyris's very popular theories (Argyris, 1962), which contrasted rational/technical competence (being open about one's ideas and arguments, reasoning, and persuading) with emotional competence (being open about feelings, expressing vulnerability and uncertainty, supporting, caring, and the like). Barry and I designed the Organization Behavior Description Survey to include items representative of all Argyris's behavior categories, and then I performed a factor analysis on the correlations among the items in order to see whether the underlying relationships confirmed the theory. What Barry and I found was that some of our rational/technical items had the same patterns of correlations as items describing being expressive of emotions. Both of these sets of items were negatively correlated with a set of emotional openness items that described showing vulnerability. Also, other participants in the T-groups gave the people who were high on emotional expressiveness relatively low ratings on being constructive and helpful group members. From the patterns of correlations among the items, it became clear to us that group members saw emotional expressiveness and willingness to confront as aggressive and unconstructive, even after (or perhaps *especially* after) they had been through a T-group in which such expressiveness was promoted and valued.

In contrast, group members valued as helpful and constructive by others were seen as showing such behaviors as active listening, caring, and supportiveness. Again, we found no evidence that group members found a person's being open about feelings constructive. This finding seemed to be a clue to the deeper structures of trust in interpersonal relationships.

That was the last serious attempt I made to conduct research in the way I had been taught in graduate school. I came to feel that kind of empirical work was like picking up crumbs that fell off the table of knowledge; I was impatient to learn more and to learn faster and, above all, to learn things that could make a difference in the world. My story since that time is in part the history of my effort to find trustworthy ways of learning and knowing that go beyond the methods of Newtonian science that we psychologists were saddled with in the early sixties. At first, I knew only that the research done by me and others on T-groups somehow missed the point. By the time I had reduced the T-group experience to testable hypotheses and statistics, all the juice had gone out of the experience, and the questions I was able to answer seemed trivial. I could not imagine that these answers would ever affect practice significantly, and I have never been interested in knowledge for its own sake. My interest has always been in the power knowledge gives people to do more things better and to make better maps and predictions in real-life situations. But at that time, academic behavioral scientists, even in business schools, were not encouraged to study real-life situations because they could not be subjected to the kinds of statistical controls that were required for academic respectability.

Since then, I have never found a good reason to change my ideas about the relevance of academic research to actual practice. No one outside academia ever seemed interested in the few academic studies I did or the many similar studies done by others. I know that my subsequent writing about ideas and practice has affected the way people go about managing change in organizations, but nothing in the world of work ever seemed much affected by the research I and others did on T-groups. (My jaundiced view has now been confirmed by the current advice of editors and reviewers that I leave out of my *Collected Papers* [Harrison, 1995] almost all the academically oriented writing I have done!)

A General Model of Consciousness Development

In 1965 or thereabouts, while I was still engaged in academic research, I applied for and was granted a small Ford Fellowship to support that research, and I used the time it gave me to attempt to gain promotion and tenure at Yale. I wrote a long monograph, titled "Cognitive Models for Interpersonal and Group Behavior: A Theoretical Framework for Research" (Harrison, 1965a). This paper articulated the first elements of what eventually became my general model of the development of consciousness, first, in individuals and, later, in groups and organizations. As in all my work, the basic ideas were not original with me. My forte is not creating ideas but arranging them in new patterns. There were four fundamental ideas arranged in a new way in my model.

The first idea is that cognitive development proceeds from simple, concrete, undifferentiated, crudely articulated concepts to abstract, complex, highly differentiated, elaborately articulated concepts. The work of Witkin and his colleagues (1962) and of Harvey, Hunt, and Schroeder (1961) greatly influenced my thinking about these matters.

The second idea is that there are a few fundamental *domains* of human functioning about which all of us develop our consciousness and that this development proceeds unevenly. We can be highly developed in one domain and underdeveloped in another. The domains I have worked with are *power, achievement,* and *affiliation.* I got these from David McClelland's work on motivation (1953). Obviously, one could differentiate as many domains as one cared to handle, but these three cover a lot of territory and are easy to work with.

The third idea is that all individuals learn dialectically. We adopt a way of seeing the world, a *thesis,* use it to cope with our lives as long as it works for us, and only abandon it when it consistently fails, bringing us pain and confusion. Then we tend to adopt its *antithesis* and work with that as long as it meets our needs. Only after having explored the extremes of thesis and antithesis do we fill in middle positions on the bipolar dimension that links thesis and antithesis. Later, the dimension formed by the thesis in opposition to the antithesis itself becomes a new thesis, against which is set up yet another antithesis, and so on. From discussions with radical friends, I believe that these ideas came from the work of Hegel and are central to Marxist interpretations of history.

The fourth idea is that as we learn and grow within any of the domains, we tend to swing between the two poles of *unity* and *difference.* When we are over toward the unity pole, we experience ourselves as a *part* of something. Our orientation is to interdependence, mutuality, loyalty, and love for others. When we swing toward emphasizing differences, we experience ourselves as *separate.* Our orientation is toward autonomy, competition, personal responsibility, and self-love. Graphically, the combination of the upward trend toward more cognitive complexity, and the movement between the two poles of unity and difference describes a sine curve. In Figure 2.1, the development of an individual in the domain of relationships is shown from dependence through to oneness, or unity with all. I believe I first came across this notion in the writing of Paul Tillich (1952).

I later elaborated upon the idea of development as swinging between the two poles of unity and separation in the article "A Practical Model of Motivation and Character Development" (Harrison, 1979).

To my mind, the significance of the model is in the ideas of a *sequence* of stages and of *readiness* for movement to the next stage. The table in the introduction showing my own evolution is an example of how these ideas can be applied, as is my work on consciousness in organizations described in Chapter Nine. With this model, I had begun the search for a way to identify where an individual, a group, or an organization is in its own process of development, so that interventions could be targeted to assist natural movement to the next stage. I believed that if I and other OD consultants could identify the next stage of growth for any living system, and if we knew how to intervene to stimulate the natural growth process, our interventions would not only be more effective, they would also, in some deeper and fundamental way, be *right.*

The idea that change should flow from within the system rather than being imposed from without has been a consistent theme for me. It has seemed important to me to work gently with individuals and systems and not to evoke resistance

FIGURE 2.1. INDIVIDUAL DEVELOPMENT WITHIN
THE DOMAIN OF RELATIONSHIPS.

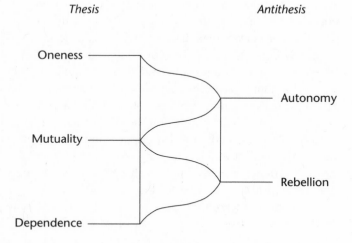

by pushing for change. Rather, I have found the minimalist approach of the aikido warrior appealing, in which one uses a system's own forces to power a systemic change. The consultant's contribution is in evoking those forces, helping to identify and remove obstacles to movement, and assisting in planning and steering the change process. In that way, we help the system evolve toward its highest flowering, its highest level of consciousness. The direction of that evolution is not decided by us, the interveners, but from within the system itself. In this way of thinking, we are not agents or creators of change but midwives for whatever the system is endeavoring to become.

The theme of minimal intervention and of working with a system's own forces crops up over and over again in my subsequent writing. Yet many of my difficulties and conflicts in relationships have been brought about in part by my trying to control and shape others. It is ironic, and it has occasioned sorrow and remorse for me, that in both my personal and professional lives I have often done the opposite of what I believe. Indeed, I observed early in my career that many of the foremost exponents of openness, participation, trust, and other humanistic values did not walk their talk, that there often seemed to be a negative relationship between espoused values and interpersonal competence. I have now come to believe it no bad thing to champion ideals we cannot achieve and, thus, to externalize the work we have to do on our own evolution. The crucial thing is to use that external work to increase our consciousness of ourselves, rather than to avoid and deny our own process. I have endeavored, therefore, to remain aware that the finger I point at the world points back at me and that my clients usually mirror my own failings and difficulties.

CHAPTER THREE

TURNING PROFESSIONAL

Characteristically, after finishing "Cognitive Models for Interpersonal and Group Behavior" (Harrison, 1965a), I wrote very little more about T-groups. Donald Taylor, a senior professor at Yale who had my best interests at heart, told me that I had the makings of a book there and that it could make a real difference to my chances for promotion if I expanded it. I replied with what now seems to me incredible arrogance that I had already written everything I had to say on the subject and that I would regard any further "padding" of my monograph as intellectual dishonesty! Thus was my fate sealed.

I was given a year's notice of my termination at Yale. I had already decided that I would not seek another academic position; not only did I feel I fit the world of affairs better than academia but also, where my work is concerned, I have never been willing to settle for second best.

I noticed the difference in my writing immediately. I now felt free to write what I wanted, the way I wanted. No one expected me to write; it became something I did because I wanted to contribute or needed to express myself. While I still had to work hard on my writing, my writing block felt like a thing of the past. I began to work on developing my own instrument rather than being wholly preoccupied with others' evaluations of my work.

When I left Yale, what I most wanted was to be in a center for applied research on teaching and learning where I could continue to develop innovative approaches to higher education. Such jobs seemed nonexistent, and I settled for a position at the central office of the National Training Laboratories (NTL) in Washington, D.C., where I was supposed to administer professional development programs. Since I could not do what I most wanted to do, I was far from sure what my second choice was, and I made the decision to go to NTL with my heart, not my head. Some of my closest friends were there at the time—Charles and Edie Seashore, Jerry Harvey, Curtis and Dorothy Mial—and I knew I would not be as lonely as I had been at Yale.

I spent the summer after I left Yale at the NTL's site in Bethel, happily engaged in training T-groups. I also took two weeks off to immerse myself in a new phenomenon, a personal growth lab. These labs were imports from the West Coast and were the vanguard of what later became the encounter group. They were characterized by a highly directive and confrontive style on the part of the trainer, the introduction of methods and techniques from Gestalt therapy, and the use of body movement and other nonverbal exercises to uncover and liberate aspects of the person that were inaccessible through talk. Rumor had it that in these groups there was considerable loosening of the boundaries we had been observing in T-groups, most of which had been brought over from psychoanalysis (for example, no touching, no acting out of primal impulses, and no sex between therapist and client). It all sounded pretty wild, and as a believer in never asking clients to do anything I would not do myself, I was eager to experience this new emotional treat.

The personal growth lab was wonderfully liberating for me. I am still enormously grateful for the gentle but powerful body movement exercises conducted by Joyce Weir, which gave me the first experience I can remember of really being *in my body*. My group experience, with Will Schutz, was equally powerful, though I do not remember it as gentle. In fact, during the first or second session of the group, another participant became angry at something I said and threw a punch at me!

I did not approve of everything that went on in that lab, nor, in fact, did the NTL Director, Leland Bradford, who shortly thereafter banned one of the trainees from further staff assignments on NTL programs. It seemed to me that participants were expected to take pretty good care of themselves emotionally at the same time as they were being encouraged to let down their defenses and trust the trainers to lead them along unfamiliar and scary paths. But nothing bad happened to me or, to my knowledge, to anyone else in our group. Will proved to be a master of his craft, and his skill provided yet another life-changing experience for me. I came away much more in touch with my own needs and feelings and clear that what I most wanted to do in the world was consulting.

The Pathos of Choice—Autonomy Versus Relationship

Unfortunately, the job I had signed up for at NTL was managerial and administrative; none of the professionals in the NTL central office had consulting as a significant part of their job duties. That did not stop me; somehow, I rationalized that NTL needed a consultant in the field and that so long as I brought in enough fees to cover my salary and overhead I was not cheating the organization of anything. I went out and hustled up work from the Peace Corps and the Agency for International Development, continued working on a project at Esso (now Exxon) that I had begun while at Yale, and tried to take care of my official duties in between trips to the field. I did not ask permission, nor did I make any secret of what I was doing; I figured if the director did not like what I was doing, he would tell me to stop it. I believed in what I used to tell my clients, "Do not ask any questions you don't want the answers to."

Wrong! NTL was not a place where people raised issues as they came up and settled them quickly. We staff members were confrontive in our roles as T-group trainers, but among ourselves, we avoided conflict and tended to let issues fester. A year after I began work at NTL, I took a Peace Corps training program to Mexico; it went sour, and I was fired by the project director. When I arrived home, sadder but wiser, NTL director Leland Bradford announced that he was putting me on probation because I had not been tending to business. Although I could see it coming, and knew I had brought it upon myself, I could not stomach the humiliation of that relatively mild slap on the wrist. I announced proudly that "I would rather be an unemployed professional than a probationary employee," and sadly took my leave from what had been the warmest and most supportive and loving work family I have ever had or could imagine having.

As I look back on the sixties, I see myself living out that decade's dream of doing one's own thing, but without the courage to own my autonomy. Whether the issue was becoming an independent professional, writing what I wanted to write and in my own style, or even my own sexual liberation, I acted as if I believed that the significant others in my life held all the cards. It felt terribly scary to assert myself, as though the cost of my autonomy would be to be all alone in an unfriendly universe without any love and support. Rather than stating that the terms of a work or personal relationship did not suit me and either negotiating a change or leaving, I would break the rules, hoping I would get away with it. In the case of NTL, I wanted to become a freelance consultant but was afraid to step out on my own. It felt less scary to provoke others to eject me from a relationship than it did to take the responsibility for ending it myself.

If I thought I were the only person who had lived out this pattern, my experience would make only a personal note that would not belong in my professional story. But I believe that many of us organization development professionals went through this process as part of a profession, as part of a nation, and as part of a culture, and that we had to go through these stages. According to the developmental model I described earlier (Figure 2.1), people do not move from dependence directly to autonomy. The alternative to dependence is rebelliousness, what in group dynamics is called *counterdependence*. It is characterized by struggle, and by an inner pessimism about the likelihood of winning. Rebellion is about not being dependent; it requires the existence of an authority with which to be in a rebellious relationship. The truly autonomous person, on the other hand, is free within him- or herself and treats authority instrumentally, that is, without feeling an emotional charge.

As consultants, we deal with a lot of people who are taking their first steps away from dependence, especially now that so many organizations are experimenting more or less seriously with programs in Total Quality Management and Employee Involvement (which, as nearly as I can tell, is what we OD consultants used to call participative management). Over and over again, I have seen managers and consultants alike struggle to understand the behavior of people whom they wish to trust and to whom they wish to give a larger measure of autonomy and responsibility. Employees' self-protective, defensive behavior sometimes puzzles me, too, until I remember those years of rebellion I lived through myself. Here is a sample of the qualities and behaviors I sometimes exhibited and which I see employees exhibiting in the face of attempts on the part of their managements to move toward a more participative workplace:

- I withheld trust from people in authority for a long time, and I only maintained that trust so long as they forbore to use their power.
- I was hypervigilant for signs of hostility or power seeking on the part of others, and I interpreted conflict in terms of power. I was insensitive to others' signs of distress, vulnerability, or neediness, especially if these others were in positions of authority.
- I was hypercritical of any unfairness, insincerity, or hypocrisy exhibited by people in authority.
- I tested the sincerity of the egalitarian values of persons in authority in ways that provoked them to use their authority.
- I pushed hard for freedom and responsibility for myself, but I dragged my feet when it came to keeping my commitments to anyone in a position of authority.
- I was competitive with my peers and resistant to their influence attempts.
- I acted manipulatively and sometimes dishonestly toward those on whom I felt dependent. When I outfoxed them it made me feel more equal. I did not believe I could win in a straight-out confrontation, so I tended to be sneaky.

Fortunately, my work in NTL exposed me to *lots* of feedback about how these behaviors affected others. It did not take me long to realize I had a serious "authority problem," and to commit myself to reducing it. My first decision after leaving NTL was to become a freelance consultant and to avoid hierarchical structures until I had myself in hand. Some of the other ways I approached this task will be apparent as this story unfolds: for example, my decision in the late seventies to endeavor to become "a good person." Today, my advice to clients who are endeavoring to move employees from dependence through rebellion to mutuality and autonomy can be summed up this way:

- As early as possible, engage in dialogue with your employees about your plans. As events unfold, have regular dialogues. Be open and forthright. Invite their doubts and misgivings and listen without becoming defensive. Continue to state your intentions, even in the face of disbelief.
- Know that their mistrust is not a rational problem, and it cannot be talked through. What you say will have impact, but only when they begin to notice your consistently congruent behavior.
- The reward system and the performance evaluation process are powerful influences on the mindset of employees. To the extent that rewards are contingent on supervisors' judgments of employee effort and motivation, the system will foster dependency and will work against the success of the change.
- Begin by giving limited autonomy within a framework of clear, measurable standards for performance. Give only as much autonomy as employees are ready to use responsibly. Be prepared for them not to come through at first and do not judge or punish them.
- Adjust the amount of autonomy given according to your experience: give more freedom as positive results are achieved. Be firm about what the outcomes must be but give employees freedom to work out how to get there.
- You have to take the first risk by showing trust. If your trust is betrayed, then you have to take the second risk, and so on. Betrayal of trust is not a sign of failure; it is part of the learning process. Make sure that you respond to betrayal in a way that builds trust (for example, by adjusting expectations) rather than by diminishing trust or by blame and punishment).
- You can have faster progress if you are prepared to take greater risks. The amount of risk you should take is the amount that, if your trust is betrayed, will leave you willing and able to risk again.
- You will be expected to be totally pure in deed and motive. No matter how hard you try, you will fail sometimes and will be harshly judged. You will need some friends who will give you understanding and support.
- Do not expect any credit or gratitude from your subordinates until long after this is over—if then.

As I look back on the sixties and seventies, they seem to me to have been for many of us in the Western democracies a time of rebellion but not yet a time of autonomy. It seemed as though all of our society was divided into rebels and authority figures. Eventually, authority was discredited. Those of us who were active in those times achieved a kind of liberation, at the cost of damaging or destroying the institutions against which we struggled, and at the end of our struggle, we found ourselves alone in a world where it seemed that everyone was so busy seeking his or her own gratification that no one had time for anyone else. All of us are now living out the consequences of that movement from a dependent and traditional ethic to one of self-expression and individuality. The challenge now, for everyone, is to attain the next stage, mutuality—to rebuild community in our lives through social structures that do not depend on hierarchical power to achieve a common effort.

The Misapplication of T-Groups in Organizations

I wrote two key papers during the two years after I left Yale, "Choosing the Depth of Organizational Intervention" (Harrison, 1970 [†]), and "Role Negotiation: A Tough-Minded Approach to Team Development" (Harrison, 1972b [†"Role Negotiation"]). I believe more people have read the former than anything I subsequently wrote and more have practiced the latter than anything I have subsequently invented. Both papers stemmed from the consulting work I was doing and reflected my misgivings about the use of T-groups and T-group processes in organizations. I like to think that these papers were influential in the shift away from those processes and in the establishment of organization development as a field of practice and a body of knowledge and technology.

At the time of which I am speaking, the mid sixties, T-groups were on the cresting wave of one of those fads for the application of behavioral science to business organizations that have been so prevalent during the past quarter century. Publications detailing the benefits of T-groups for management teams, such as Chris Argyris's *Interpersonal Competence and Organizational Effectiveness* (Argyris, 1962), were on the reading lists of forward-thinking managers. Enrollments in NTL's Management Work Conferences and Key Executive Labs (T-groups for middle and upper managers respectively) were booming. Graduates of these programs were often eager to involve their associates in T-groups in order to have others with whom they could be open and trusting at work.

My missionary zeal and that of my NTL colleagues was at or near its zenith. We truly believed that we had methods whereby organizations could be democratized and humanized and that it was only a matter of getting business leaders to understand that openness, trust, and participation are good for productivity and the bottom line. No matter that our research had so far failed to demonstrate these effects convincingly; we were sure the effects were there and that our inability to demonstrate them conclusively was due to some combination of the crudeness of our instruments, the subtlety of the effects to be measured, and the need for an entire organization to be treated if there was to be a supportive climate for the maintenance of individual changes over time.

In retrospect, we were not far off in our vision; the Japanese have demonstrated that. However, our timing was badly off. U.S. business was far too successful to take seriously the idea that anything so fundamental as the power structure needed changing in order to improve the bottom line. Even now, with the wolf at the door, many leaders would rather see their organizations die than give up their power and perquisites.

In the sixties, U.S. business was rich enough to indulge our experiments, and it did, so long as we did not challenge anything really basic like the power of the hierarchy. Our relationship with our clients was not unlike a story that had gone around when I was dabbling in sports car racing a few years earlier. It was said that the Mercedes 280SL was so finely tuned that when you bought one the dealer furnished you with a set of rubber wrenches so you could fool around with the engine as much as you wanted without changing the factory settings! Similarly, we consultants were allowed to tinker and experiment as long as nothing really changed.

The T-group was (and is) countercultural to the basic assumptions of U.S. business. Its genius is that through suspending the operation of formal power relationships and removing any task requirements, it allows the underlying dynamics of interpersonal and group relationships to emerge into the open. Normally a work group is like a black box that has energy and information going in at one end and results coming out the other. As long as it is working, no one inquires too deeply into how the box operates. When it does not work, leaders often replace some of the parts, still without understanding how it works. During a T-group, the trainer and the participants take the cover off the box, look inside, and see what's happening. If they can clean up the processes in there and make them work more harmoniously, they can often improve the performance of the system. It seemed to us at NTL that if we could conduct T-groups for work teams, the greater understanding and acceptance that are a normal outcome of the process would be good for the people and good for the work.

The catch was this. In order to create the conditions of power equality and lack of task pressure in a work group, trainers had to distort its structure and functioning markedly. Bosses had to suspend their use of power; subordinates had to engage in decidedly risky behavior in confronting others with interpersonal issues; group members had to be willing to put their task concerns on the side for a time. When we trainers were successful in creating such new rules, we often got dramatic positive changes in trust and openness. However, once the workshop or offsite meeting was over, the work group usually reverted to its previous norms. There was little support in the larger system for fundamental change, and there were lots of pressures to go back to business as usual.

The pernicious aspect of all this was that when the larger organization was highly competitive, its norms sanctioned using people's vulnerability and weaknesses against them. It was not uncommon for people in a T-group to be seduced into revealing things about their attitudes and feelings that were later used against them in the rough-and-tumble world of organizational politics. Some individuals suffered much heartache and real career damage as a result of having trusted the trainer and the group with personal revelations. By the mid seventies, such occurrences had given T-groups a sufficiently bad name in business organizations that some of us felt it imprudent to acknowledge our connections with NTL when dealing with prospective clients.

Family groups, consisting of a manager and his (never her in those days) di-

rect subordinates, were notoriously hard to work with. There was usually great resistance on the part of subordinates to becoming open, the manager often failed
to play the game and used his power in subtle ways, and sometimes the groups
never did get off the ground. Faced with these difficulties, many of us began to
look for ways to help work teams that did not evoke so much resistance. Robert
Blake and Jane Mouton's managerial grid was one such approach (see Blake, Mouton, Barnes, and Greiner, 1969/1991). Those of us who loved T-groups tended
to scorn the grid as overly mechanical and impersonal, but I believe it outlasted
T-groups as an organizational intervention just because it intervened at less depth
than the T-group. It combined utility and safety, and it expanded people's awareness of their own interpersonal styles without frightening them to death.

As T-group trainers, most of us subscribed to the notion that the deeper the
group went, the more value had been obtained. I think this assumption stemmed
from the roots of our work in psychoanalysis. A premise of psychoanalysis is
that the basic cause of psychological malfunction is deep in the unconscious and
that to treat a symptom without getting to its root cause is ineffective. The symptom will recur, or another symptom will grow from the still active cause. We took
on this theoretical baggage without questioning it very closely. There always
was, and still is, a tendency on the part of consultants to dismiss clients' diagnoses
of their own organizational problems as overly simplistic.

What I wanted to say in writing "Choosing the Depth of Organizational
Intervention" was that the further below the intellectual surface we probed in our
search for the root cause of problems, the more resistance we would encounter,
the more powerful the emotions we would evoke, and the more unpredictable
would be the outcomes of our work. I questioned the idea that deeper is necessarily better. Privately, I believed that a reason why many consultants and trainers
like to go deep is that it is exciting and makes them feel powerful, but I did not say
so in the paper. What I did say was that if an organizational problem can be sat-
isfactorily solved by changing such surface arrangements as the way work is organized, it is overkill to probe deeply into the psyches of the people doing the work
or even into their feelings about one another. It is also an invasion of their privacy,
and it creates an unhealthy dependency on the consultant, because few work
groups can manage that level of self-examination on their own.

In writing the paper, I was calling for us to let go of, or at least question, our
roots in depth psychology and T-groups and for us to address our clients' problems on their own terms, without preconceptions as to the appropriate treatment.
Others around this time were also providing new technology that became the foun-
dations of the OD field. For example, Edgar Schein (1969) published guidelines
for conducting process consultation with work teams, while my paper provided
support for developing approaches focused on task issues rather than on interpersonal ones. And of course, it continued my theme of honoring clients' emotional defenses rather than endeavoring to penetrate them.

I like the paper well enough, but I have never quite understood its popularity with others. I have had more complimentary feedback on that one paper than on any of my other early articles, and it has been more often reprinted than any other except the next one I wrote. In that next paper, "Role Negotiation: A Tough-Minded Approach to Team Development" (Harrison, 1972b), I took another step along the path away from the emotional swamp. Role negotiation was my first attempt to create OD technology, and I invented the method in the course of two difficult but very different consulting assignments.

The essence of role negotiation is that people who work together meet to share information about how their work is hindered or helped by the way others in the group do their own jobs. Group members give each other written messages about what they would like the others to "start doing or do more of; stop doing or do less of; and continue doing the same." Then they negotiate agreements of the form, "If you will do this thing that is helpful to me, then I will do this thing that you are asking of me." The idea is to negotiate a quid pro quo, a something for something else, in which each party is getting something of sufficient value in return for what he or she is giving so that he or she will keep the agreement out of self-interest.

I had already observed that in the spirit of cooperation and mutual good-will often engendered in team development sessions, people would make agreements to be helpful to one another or to change annoying interpersonal behaviors, but the changes did not appear to be very lasting. As I mentioned earlier, it seemed that the altruistic motives which emerged during the group session tended to decay when participants returned to the workplace. Under the pressures of normal organizational life, people reverted to their usual self-oriented ways of behaving toward one another. This observation, then, was the background for my invention, the details of which arose, as I said, in response to a couple of actual consulting problems.

The first of these problems came to my attention at a weekend workshop led by Jim Clark for a group of administrators in a southern California school district. I was asked to join the consulting staff for the second workshop in a series, taking responsibility for one of several family groups (each family group was made up of people who all reported to the same organizational superior).

From the beginning, my group appeared especially gun-shy of giving and receiving personal feedback. There were several anxious queries about whether they were going to be asked to do more of that "personal stuff" they had been exposed to at the last meeting. Several expressed strongly their fears that more of such personal attacks would damage working relationships among the group members. I saw stretching ahead of me a most uncomfortable weekend, in which I, against my own sympathies but in the name of open communication and teamwork, would endeavor to persuade or seduce them into going contrary to what I felt was probably their better judgment. It did not feel good to me, and I was suddenly inspired to say, "As far as I'm concerned, I don't care whether you express a single feeling the whole time we're here together. What I would like you to do is to talk about your work—about what kinds of things others do that make it easier or harder for you to do a good job. If feelings come up in the course of the discussion, that's up to you; I shall neither encourage nor discourage it. As far as I'm concerned, we're here to talk about work, not feelings."

The group heaved a great collective sigh of relief, and group members immediately dropped their resistance to working. They spent a productive and involving weekend talking about work. Of course, feelings came up, but personal attacks were few or nonexistent. I went away afterwards with the belief that by reframing the discussion as I did, I had changed the territory to one with which they were much more comfortable. They did not know how to talk about feelings; they did know how to talk about work. The former was not legitimate in their organization's culture. The latter was acceptable and appropriate.

I also came away intrigued with the possibility of creating a context and a set of rules that would facilitate people's working their issues in a way that would feel appropriate and safe to them.

Not long afterwards, I had another, seemingly quite different experience that brought me to the formula for role negotiation. I had been asked by some old NTL friends to conduct a team development session in a department of the University of Puerto Rico. The participants were all NTL trained and hence quite sophisticated and comfortable with working on their interpersonal processes. In talking with the members of the group privately about previous group sessions, it became apparent that they had used the sessions to vent feelings that arose around work problems, particularly the use of authority by the department chairperson. Nothing had seemed to change as a result of the sessions, but people had felt better for a while. I was struck by how this group seemed to take flight into feelings to avoid dealing with work while the group of school administrators had taken flight into work as an escape from feelings. To me, both groups seemed to need the same intervention if group members were to make any lasting improvements.

I began the session with the Puerto Rico group by asking them to agree on what important decisions were made in the group, and how those decisions were made. Then members of the group identified aspects of the decision-making process they were not happy with, such as the fact that the chairperson frequently made important decisions concerning areas of their responsibility without consulting them. The group members and I proceeded to address these areas of dissatisfaction, but I got the group to agree to a rule that they were to discuss the issues only in terms of concrete proposals for change. In other words, no feelings, only facts.

At the end of the session, group members seemed pleased with their work, reporting that they had made more solid progress than in any previous team development meetings. I wish I could report that the agreements they made stuck, but I never went back to find out. I had all I needed to convince me that I had found something my OD colleagues could use, and the next time I was at Bethel, I presented the method in a program for OD specialists. Not long afterwards, I published the article.

Over the years, I have received much gratifying correspondence on how people have used role negotiation. Uri Merry wrote from a kibbutz in Israel that he had used it there with great success. Richard Hill used it for a companywide program at Diamond Shamrock, developing a role negotiation workbook for the project. (The workbook is gone now, but see Louis, 1976, for a description of the process.) I was pleased and proud of the adventures of my brainchild, but I never used it much myself. It always seemed a little too mechanical to me, and it did not fit my own intuitive go-with-the-flow style of working with a group. I thought it a pity I never learned to use it properly, because it seemed to work so well for others.

I was caught up in the passions of the sixties more than most members of my generation. I believed in the Peace Corps, the Great Society, foreign aid, experimental universities, feelings, flower power, doing your own thing, and loving freely. To me, these things seemed implicit in the philosophy behind the work we OD consultants were doing with T-groups and in consulting to organizations. I had my reservations about the darker side of some of our beliefs and practices, but fundamentally, I was joined up. I hoped a new day was dawning during the course of which we would see a better world, and I wanted to be an architect and prophet of that world. Much of my story since then is the chronicle of the decline and fall of that ambition and those hopes. Although I have some sadness about the dashed hopes, I do not regard my story as a sad one but as one of personal and professional transformation.

Leaving Home

The period between my leaving Yale in mid 1966 and my departure for Europe in May 1968 was very turbulent. In retrospect, it seems that I was driving very hard to become autonomous but that I defined autonomy as doing the opposite of what others expected of me. During that period I lost, left, or divested myself of most of what defined me socially: my academic career, my quasi-family ties with NTL, my marriage, and my country. When I arrived in Holland in May 1968, it was to begin a new life. Here is how I got there.

After having decided during my 1956 trip to Europe that I wanted to come back but not as a tourist, it took me more than a decade to find the way; now, a project with a major oil company provided the means.

I am not good at the hard sell: I am shy, I hate "cold calls," and I dislike intruding into anyone's space uninvited. Once I am invited, however, I seem to have a gift for making the most of my opportunities. This particular opportunity started with a request from an internal consultant with whom I had been working in an NTL project to do team development in the engineering function of one of the large oil companies. He suggested we team up to conduct a team development session (read T-group) for a group of technical advisors going to work on the startup of a big chemical plant in the Netherlands. The session went well, and afterwards, I asked the leader of the group whether he thought there might be any interest in joint team training for the host country staff and the U.S. advisors. We were soon asked to come to Holland to talk to the local plant management about the idea, and my internal colleague and I ended up with a contract to both facilitate the startup and do research on how to improve the startup process. I felt like the cat that swallowed the canary: it had been so easy and natural to expand the client's original interest in building a cohesive team into a major cross-cultural project!

It was a perfect time to go. My independent practice was going well, but I did not have any commitments that would keep me from being away for a half a year. My marriage was coming unstuck, and I had separated from Barbara shortly after my initial visit to Holland. I was having a very tough time emotionally with the separation, and I felt I was making such demands on the time and support of my friends that soon they would dread hearing my voice on the phone. I despised myself for my emotional dependence and neediness, and I hated the idea that people were perhaps being nice to me because they felt sorry for me. In short, I was being rather hard on myself. I had a fantasy of being somewhere new where no one wanted to help me or felt sorry for me, and where I could make some new friends who were drawn to me just for who I was right now, not out of loyalty to a friend who was down on his luck. I did not seriously consider that my friends still loved me for who I was right now; to me, being weak and emotionally needy was the same as being worthless.

It felt good to leave. As my plane left Washington, D.C., banking steeply over the green hills and fields and straightening out on its course toward the sea, I felt like Columbus setting out to discover the New World. I was leaving doubt and despair behind, and there were bound to be exciting adventures ahead. I thought with a thrill that I did not know when I would be home.

CHAPTER FOUR

EXPATRIATE'S WAY: MY SOJOURN IN EUROPE

The period between my departure for Europe in the spring of 1968 and my return to the United States in the summer of 1976 was one of adventure, excitement, creativity, and professional and financial success. This was the time in my life in which I first experienced to the full my personal autonomy and power.

The startup project was the most difficult I had undertaken up to that time, and I can now see that it was close to the most difficult of my career. It had a more significant impact on my thinking about consulting than any other project I have worked on, before or since, because it challenged the assumptions I had learned to make about what organizations need in order to grow and change. Then, having found working in a foreign culture to be such an intense learning experience, I felt as the project drew to a close that I did not want to go home. I decided to stay on and learn more!

The project was a green-field startup. Except for a few expatriate managers and the U.S. startup advisors, almost everyone was new to the chemical process business. The plant was being erected in a muddy field out in the middle of nowhere. Construction was behind schedule, so the decision had been made to conduct some of the commissioning activities while the remaining construction work was being completed. Thus, there were two separate and somewhat antagonistic organizations working on the same plant and equipment at the same time: the contractor's people and the company's startup team.

I worked with an internal consultant whose background and orientation were similar to my own. We had two Dutch counterparts from an Amsterdam consulting firm. Due to delays in the approval of our project, we did not arrive onsite prior to the beginning of the startup. When we did get there, things were already heating up, and the department managers only reluctantly took time to participate in our team development meetings. We proceeded much as we would have with any new client: we interviewed everyone to find out what organizational and interpersonal issues were hot, summarized the results, presented them to the group, and asked them to tell us which were the ones they wanted us to help them work through. However, our offer of help was seen as less than helpful because everyone already knew things were in a mess; it would not have been a startup if they were not. People were stretched to the limit just dealing with their jobs. To them, worrying about their communication links with other functions or about something as vague and abstract as team functioning was just not on.

We did not catch on right away; we thought that there was something wrong with our presentation or that the group was defensive and resistant or that we had not identified the right people to champion our activities, so we persisted in our course for a couple of weeks. Then the assistant plant manager warned us that we were becoming part of the problem rather than part of the solution. He strongly advised us to move our offices from the administration building to a Quonset hut out in the middle of the mud where the startup engineers had their cubicles. He told us to find some problems we could solve and become part of the team by solving them.

We were a bit chagrined to be told our business by our client, but we took his advice. We started to spend time with the people in the field, learning how they interfaced with one another, what their organizational problems were, and how they did their work. We attended all sorts of meetings, sometimes facilitating the process, sometimes coaching the meeting leader if he would hold still for it. When individuals got into conflicts, we tried to mediate. We gave up criticizing the system and devoted ourselves to trying to make it work.

Now, in the nineties, many organizations are in such flux that every day is like a startup. In the sixties, many managers resisted coming to grips with problems, acting as though they had forever to solve them. We had come totally unprepared for the fluidity and chaos of a startup; we were used to working with rigid bureaucratic organizations in which the model of *unfreeze*, then *change*, then *refreeze* (Schein and Bennis, 1965) made perfect sense. We had not seen organizations that had never properly "set." A plant startup is like a war: once it begins, the time for planning, training, and tuning up the organization is over. Everyone's thinking becomes very short term, and if you take a longer view, others think either that you do not care or that you do not understand reality.

At home, I had become something of a champion for individual freedom against the constraints of authority and a rigid bureaucracy. Now, it was both challenging and exhilarating to be in an organization where people had autonomy but were disempowered by the lack of systems and by unclear roles and responsibilities. I learned a powerful lesson there: that I should endeavor to suspend my assumptions about how organizations work and how they should be treated. I learned to see each organization as unique, as worthy of being understood afresh from the inside out.

We learned to stick close to our clients and to help them with whatever seemed to be needed. My own credibility was enhanced when I was crawling around inside a refrigeration unit with some engineers and I found the gas leak we were all looking for. That story went all over the plant in about half a day!

So we learned a lot, and we were able to do useful work during the seven months we were there. Mainly, though, the success of the project was in our learning. My own special assignment was to study the startup process to learn how it could be improved. I asked each of the three other consultants on the project to keep a log of everything of interest that happened when they were on-site, and I kept a similar log. At the conclusion of the project, I went through all these journals, looking for themes and issues and finding about fifteen of them. Then, I went through the journals again, assigning comments to themes. This process was unexpectedly exciting. I started out with what seemed a complete mess and with little idea of what we might have learned. As I painstakingly rewrote each entry into my notebook under its theme, a rich and meaningful picture emerged. It was fuzzy at first but then increasingly sharp and definite. It was my first experience with a hologram, a word I first heard years later, and it seemed like magic to me. I was so proud of what I had discovered in our logs and so certain we could dramatically improve startup processes by using our findings that I could hardly wait to share my report with my clients. This, I felt, was *real* research—*action* research! I felt I was fulfilling my mission in life, bringing light out of darkness, and what more satisfying arena in which to have that success than the chaos of a new plant startup!

I saw my report to the company as a very significant contribution to their competitive advantage. It never occurred to me that they would bury it, but bury it they did—for fifteen years. I heard later that, after it had moldered that long in the files, it was finally exhumed and used for some training and planning purposes. Unfortunately, this startup had not gone well, and according to the inexorable laws of traditional bureaucracy, no one involved with it gained any credibility from his association with the project. There were endless delays and equipment malfunctions, and the plant was behind schedule and over budget for a long time. The people for whom I had written my report apparently believed there was nothing reliable to be learned from such a mess. Or perhaps no one wanted to draw attention to what had happened there or be associated with it. I never knew for sure because communication just ceased with the people for whom I did the work.

I was hurt and deeply disappointed, and I vowed that I would prove them wrong somehow. I took my savings from the project, which after my divorce were my entire capital, and went to London in search of more appreciative clients.

Learning on the Dark Side: Embracing Failure

It has always frustrated me when organizations do not seem to want to learn from failures. I remember hearing that one of the significant findings of Robert Blake and Jane Mouton's work on intergroup competition is that losing groups learn more than do the winners (see Blake and Mouton, 1984). Losing groups spend more time analyzing their performance, and they are more likely subsequently to experiment with new behavior. In most organizations I have worked with, however, there have been strong pressures not to look at failures in depth. Instead, organizations often deal with their unsuccessful projects by covering them up or by blaming a convenient scapegoat. Once honor has been served in this way, the incident is often forgotten, and its lessons remain unlearned.

It is also my own experience that I and others learn more from difficulties than from successes if we can bring ourselves to face the difficulties squarely and honestly. That is the reason this professional memoir dwells so lovingly on the ragged and awkward parts of my own journey. Although I am proud of my successes, only wishing there had been more of them, perhaps I am a little uncomfortable with them as well, having been raised to value struggle more than success. I tend to take success somewhat for granted, as though once I have arrived, there is nothing more to be said or learned from the journey.

Whatever the reason, I tend to look back with more affection and gratitude to the projects that did not turn out as expected. That emotion is born of the loving attention I have given to learning from the difficulties and barriers I encountered in these projects. Whatever I now possess of depth, wisdom, and courage is due in large part to my determination to look each project in the face, evaluate what worked and what did not, and stay with the process until I believe I have gained all the learning that is there for me. Moreover, one not only learns from the analysis of specific failures but there is a meta-learning as well. When I meet young executives who have an unbroken record of success and who are perhaps on the fast track in their company, they often seem more self-conscious, afraid of failure, and in some subtle way less confident than those who have seen their share of personal ups and downs. The latter know they can survive failure; the fast-trackers often seem insecure—they know there are others hot on their heels, and they do not know how they will cope with the inevitable end of rapid promotion.

To have lost or failed publicly and then to go on and overcome the setback and learn from it seems to strengthen a person or an organization. It has always seemed a pity to me that we consultants usually feel constrained by ego or custom to share only our successes, when there is so much to be learned from things that do not go well. Would not it be exciting to set learning from failure as the overall theme at one of the annual Organization Development Network Conferences? We would not only learn a lot, but I am quite sure that a strong atmosphere of nondefensiveness and mutual support would develop in the conference that would encourage all who participated to dare more in the pursuit of their own dreams of excellence.

How to Succeed in Business Without Having Fun

Certainly, I learned a great deal in the Netherlands startup. I used what I learned to put together a seminar on new plant startups after I moved to London, and I acquired another client on the strength of it. This next (and last) startup project was a brilliant success, albeit nowhere near as interesting as the prior one. The team of internal and external consultants that I was a part of got in early enough in the process to influence the planning and training of the startup team and to do a lot of team building with the management group. In particular, we successfully used role negotiation to define and clarify the responsibilities of the key players and to reduce the overlap and gaps between roles. We gave team training in problem solving, and we conducted contingency-planning sessions until everyone was bored with preparation. When the startup finally came, it was an anticlimax. The plant went to 120 percent of capacity in four days and never looked back.

In the paper I wrote based on my startup experiences, "Startup: The Care and Feeding of Infant Systems" (Harrison, 1981 [†]), there is little that was learned in this second experience because only the first one was rich in learning. One thing that did surprise me in the successful startup, though, was how reluctant the engineers were to support activities designed to ensure success. The sophisticated critical path planning system that was to manage the startup process was sabotaged by the startup team, who failed to feed it timely information (thus breaking the heart of the planning manager—he did actually die of a heart attack during the startup). After the startup was over, some of these same engineers complained to me that I had taken all the fun out of the startup with the team preparation and contingency-planning activities I initiated. They said I had made it tame and bureaucratic, and I had to admit it had not been much fun for me, either. Perhaps something in those of us who like startups longs for the excitement of combat and the opportunity to decide quickly and intuitively. There is a fine camaraderie in giving everything one has to overcome a shared challenge. I know myself as a startup type, and I certainly became as bored with our meetings as the engineers did. But I was surprised that it was the engineers who missed the chaos of the "normal" startup so keenly, because these are people who have chosen to live their working lives in a world of facts and reason.

I see the same process going on in some high-tech companies today where people often seem addicted to chaos and crisis. People may avoid the work of understanding complexity because it feels overwhelming to deal with it rationally and analytically. They do not know how to comprehend complexity through deep reflection and dialogue, so they avoid understanding in favor of action. I agree that the contribution of rational planning is limited in fast-changing complex situations. But to make a virtue of muddling through, of making up for lack of foresight with energy and hard work, is not the answer. Instead, I believe we consultants must learn to practice either the *way of the sage* or the *way of the shaman*, if not a combination of the two.

The way of the sage involves deep reflection and the practice of something akin to David Bohm's Dialogue (Briggs, 1993). We provide time and space for the group to come to a deeper and more inclusive understanding than is possible for any of the individuals in the group. The way of the shaman involves practicing centeredness and stopping the mind's chatter, along with cultivating a deep spir-

itual connection with nature. The adept acts intuitively, out of her or his participation in the flow of events, always remaining balanced and acutely aware. The
way of the shaman has much in common with Asian martial arts. I prefer not to
call it the way of the warrior because, in our culture, the word *warrior* implies neither deep connection with nature nor cooperation between nature and humankind. I see both as essential to personal mastery in a time of chaos and change.
Managing effectively will require something akin to a spiritual practice, and that
idea is as yet a pretty big stretch for most people in business.

From Culture Shock to Cultural Awareness

I have jumped ahead of my story in order to complete the discussion of my learnings from my startup experiences, but there was more to my sojourn abroad
than those projects. In Holland, when I was not working on the startup there, I
was exploring Europe, meeting other consultants, and building a network of contacts that I hoped would bring me additional work in Europe. And I was looking
for love in my life. In September of 1968, I traveled to Vienna to deliver a keynote
address to an international conference on group therapy, as a stand-in for my former boss at NTL, Leland Bradford. On the flight from Amsterdam to Vienna, I
met Diana, an Englishwoman who at that time was working as a travel agent in
Johannesburg. In 1970, she was to become my second wife.

As my contract in Holland neared its end, I found myself reluctant to return to the United States. I felt I was learning things about consulting that I could
only learn in a culture other than my own. I was discovering that many of our
cherished notions about how people think and feel and behave in groups and organizations are culturally determined. I found living in a different culture exciting and also liberating. Without a partner, and living far from anyone who had
known me, I felt I did not have to be anyone I did not want to be. I was free to
construct a new life and a new persona. I figured the money I had saved from the
startup project would last me a year while I saw whether it was possible for me
to make a living as a freelance consultant in Europe. I settled on London as my
base simply because people spoke English there.

In January 1969, I took a few weeks holiday in South Africa to visit Diana.
On this trip, I combined writing my paper "Classroom Innovation: A Design
Primer" (Harrison, 1969 [†]) with sightseeing and professional networking. Then
I started to look for clients and for a place to live in London. Initially, I found working with British organizations very frustrating. I came up against qualities, assumptions, and values so deeply imbedded in me that I did not know they were
there until I experienced that other people were not the same, usually through
some misunderstanding or interpersonal disconnection that took me by surprise.
For example, in the United States, I usually could guess during an initial interview
with a client how likely it was that a project would go forward. In Britain, I frequently had the experience that a potential client who seemed quite interested

during that critical first interview would never call me again; however, it also oc-curred more than once that someone who had been probing and questioning al-most to the point of being rude would later develop into a client. In meetings, too, I found myself feeling inept and clumsy because I did not have the sensitivity to nuance and to deeper structures of meaning that I naturally and only semicon-sciously made use of in my work in the United States.

I remember one incident that occurred in a European T-group laboratory sponsored by INSEAD, the international business school at Fontainebleau, France. I was part of a multinational staff for the laboratory. The others were Claude Faucheux and Max Pagès from France, David Hall from Canada, and Traugott (Doc) Lindner from Austria. Midway through the lab, we asked the participants to conduct some social research on the laboratory as a community. For the staff contribution, we did a sociogram in which we diagrammed the social choices of each staff member: whom we would prefer to work with or spend social time with, whose ideas we were most likely to accept, and so forth. On every question, I came out a "social isolate," having been chosen last by everyone or all but one.

I had been feeling already that something strange was going on: I had trou-ble getting the attention of the group; my ideas were ignored but later accepted when others introduced them—that sort of thing. Now, I spoke up and asked what was going on, and Max responded with a long polemic about "American behav-ioral imperialists" who came to Europe only to spread their supposedly superior culture to the naïve Europeans. He got quite heated about it, but I did not see what that had to do with me. I pointed out that I had decided to stay in Europe because I thought I could learn from Europeans.

Immediately, Doc Lindner turned on me. "Who do you think you are," he said, "to expect to be treated as an individual? We Europeans have been spilling our blood for centuries over lines drawn in the dirt between one nation and an-other, and now you come here, expecting not to be misunderstood because of your uniqueness." I got the point. The memory of that incident informed my thoughts and actions during the remainder of my eight-year sojourn in Europe. I always expected prejudice, and I was determined to overcome it where possible. I was pleasantly surprised on the many occasions when I did not experience it. I worked hard to fit in, to do the done thing. Later, I learned how constraining it is to fit in and what a barrier to one's own growth it can be. I learned that there is a time when it no longer serves a sojourner to adapt—that further integration and ac-ceptance can be won only at the cost of boldly stepping into one's selfhood. But I did not learn that in Europe; I had to return home to achieve that last insight.

I feel a deep pride in what I achieved in my eight years in Europe, where I found both recognition and success. However, the inner experience of living with those cultural barriers is difficult to share with those who have not been expatri-ates themselves. I certainly learned on visits to colleagues in the United States that I could not communicate meaningfully about my experience and that I would do best to keep to myself any unfavorable comparisons between our culture and that of the Europeans. After a while, I discovered that I felt easier and freer when I was with expatriates of other nationalities than I did when I was with my fellow citizens. Even though the places we expatriates had been were different, a shared process brought us to an easy intimacy about our cross-cultural experiences. It was not that I did not feel just as American as anyone who had never left home. To live and work in another culture is, if one is the least bit aware, a powerful mirror in which to see one's own cultural qualities and know that they are bred in the bone, less easy to change or erase than a tattoo, though they can be covered over to a degree. When I had lived in Europe for a couple of years, I felt I knew for the first time how thoroughly American I was, and that knowledge has never left me. But people who have not had that experience of living abroad seldom want to know about it, and overseas experience is not that highly valued, either by friends or by potential clients. For example, no one on either side of the Atlantic has ever offered me the opportunity to consult on cross-cultural issues between North Americans and Europeans, and I have always felt a little wistful that I did not have a chance to show the usefulness of what I learned!

Surprisingly, I found that communication with people from North European cultures (Dutch, Belgian, Scandinavian) was easier than communication in Britain, at least for me! When people communicate in a language not their own (I and my Northern European colleagues always spoke English), they tend to put things more simply and to be more straightforward than when using their own language. It is hard to dissemble adroitly in another language. One first learns to express oneself in a language—only later does one learn how to hide the truth.

I had the good fortune to arrive in Europe at a time when the United States was very successful economically and people abroad were looking to my country for the secrets of management. There was a growing interest in applications of behavioral science to organizations, and I walked into a receptive market. People were very interested to hear what I had to say, and quite a few of them were eager to learn my trade. A good deal of my work came to be coaching and training people in the principles and practices of organization development. I soon got to know many if not most of the people in Britain who were then or later became well known in the field. Early on, I was befriended by Dean Berry and Charles Handy at the London Business School, who gave me opportunities to present my work to their students. Charles, especially, became a close friend and colleague, and our conversations about the frustrations I encountered when working in Britain led both of us to publish some of the earliest work on organization culture (Handy, 1985; Harrison, 1972d [†]). Charles, in particular, wrote a fine book on the model we dreamed up together (Handy, 1985).

A number of internal and external consultants associated with Imperial Chemical Industries (ICI) became friends and helpers, people like Arthur Johnston and Philip Gray of ICI, and Mike Reynolds at Durham University. It was fortunate that I had the advice and counsel of these colleagues and clients because I found it difficult for quite a long time to have any sense of confidence in my face-to-face relationships with the British.

Disillusionment About Making a Difference

For me, one of the major differences in working in Britain was getting used to a different sense of time. If I learned anything from my sojourn in Europe, it was that pacing and timing are of the essence in intervening effectively as a consultant. One experience brought that issue into focus. I worked for two years with a group of internal consultants who were endeavoring to create a more participative climate in their organization. I became very frustrated and judgmental about their reluctance to take risks and their tendency to procrastinate, and I decided they were using their relationship with me as a way of convincing themselves that they were on the leading edge and engaged in meaningful change work when they were not. After long thought, I decided it was a matter of principle not to continue to collude with their defenses. I wrote the paper "Strategy Guidelines for an Internal Organization Development Unit" (Harrison, 1972c [†]) as a kind of final test. It described what I did not see them doing and what I thought they ought to be doing. I wrote it as a letter to the group, and I was not at all direct with them about the meaning of the paper to me. They read the paper and were very complimentary about it, but I did not sense they were going to change, so I terminated our consulting arrangement without further confrontation. Three years later, I visited them again and discovered the group had accomplished substantial changes. The members of the group had had a better sense of the organization's readiness for change than I did. Their style of quiet persistence and gently bringing up issues and moving them along was well suited to most British organizations.

"Strategy Guidelines for an Internal Organization Development Unit" was my first attempt to codify the principles of practice in organization development, and as I look at it now I am pleased that most of it still seems valid and worthwhile. Some of it was taken from a talk I heard Herb Shepherd give at Bethel. I do not suppose the paper took me more than about two hours to write, and I remember that all of it seemed to come to me at once, fully formed. When I look at it now, I am struck by how right the precepts are and how seldom they are followed. An example is the principle of working *with* forces in the organization. Another example is the principle of avoiding systemwide or across-the-board changes when there are limited resources in order to concentrate energy and people where the possibilities for positive outcomes are greatest.

The principle of keeping the limited resources for change together and focused is fundamental to creating change in systems that are much stronger than the resources that you can bring to bear, and this principle applies to everything from organization development work to creating a revolution in a nation. Somehow, I have always known this; it is not something learned from experience. I was, of course, delighted later on to find strong support for these ideas in revolutionary literature, such as the infamous Little Red Book, *Quotations from Chairman Mao Tse-Tung* (Mao, 1967). Mao counseled that when one's force is weak, one should not take on superior forces, should avoid battles whenever possible, and should seduce hostile forces rather than trying to overcome them. I have heard that when Mao's Chinese Communists captured members of the Kuomintang, they fed them well, treated them hospitably, and then sent them back to their own army. The Communists could not afford to feed prisoners on a long-term basis; they either had to kill them or send them back. By treating them with kindness and respect, the Communists created emissaries for their cause and spread doubt and dissatisfaction among the opposing forces. Later, when Mao was firmly in the saddle, he could afford to change his strategy and to crush those who opposed his will. His kindness for the enemy was based on shrewd policy, not principle.

From Organization Development to Management Self-Development

My observation of cultural differences between U.S. and European T-groups eventually led me to develop a new form of experiential education, the Autonomy Laboratory. In the course of this work, I learned a great deal about how people learn, and I now count these learnings as among the most significant of my career to date. They enabled me and my colleagues to design a number of very effective programs for training managers in interpersonal skills. Moreover, they have important implications for the management of organization change, implications that are of particular relevance when change is rapid and traumatic. Many if not most of the major changes presently going on in organizations appear to fall into that category.

My early work in Britain and Europe had been focused on organization development consulting; then, two or three years later, I radically shifted my practice. I abandoned the attempt to change organizations as whole systems and focused instead on helping individuals to change. I found European organizations very difficult to change. I doubt they were more so than U.S. organizations, but they had a sense of conservatism and a slower pace that made me think they were more difficult. Although it was easy for me to get enough business, I was disappointed in the lack of visible results. However, with my development of the Laboratory in Initiative, Autonomy, and Risk Taking I felt I had an approach to management education that was very powerful. I believed I could do more good helping individuals who wanted to change than I could failing to help organizations that did not want to change.

The initial stimulus for my innovations in management education was a cultural difference I had noticed when, early in my sojourn in Europe, I was asked to conduct some T-groups. I was disappointed by the low level of excitement and movement I experienced compared to North American T-groups. European T-groups seemed to require a great deal of skill and provocation on the part of trainers to stimulate the energy needed to make the group a good learning experience, and my impression from talking with European trainers was that their experience was similar to mine.

I found this difference very curious, and I spent a lot of time trying to understand it. I concluded that, in North America, the T-group's process was fueled in part by the existential isolation and loneliness we North Americans carry as a people. The T-group appealed to us at a time when we were acknowledging needs for love and intimacy that were not readily available in our culture, and we were beginning to explore a variety of ways to meet those needs.

For the Europeans, loneliness and alienation did not seem to be a major issue. I theorized that, instead, initiative and autonomy might be issues for them. What a coincidence that this was the issue *I* was working on so diligently for myself during those years! The European managers I met seemed enmeshed compared to their U.S. counterparts. They seemed caught in a matrix of family, community, and organizational *expectations*, which they seldom questioned. They were less geographically mobile than Americans—they tended to live close to their families of origin and to continue a rich family and community life; in their organizations, they tended to stay within the same department or function throughout their careers, and they usually stayed with the same organization.

Of course, there is far more overlap between European and North American cultures than this stereotyped analysis suggests, but at this point I was looking for differences, not overlap. I wanted to invent a learning process that would be as deeply impactful for Europeans as I knew the T-group could be for Americans. I asked myself what the experiential learning process might be that would evoke for participants the issue of autonomy, of thinking and acting for oneself.

I found a client and colleague: Jacques Mareschal, management development manager at IBM Belgium. He was intrigued by the question I raised and had the freedom and resources to explore it. He and I decided that we would create a learning experience that would address the issues of autonomy, risk taking, and taking initiative. We would get people to ask themselves what they wanted in the world, who they were as individuals, and what their own needs were as differentiated from those of other people.

It is not uncommon for me to sell my clients a program or a process on the basis of pure vision and to commit myself to creating that program or process. I see the ideal so clearly that I just know that I can find a way to implement it. In this case, too, I committed myself to developing this innovative new vehicle before I realized what a formidable design problem we faced. It was clear to me that we could not use the small group as the learning "engine" because groups provided the safety and comfort we wanted to remove. But when I thought about this further, I realized that all my experience was in using groups to create emotional effects. I had not a clue how to produce the creative tension of the T-group lab without using groups.

I went through a very anxious period in which I felt sure I would have to admit defeat. Often when I am in such a state, the universe seems to conspire to send me what I need. In this case, I read a paper by Richard Byrd (1967) that described a "non-group" experience he had conducted. In a sensitivity training program, he had given the participants no group, only open space and time. There were no schedule, no assigned groups, no prescribed activities, and no real boundaries, and the trainers were unwilling to provide any of these comforts.

Byrd's design was very confrontive and anxiety provoking for participants partly because his staff refused to meet people's dependency needs by telling them what to do or providing any structure. I sensed that would create so much anxiety for participants that most of their energy would go into anger at the staff rather than into learning how to create their own experience. Byrd had the emotional engine we were looking for in his radical destructuring of time and space, but we needed some kind of gear box to translate that power into the sort of learning we wanted at a level of anxiety that would facilitate, not inhibit, learning.

Jacques and I came up with a fairly elegant solution to managing optimum anxiety. First, we destructured time and space much as Byrd did, giving participants twenty-two hours out of every twenty-four to use as they chose. We hoped thus to remove outside constraints and demands, so that participants could tune in and listen to the quiet inner voices that tell individuals who they really are and what their true path is. Next, we approached the issue of managing anxiety by balancing the missing structure with rich content. Jacques and I ransacked our files for all the structured exercises, diagnostic instruments, and reading materials we could find for learning about human behavior at the individual, interpersonal, group, and organizational levels. Jacques brought an early version of a videocassette recorder to the program so that people could record and process the activities they chose to do. We included recently published books of structured exercises (Pfeiffer and Jones, 1969–1971). The centerpiece of our learning cafeteria was a wonderful set of self-development tools called the Blocks to Creativity that had recently been developed by Sonia and Ed Nevis of the Cleveland Gestalt Institute together with a colleague. Along with this rich library of learning resources, we provided ready access to a supportive staff. We had created a situation that participants would find tremendously confronting, but instead of letting them struggle with it unaided, we resolved to move forward and be as supportive as the participants needed. Once they identified learning projects and got their own learning engines going, we would pull back and give them space.

We took fourteen managers from **IBM** Belgium off to a hunting lodge in the Ardennes forest and spent five days with them on the first of these labs. It was a great success. The participants floundered a lot during the first half of the week, but most eventually found activities they liked and felt they had learned a lot. Our combination of low structure and high support kept participants at an appropriate level of anxiety. They were energized and motivated more than threatened. They saw us as helpful to them when needed, but they did not become overly dependent on us. Later, a researcher from a Belgian university conducted follow-up interviews with all the participants to assess whether such a radically different experiential learning lab might produce outcomes different from those of a T-group. He reported that our participants achieved a degree of self-insight similar to that which people achieved in T-groups, and he was excited to find that the level of stress in our lab was much lower than the level he had found in T-groups.

The latter finding was unexpected, and I thought a lot about how we could build upon it. A way of thinking about learning and stress began to emerge that was new for me, and it formed the basis for my subsequent successes in designing training to be high on impact and low on anxiety-induced resistance. Today, as I turn my attention to the healing of organizations and individuals traumatized by change, I find that way of thinking still bears fruit.

I began with an observation about how anxiety is managed in most structured learning situations and in sensitivity training groups and the team development activities that grow out of them. People are constrained to stay physically present in the situation and deal with whatever comes up. Because group members cannot leave the scene at will, much of the group's time is spent struggling over the level of stress and anxiety that members will be required to tolerate. What seems exciting and productive for some is frightening and even paralyzing for others.

In the Autonomy Lab, people choose their own activities, pace, timing, and partners. They come and go as they please, and so each chooses the level of stress and confrontation at which he or she wants to operate. People feel free to take greater personal risks than I as trainer would push them to take, presumably because they know they can stop or reduce the stress at will. People work very intensely and confront themselves strongly, and they seem to do fine. In these groups, I did not see the kinds of emotional distress that I saw in sensitivity training groups.

Instead, the pattern went something like this. Participants were rather anxious and uneasy at first because they were not used to thinking about what they wanted to learn and taking the initiative to create their own learning experiences. With help from the staff and their more adventurous colleagues, they eventually found things they wanted to do, and by the middle of the week, I found myself experiencing a bittersweet feeling, much like a parent whose children have left the nest. People stopped asking me for advice and counsel; I stood alone in the midst of a buzzing hive of activity, feeling unwanted, unneeded, and a little lost. At the same time, I experienced a profound satisfaction in having created a situation in which others could experience a significant increase in empowerment, if only for a while. I felt at those times that I was really on track, doing what I had come here to do in this lifetime.

Deeper Learnings about Learning

From watching people manage their own learning in Autonomy Labs, I received a powerful insight into how people paced themselves and managed the anxieties and stresses of learning. It was very different from the way management educators designed training programs. I became curious to know what the *natural* process of pacing and managing stress in learning is, a question that I had never thought to ask seriously in all the years I had been a thought-prisoner of the implicit assumptions by which we consultants worked.

For as long as we lived together, and often even now, my daughter, Susan Jane, was one of my best teachers at the spiritual, mental, and emotional levels. She is so open and her process is often so clear and clean that she has been the source of many of my insights about how people learn and grow and how they overcome the difficulties and barriers placed in their way. Susan Jane was about two and a half when I was doing these labs, and I observed that her process was very similar to what I saw in participants. As she played around the house, she would often involve herself in something that felt risky to her, climbing up on a window ledge for example. When she succeeded in scaring herself by this activity, then she would run to her mother or me for comfort, or perhaps she would go off in a corner and suck her thumb for a time. Her learning process, and that of the participants in my Autonomy Labs, was *cyclical*, not linear. It involved a pattern of alternate advance and retreat, which was reminiscent of the notion of the castle and the battlefield that had come to me some ten years before. I already had the idea that the most effective emotional learning took place in the space between safety and nurturance on the one hand and stimulation and challenge on the other. I was now seeing what happened when people were allowed to pace themselves in that process. They adopted a natural rhythm of expansion and contraction, of going out and returning, of emotional arousal followed by integration, as illustrated in Figure 4.1.

Most of the time, we OD consultants do not provide for the cyclical flow of energy in the way we design training and education. When I originally learned to create experiential learning designs, we did our work much the way an author writes a play. We created emotional problems for participants, and then we provided ways to resolve them in a dramatic burst of energy, in the last act, so to speak, after which everyone went home. In watching Susan Jane and in watching participants in the Autonomy Lab, I discovered that this design is not the way people naturally learn. It is unnecessarily stressful because it works against the need of mind and body to take downtime. It does not make for optimum learning because it does not provide for integration after an emotional experience. And it is probably one of the reasons why training programs in interpersonal skills have such a poor track record in changing behavior.

Savoring a Job Well Done

I felt that I had achieved an insight of real value in my work with Autonomy Labs, and they gave me a great deal of satisfaction. I became convinced that they had more impact on the personal lives of the people who attended them than anything else I had ever done. I had succeeded in creating a learning experience that ri-

FIGURE 4.1. THE NATURAL RHYTHM OF SELF-DIRECTED LEARNING.

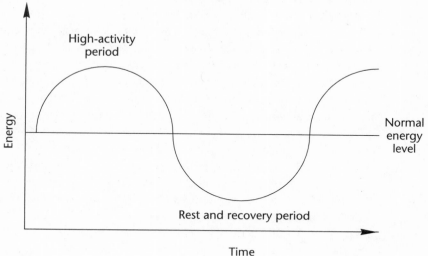

valed the T-group in impact, and I was proud of that. I also felt a deep sense of connection with people as they went through this program, and I made some committed friendships that have lasted a long time. That did not tend to happen in T-groups. In Autonomy Labs, however, there was plenty of time for people to discover others with whom they had some special connection or empathy and to go as deep with those others as they were able to sustain. The level of intimacy was not forced by the group context, and there was no norm that one had to live at a high level of emotional intensity.

I ran these Autonomy Labs all over Northern Europe: Belgium, Holland, Sweden, Ireland, England. For the most part, the participants loved them. There were sometimes one or two people who might have been sent unwillingly to the program and who tended to resist becoming involved. If these individuals did dig in their feet, there was not a lot of peer pressure on them to become involved against their will, and they just drifted along till the end. People who came because they wanted to come generally had a great time and went home feeling their time and money had been well spent.

I had great times with this work and many adventures and, as I said, made some deep friendships which I still treasure. In time, I developed a little international network of friends who were interested in self-managed learning, all of whom I had met in autonomy labs: David Megginson from Sheffield, Gert Graverson of Copenhagen, Arne Ebeltoft of Oslo, Pieter Kruijt of the Hague, Thore Sandström and Björn Dahlback of Stockholm.

One of my best Autonomy Labs was an early one in which I was prevented from playing an active role. It had been organized by Thore Sandström and Arne Ebeltoft and was to be held at a conference center in Sweden. I arrived at the airport the day before the lab, but as my colleague and I drove from the passenger terminal to the freight depot to pick up the great load of learning materials that I carried to all these affairs, we had an accident with an airport bus in which our car was pretty well destroyed. My colleague was unhurt, but because I had been sitting on the side of the car the bus hit, I suffered a broken clavicle and a hairline fracture of the skull. I also had a light concussion and so remember nothing of the accident to this day. The next day, we went on with the lab, but I was in some pain and not functioning well mentally during most of the five days. We trainers turned that into an advantage by announcing that the visiting expert was not fully operational and that participants would *really* have to make their own learning if they were to have a successful experience. They rose brilliantly to the occasion, and it was one of the best labs I ever did not conduct. I thought this probably would be a great way to begin all the labs but decided against putting the idea to a test!

Unfortunately, the Autonomy Labs gave me more professional and personal satisfaction than they did commercial success. There was a lot of sales resistance on the part of training managers in European companies. For one program, sponsored by a colleague in Belgium who had a lot of enthusiasm for my work, thousands of brochures were sent out, and only one person signed up. The colleague and I looked over the brochure copy and tried to put ourselves in the shoes of training managers being asked to send people on courses to learn to be autonomous and to take risks and initiatives. We decided our brochure would sound to managers as though we were fomenting revolution or anarchy or at least an unmanageable individualism among their staff. I had come across a technology that was very powerful and very humane, but I did not know how to sell it effectively in Europe. In an attempt to stimulate others in Europe to work with it, I wrote the paper "Developing Autonomy, Initiative and Risk-Taking Through a Laboratory Design" (Harrison, 1972a [†]). When I came back to the United States, I followed that paper with another one: "Self-Directed Learning: A Radical Approach to Educational Design" (Harrison, 1977 [†]). Neither paper attracted the degree of interest I had hoped for. I did feel, however, that I had made a modest contribution to the development of self-managed learning in Britain through the management educators who attended my Autonomy Labs.

Making Management Self-Development Commercially Viable

My intuitive market analysis told me that I was probably never going to do very well with my Autonomy Labs as long as I was selling a *process*. People who bought management training were looking for specific content; they wanted programs whose aims were couched in terms of what participants would know and be able to do after they completed the program. I had discovered a way of designing learning situations that would enable much faster learning of emotionally loaded material than was possible in more rigidly controlled and structured designs, situations in which the learning could occur with less stress and trauma. Moreover, I had for many years held very dear the Hippocratic imperative, "First, do no harm," so I was strongly motivated to find applications for what seemed to me a powerful and benign new learning technology.

My first excursion into fitting content to my process was in collaboration with Fritz Steele, a colleague with whom I had taught at Yale University. We conducted the first of six weeks of the NTL Institute's Program for Specialists in Organization Development at Bethel, Maine, in the early seventies. Previous versions of that program, which I had staffed in both Britain and the United States, had been built around T-groups, with the addition of lectures, group discussion, case studies, and sometimes fieldwork, all focused on consulting issues. Our idea was to create the process of self-directed learning around the content of organization development consulting. We felt it particularly appropriate that this specialists program be offered in a self-directed format because being an effective internal or external organization development consultant requires a high degree of autonomy, initiative, and personal risk taking.

Although the Autonomy Lab and its relatives appear quite loose and unstructured, their design requires much hard work to provide participants with a wide variety of appropriate *content*. In this case, again, we went through our books and our files of articles, instruments, and exercises and pulled out anything that we judged relevant to understanding and practicing organization development consulting. We then developed categories and assigned materials to them.

The idea was for participants to use the first week of the program to identify both their strengths as consultants and their less well developed sides. Participants were asked to identify an organizational change problem for which they had some real responsibility; then, they were supposed to use the staff, the resource library, and their fellow participants to assess what they needed to know and to be able to do to carry out their project. They were to create a self-development plan that they would work on during the remainder of the program, each week of which was to be conducted by a different staff. Thus, we made the structure of the first week almost identical to that of an Autonomy Lab, with free time all day every day, except for two hours during which participants met in small groups with either Fritz or myself; shared their learning experiences, difficulties, and triumphs; and gave and received help amongst themselves. When we were not in session with these review groups, we had time to work with participants, individually or in groups, around topics of our interest and their choice, or to consult with individuals on their development.

The program met its objectives very well. Most of the participants were well satisfied, with the exception of a minority who had, in spite of our preprogram communications, come expecting the intensive T-group experience that was the traditional first week of the Program for Specialists in Organization Development and who were unwilling to shift their frame of mind to take advantage of what we were, in fact, offering. Also, some of the staff members who had the group during the remaining five weeks of the program were not happy with our design. We had had to create that design without their input, and they found the participants unusually demanding and unruly after we had liberated them! I believe that was one reason we were not again invited to offer our version of the opening week.

I was elated with the experience, however, not least because the design offered me a lot of time and scope to do one-on-one *shadow consulting*, which always gives me great pleasure and satisfaction and is well received by clients. Shadow consulting is consulting to a consultant about the latter's project. I prefer that term to the one used in psychotherapy training, which is *supervision*. The process is similar, but the relationship is more equal.

For my next project, I invited Ian Mangham of Bath University to join me in offering European versions of the self-directed consultant development work, and we launched The Program in the Management of Change, a course that covered eleven days stretched over three months. We endeavored to limit program attendance to participants who could bring a genuine change project to work on, and the work began with a five-day intensive session in which we had participants spend one segment of each day working together in six-person coaching groups, helping one another define the projects and plan their learning. They spent the remainder of that first week in individual study with the resource library, informal interactions with other participants, and individual consultations with the staff.

We divided the remaining six days into three segments, asking participants to meet for two days every fourth week. The participants spent part of that meeting time with their coaching groups, part of it with the resource library, and part in individual sessions with Ian and myself. In between sessions, participants occasionally also visited one another's sites for coaching and planning. A unique feature of the program was that we organized a panel of experienced consultants who agreed to serve as resources to our participants at something less than their normal consulting fees. Each participant was given a rebate of part of his or her fee to spend on such consultations, and participants could and did pool their financial resources to make them go further.

It was in conducting this program for different groups that I experienced the most successful development of the learning principles I had taken from the Autonomy Labs. The program was moderately difficult to recruit for, but it was financially successful, and once the materials had been assembled, it was easy to run for different groups and extremely satisfying to participants and staff alike. I only abandoned the Program in the Management of Change when the Positive Power & Influence Program began to absorb all my time after I moved to California in 1976.

Domestic Delights and Discontents

In this section, I backtrack, reviewing parts of my personal life and relationships during the time I lived abroad, in order to expand the reader's sense of the context in which I worked and my development as a whole person. As soon as I arrived in Holland, I began contacting European members of the NTL network. I sought little contact off the job with my clients and colleagues in the startup. I followed this pattern during my entire time in Europe, seeking out connections with Europeans, because I was there to learn from their culture, not to be with other expatriate Americans.

After my first startup project had been completed and I had settled in London's West End, I connected early on with members of the fledgling Association for Humanistic Psychology and also with members of the Group Relations Training Association, an organization that conducted T-group labs in Britain. The people in these groups were very diverse but drawn together by mutual interest in personal growth and new ways of learning. A number of the people taught in the North West London Polytechnic, which was experimenting with just the kind of innovative classroom learning that I had been interested in when I was at Yale. The group members were also considerably less mainstream than were most of the people I associated with in the United States, and they included quite a few radical leftists. As a fringe person in London myself, I felt at home with them and found their life-styles and politics liberating to my mind and spirit. The London of the sixties and seventies seemed a tolerant and accepting place, where people were more interested in me as a person than they were in what I did for a living or the money and possessions I had, or lacked. Part of what I was enjoying was the freedom of being an expatriate—I was not expected to be like everyone else or to know all the rules. But the British have always separated their public and private lives more than we North Americans do, and they had a genuine tolerance for diversity and even for eccentricity.

In the fall of 1969, Diana came from South Africa to join me in London, and we were married the following summer, the year I turned forty. Not long ago, I wrote to my friend Sabina Spencer on her fortieth birthday and shared with her what my forties had meant to me:

> It was, for me, the entry to my own power and the beginning of my flowering as an adult—late bloomer that I have been. That decade was the time when I truly became a man. I realized at forty that I wasn't going to live forever, but life still seemed long, and there was plenty of time ahead to do anything and everything I wanted to do. I began to give attention to taking care of my physical body, gradually outgrowing the carelessness with which I had always treated it, and my body responded to that attention by becoming strong and more vital. I realized, too, that I could no longer be a promising young man—that I had to deliver on that promise in the decade ahead if I was to achieve my dreams of making a difference. I had always cherished the idea that I was somehow chosen to make the world a better place for the human spirit, and during that decade, I tried very hard to make good on that promise. So it was not only a decade of hope—I have always had hope. It was a decade in which I

translated my wish to make a difference into forms and activities that I believed could manifest my dreams in the real world.

It was, too, a decade of adventures. I traveled everywhere I had always wanted to go. I entered into a committed relationship, transcending the fears and uncertainties which had kept me ambivalent about that state for so long. I changed the direction of my professional practice two or three times, and my world changed with me, validating those risky shifts. I found the inner guidance to know when I was on my spiritual path and when I was off, although, in that time, I was more often off than on!

It was, indeed, an exciting time, but in some ways, it was a bit lonely. As a couple, Diana and I found it difficult to create a full social life for ourselves. London seemed to be made up of tight networks of people who had known each other for ages. It was not that they were unfriendly or exclusive, but their free time was taken up with each other or with their families. During our time in Europe, we traveled a lot and through our work we made good friends in Holland, Denmark, Norway, Ireland, Sweden, and the north of England. But when we were at home in London and wanted company for an evening, we usually had to content ourselves with ourselves. As a result, we lived a somewhat isolated life, punctuated by brief periods of intense and deeply satisfying interaction. I sometimes missed the company of good friends that I had enjoyed in Washington, D.C., just prior to leaving the United States.

After Susan Jane was born in 1971, watching her grow and learn both nourished my soul and fundamentally shaped my thought regarding psychological and professional issues. I was fortunate not to become a father until I was forty-one, a time in my life when the passion for achievement and success that had so animated me early in my career had abated somewhat, and I was ready to take on parenting as a freely chosen commitment. Because I was often at home, and because Diana made space for me and coached me in being the best parent I could be, I was able to share almost all aspects of Susan Jane's care and nurturance. I quickly came to regard her as a spiritual teacher who had been sent to open my heart and connect me with my soul. At that time, I could not easily open my heart to give or receive love from other adults. In Susan Jane, I found both a model and an irresistible playmate. Her heart was so open, both to other humans and to the divine, that it became constantly easier for me to step into loving, reverent feelings of which I had not known myself capable.

In other ways, too, my learnings as a parent have greatly influenced my practice as an educator and consultant. They have especially affected my thinking about leadership, conflict, and the management of change in organizations. Diana and I are both strong-willed persons, as is Susan Jane. If one or both of us had consistently taken a heavy-handed approach in parenting Susan Jane, we would have had one pitched battle after another, and the danger in each would have been that Susan Jane might have been broken and the force of her will turned into passive aggression, resentment, or self-hatred. However, Diana and I also could not be completely permissive. We believed in influencing our child's development and setting limits on her activities. We wanted to maintain an orderly and attractive home, and we had strong preferences for values such as mutual respect and courtesy.

Two important personal themes or metaphors in my life have been the warrior and the lover. When my heart and my assertive will are split off from one another and one of them is dominant, I tend to be incomplete and unfulfilled. When they dance together, magic enters my life. So it has been for me as a parent, and so it is in my other relationships, personal and professional. With Susan Jane, I learned to think of the conflict of wills between parent and child as a series of tactical withdrawals, ending in adulthood. The warrior part of me wanted to have an impact, to make a difference in my daughter's life, and to achieve that with mutual respect, not fear. I wanted to enable her warrior qualities, too—to strengthen, not weaken, her own will. The lover in me never wanted to be out of relationship and wanted to stay in dialogue at all times. After Susan Jane reached the age of reason, the essence of my use of parental authority was to invoke that authority only when persuasion and inspiration failed and when the issue seemed crucial. Even then, if I sensed I could get compliance only by evoking fear, I would usually back off and negotiate, trying to find some sort of win-win solution. I was not very good at this balancing act at first, but I got better as I went along.

The same model now guides my work as a consultant to leaders in organizations. To shape the direction of an organization and at the same time empower its members requires just such a balancing of assertive thrust and receptivity. I help my clients to understand and find that balance. Most organizational members are, as is my daughter, reasonable people who are capable of both respect and love. When they are not, the incapacity is usually not inherent in the people. Instead, their incapacity for cooperation stems from the fear, mistrust, and passive resistance that arise in organizations in which authority and control have been considered the way to overcome resistance and make things happen.

In London, I also experienced an intensification of a pattern of work addiction that had started when I was at Procter & Gamble. Although I give my own unique qualities to that pattern, work addiction is not uncommon among my colleagues, especially those who work for themselves. For the first two years I was in Cincinnati, I had worked pretty much a nine-to-five schedule and became quite involved in sports car racing as a leisure activity. Then, I decided that it was time to get my academic career underway. I sold my Austin Healey and ceased do-it-yourself projects around the house. Instead, I spent my free time working on the publication of my thesis research, a task I hated but felt was essential to getting a position at a major university. When I went to Yale in 1960, it was expected that one would work long hours in research and writing. I spent a lot of those hours staring at the typewriter, blocked, and I dealt with my lack of productivity by putting in more time. Since my writing was not going well, I felt guilty whenever I took time away from it for my new leisure enjoyments, waterskiing and scuba diving. For many years, the only times I could play without guilt were when I was on vacation and when I was working away from home. During my working travels, I allowed myself to enjoy the little free time there was because the work was so intense that it completely met my need to convince myself I was working as hard as I could!

After I married Diana and had a child, it seemed natural to work as hard as possible in order to catch up after having left my first marriage with next to no money. For years, I was obsessed with the need to make as much money as possible, without any clear sense of how much was enough. As a consultant in some demand, my income was limited primarily by my willingness to exploit my time and periodically to raise my fees. I did both. Exploiting my time severely impacted the quality of my life and family relationships. Raising my fees caused me to be more perfectionist than was appropriate. In Europe, I charged a lot more than local consultants, and I felt I needed to be impeccable to justify my fees. There are times when I am impeccable, but when the conditions were not right, I tried to make up for that by hard work. Impeccability and hard work are not at all the same thing. Impeccability flows from a oneness between one's very being and the work to be done, while hard work frequently involves forcing oneself to do more and more of something that is not very effective.

I also used my office work as a way of being by myself, to balance the interaction with family that can become intrusive when one works at home. As an flaming introvert living in an extroverted society, I had never, until recently, legitimized my being alone. The periods of intense loneliness I had previously experienced left me afraid of solitude, not consciously craving it. The office work was a poor substitute. What I needed was more contemplative time, but with no role models or guidance to support such behavior, I just did not get the message.

The Seeds of Spiritual Awakening

Whatever the antecedents and contributing factors were for my workaholic patterns, I now believe that the root cause was an unrecognized spiritual hunger, which I tried to assuage by finding the meaning and purpose of my life in work. One reason that looking to my work for fulfillment has not worked well for me is that it is in my nature to look for the ideal behind things, events, and processes. Once I see the ideal, it often becomes for me more real than what others think of as reality. In each of the professional enthusiasms that have given me a sense of passion and deep meaning in life, I have pursued an ideal that has proven unattainable. When perfection eluded me, I then moved on to something else that held out new promise. I could believe in that promise as long as it remained at the level of the ideal. Then, the pattern was repeated, and the new ideal, too, brought disappointment. Thus, doing my work well never brought the fulfillment I was looking for.

There is now a broader spectrum of meanings in my life. Not long ago, I was asked to write a personal mission statement, and one came to mind quite easily: "I bring love, light, and learning to all my relationships, personal and professional." Twenty-odd years ago, I was still stuck in a cycle of enthusiasm and disillusionment, and it greatly contributed to the abrupt career changes I have described, such as the abandonment of my academic career and my move from organization development consulting to management education. An experience I had in 1971 reflects the state of mind that would initiate one of these periodic changes in my life. I was flying from London to New York, and I was enjoying the feeling that, after years of having had a fear of flying verging on terror, I was now quite comfortable on airplanes. I was also reviewing my life, feeling rather satisfied with myself in several ways: I had overcome the distressing anxiety attacks that had made my life a frequent misery in my twenties and early thirties, and I was as mentally healthy as years of therapy capped by six years of classical psychoanalysis could make me. I had become a successful independent consultant; I had no trouble making more money than I needed to live on; I was married to a woman I loved deeply; I had a baby daughter whom I adored.

In my reverie, I understood that if the plane were to fall into the ocean at that moment, I had done everything in my life that I had thought I wanted to do, and either it had worked out well or, as in the case of my academic career, I had decided that it was not my true calling. I felt as though I could die relatively content at that moment. I was forty-one years old, and I did not have any pressing ambitions or dreams. Until that time, I had focused all my will and attention on overcoming whatever deficit, shortcoming, or barrier was making my life difficult at the moment. I had a strong will, and it was schooled to battle, not peace. Then, as I looked ahead, I experienced some dismay. I thought, "Is this all there is, just doing this stuff for the rest of my life? How am I going to keep myself excited? How am I going to have a sense that what I am doing is really worthwhile?"

As I have mentioned, I had the rather grandiose idea that it was important for me personally to make an impact on the world's becoming a better place, and not in a small way. Perhaps it was the zealous sense of mission that I shared with my fellow T-group trainers during the high tide of optimism we experienced in NTL. Perhaps it was the influence of the Kennedy years. Then, it seemed that the world could be made a better place just through the application of money and knowledge by people of goodwill. Perhaps it was the oft-repeated affirmation by my parents that "you can do anything you want to do."

When I looked back on the things I had done prior to that airplane ride, I could not say I had achieved much in the way of world improvement! I had had hopes of making an impact, first with sensitivity training, then in my work of trying to reform university education. But my hopes of making a difference in higher education had died with the antiwar movement. The energy for university reform was co-opted by that movement and left the classroom to take to the streets. Then, I had devoted the next few years to making the world of work a more human place, but I was finding that organizations were more interested in appearing to be up on the latest management fads than they were in really changing. Nothing I had done was a success according to my criteria for a worthwhile life, but I was not yet able to give up those criteria.

Now, as I look back on the projects I have engaged in over the more than thirty-five years I have worked in consulting, research, and management education, I can point to no more than five in which I believe I personally made a significant difference in the life of an organization, and of those, there were only three where my influence was transformative in the sense that my presence and activities led to changes in significant values, beliefs, and ways of working. Of those three, there was only one in which I believe that the transformation was not reversed later on.

Thus, carrying my exalted ambitions has, at times, been a heavy burden. Because I am one of the rare full-time consultants who also writes regularly about practice, I have a reputation in my profession that is based more on what I write than on the work I do. Often, the gap between the two has caused me to feel like an impostor, knowing that the impact of my work has seldom if ever matched the depth of my understanding. I spent many years feeling that I was really not a very good consultant, and my appreciation of the compliments I received on my work was marred by an inner sense of shame. When I compared my achievements with what I could learn of others' work through their writings, their presentations at conferences, and their conversations, I generally felt myself to be lacking.

My response to a gap between my inner imperative to make a difference and the reality of my experience was to look for more powerful ways to change organizations and the individuals in them. That is what I did when my airborne reverie left me with a feeling of emptiness. Having become disillusioned about the amount of change I could create in organizations, I began to look to new ways of management education as offering opportunities to make a difference in the lives of individuals. However, behind my dissatisfaction with the amount of impact I could make in my profession, there was another, deeper sense of dispiritedness in my life, a sense of something missing, a sense of sterility, and an increasingly lower level of energy. Creating ever more difficult professional challenges temporarily enabled me to ignore this feeling. I had come to Europe and started from practically nothing to build a consulting practice. Once the consulting practice was going well, I abandoned it and reestablished my practice as a management educator but around a technology so radical that it was really hard to sell. In retrospect, it seems as though I kept trying to engage myself in my work by taking bigger risks and challenges. Each such transition worked a little less well than the one before. I was living out a pattern of addiction, in which I required ever larger doses of excitement in order to keep the underlying pain at bay.

I have seen clients dealing with an increasing sense of meaninglessness in their lives and work in much the same way I did. It is often called a midlife crisis, but I feel that label trivializes the experience. I think of it as a crisis of meaning and spirit. My story up to the early seventies is about my getting my act together and discovering how to function well. The story of the twists and turns in my work since then is the history of my response to spiritual crisis in my life and the search for enduring meanings that do not depend upon external success or impact.

CHAPTER FIVE

MY LOVE AFFAIR WITH
PERSONAL POWER

In 1971, I had begun a collaboration with David Berlew. We had known each other for about ten years, first through NTL and later through Development Research Associates, my employer in Boston for tax purposes while I lived in Britain. We liked and respected each other but had never worked together. However, we had both become dissatisfied with the leadership skills training that was then being offered by people like ourselves. The experiential learning materials that were available (mostly through the publisher University Associates) had their roots in T-group training, and they were strongly oriented to T-group values: openness, trust, listening, authenticity, and the like.

That was fine as far as it went, but in organizations, people need and use a much wider range of skills. People use their authority; they use threats of punishment and promises of reward; they use rational argument; and sometimes, like John F. Kennedy and Martin Luther King, they inspire others with dreams of a better future. There was nothing available that filled the need for skill development in all these areas or that gave people help in choosing what skill to use in a given influence situation. David and I became quite excited, imagining that we had found a gap we could fill with our creativity. We undertook the development of a training program that would enable participants to explore whatever skills they most needed to learn. The tough, aggressive people could learn to make themselves vulnerable, to build trust, and to listen with empathy; the soft people could learn to use authority, pressures, and incentives to induce compliance. The charismatic individuals could learn to back up their visions with reasons and facts; the rational thinkers could learn to spin stories and dreams of a better future. I was especially excited because I saw in this project the possibility of harnessing the motivating power of the *process of choice* in self-directed learning to a *content* that customers would see as relevant and valuable. I hoped in this way to make a contribution to the art of educational design that would go beyond the particular program that Dave and I might design together.

Dave and I originally approached this design in a spirit of play. We certainly had no intent to create a business. But our product, the Positive Power & Influence Program, was a very successful job of educational social architecture and it has proven extremely durable. We conducted the first Positive Power & Influence Program in 1973. The program is still being run in several countries and many organizations twenty years later, and it shows few signs of going out of date. I trace its longevity to the way in which its design brought together everything that Dave and I both knew about designing training, although credit must also be given to the many skilled practitioners who have sold and delivered the program down through the years.

A Design Template for Self-Managed Education

The first decision that Dave and I made was that we were going to cover the entire range of interpersonal styles that we saw people using out in the world of work and that we would provide an opportunity for people to learn to use and practice whatever skills they believed would enhance their effectiveness as managers. We countered the strong bias among our colleagues for the kinder, gentler styles by trying to honor all styles equally. However, we did decide we wanted our program to focus on positive power rather than negative power, and we defined positive power as including all influence behaviors that achieve one's objective without weakening or damaging the other person, that leave the other intact, as it were. We were not interested in teaching people to destroy or damage one another—they were on their own if they wanted to do that. Beyond that, we did not mind whether they were tough or nice to one another, so long as they learned to be effective.

Next, we mapped the area to be covered. Our mapping was intuitive, based on what we saw people doing with one another in the organizations with which we worked. We divided influence styles into "hard" and "soft," and then we named two hard styles and two softer ones, as illustrated in Table 5.1.

We easily agreed on the first three style categories, but we were stuck for a while on the fourth. I had and still have a firm belief that the fewer categories we asked people to learn and use, the better our model would stick with them; it would be good if we could get away with two and certainly not more than three. Because of his experiences as both a Peace Corps administrator and a consultant who worked with top executives, Dave was very interested in leadership, and he had concluded that a fourth style, visionary leadership, was the wave of the future. At the time, no one else that I knew about was talking this way, and I was little

TABLE 5.1. CONSULTANT'S JOURNEY.

Hard, Competitive Styles		Soft, Cooperative Styles	
Rewards and Punishments	*Assertive Persuasion*	*Participation and Trust*	*Common Vision*
Assertive, demanding behaviors: using positive and negative incentives to achieve compliance; bargaining and negotiating; using pressure tactics	*Reasoning behaviors:* using rational arguments, facts, and opinions to convince and persuade; appealing to reason and to the authority of knowledge, expertise, and experience	*Trust-building behaviors:* listening and drawing the other out; making oneself vulnerable by acknowledging weakness, wrongdoing, and inadequacy; showing trust and confidence in others; appealing to the other's positive qualities and values	*Inspirational behaviors:* sharing and evoking hopes and dreams of a better future; invoking shared ideals and values; using colorful images and metaphors

moved by his arguments. However, I was impressed by his passion for the subject, and I went along, more to avoid strain in our working relationship than from any sense of inner conviction. Of course, I could not have been more wrong in my judgment about the importance that visionary leadership behaviors would come to have in the future, and thanks to Dave's own vision, we were probably the first to offer training in that skill set.

My own passion around our design was for self-directed learning, and we agreed that there would be a significant component of self-development in our program. We knew from my experiences with the Autonomy Labs that people can take two or two and a half days to get to the point where they are learning under their own power. That was half the time we allowed ourselves in our design, and we asked ourselves how we could move people into an active learning stance more quickly. The answers and insights we came up with are set forth in the paper I wrote several years later, "Self-Directed Learning: A Radical Approach to Educational Design" (Harrison, 1977). Our fundamental design principle was to give participants maximum feasible choice: wherever there was a choice of activities to be made, trainers would delegate as much of that choice to the learners as they were ready to take. Being ready to make a choice implies that the learners have enough information to choose in their own best interests, that the act of making the choice is sufficiently comfortable that they do not avoid it out of anxiety, and that the learners are motivated to choose by a personal interest in the outcome. As we designed the learning process, at each place where a choice had to be made we asked ourselves, "Why can we not delegate this choice to the learners?" At the outset of a learning process, the answer to that question is usually that the learners do not understand the model we are working with well enough to make a completely informed choice. Then we must include activities that will inform the learners, so that we can pose the choice later on.

In designing the Positive Power & Influence Program, Dave and I came up with what I think of as a *design template,* which we later found could be used to create maximum feasible choice for people engaged in learning almost any kind of content. We have found the design template to be especially powerful when one is designing for the learning of content that is loaded with value and emotional connotations. As Figure 5.1. shows, the educators in the Positive Power & Influence Program make all the choices about preprogram work and most of the choices during day one. During days two through four, participants assume an increasingly greater degree of choice until day five, when they are preparing to take their learnings back home.

Table 5.2 shows how the design template opens up choice over time, again using the Positive Power & Influence Program as an example.

The Power of Commit Pits for Motivating Learning

Part of the power of our program's design, and other designs based on the same template is the way in which we create *commit pits* for the learner. The metaphor captures an element of (I hope benign) trickery in my approach to design. In trapping elephants, hunters used to dig a large pit in the middle of a much-used trail and cover it with brush and leaves. When an elephant took that trail to go to food or water, it fell in the pit. In my training designs, I always assume that participants are bigger and stronger than I am and that in a contest of wills about what and whether they will learn they will win. Like elephants, they will pretty much go where they want. Therefore, I design the choices I ask participants to make among learning activities (trails) so that no matter which of the alternatives they choose, useful learning will occur. Since the act of choosing activates the will to carry

FIGURE 5.1. LEARNER CHOICE VERSUS EDUCATOR CONTROL IN THE POSITIVE POWER & INFLUENCE PROGRAM.

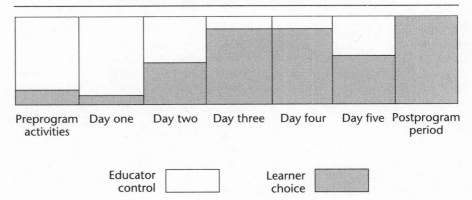

TABLE 5.2. HOW LEARNER CHOICE INCREASES IN THE
POSITIVE POWER & INFLUENCE PROGRAM.

Time	Design Phase	Activities	Design Rationale
Preprogram activities	Collect data on own influence style	Complete self-scoring Influence Style Questionnaire, distributed by the participant to supervisor, peers, and subordinates; write out an unresolved, real-life influence situation that one would like help on during the program.	The participant does not know the influence style model at the outset and is led to begin to learn the model by collecting data about his or her own influence style and interpreting the data according to the definitions and directions given. The participant chooses the colleagues who will provide the most useful and interesting information.
Day one	Learn the model and map one's influence strengths and weaknesses on it	Review questionnaire results; take part in videotaped exercises in group problem solving, negotiating, and presenting ideas; categorize own influence behaviors from videotape.	The educators provide exercises that will give each participant the opportunity to demonstrate skill in all four styles. Participants follow instructions and learn the model through applying it to their own and others' videotaped behavior.
Day two	Experience underused styles	Review own influence profile and choose the two least-used styles; take part in two "tracks" consisting of short, intensive role-plays in which only one of the four styles is used and used in an extreme and overstated way.	Having mapped their own patterns of style usage, participants are asked to commit themselves to experience intensively two styles that will stretch them to use unfamiliar behaviors. They are asked to commit only to experiencing the new styles, not to learning to use them.
Days three and four	Experience self-directed learning	Having experienced both familiar and unfamiliar styles, choose to develop one or two further; freely select from a cafeteria of experiential exercises those best suited to one's own learning needs; use initiative to enlist other participants in one's learning project.	Having experienced how much innovation and stress tolerance it would take to acquire some skill in underused styles, participants are ready to choose either to further develop familiar styles or to begin the acquisition of skill in using previously avoided behaviors. The

			free-range learning situation provides opportunities for empowerment by offering participants scope for initiative and self-direction in enlisting others in their learning projects.
Day five	Practice using learning in real-life cases	In three-person groups, participants role-play and record the unresolved, real-life influence situation of each member; review the tapes; consult with observers; and redo, until satisfied with the result.	The educators, who assume that participants do not know how best to prepare to apply their learning back home, provide a framework for working on back-home cases. Participants choose whom they work with, whether to work on their original case or present another one, and how they will work together on their cases.
Postprogram activities	Apply learning to life	Carry out the strategy and tactics practiced on day five in the back-home influence situation; devise and carry out further learning activities to enhance skills.	By ensuring that participants have spent some time practicing the application of their learning to a real-life case with the coaching of their peers and of the staff, the educators hope that each participant will have at least one success experience in using learnings from the Positive Power & Influence Program. Beyond that, participants are on their own.

through the consequences of the choice, when I can entice participants into making a choice of what or how they learn, they will find themselves committed to learning. There will then be little or no resistance to carrying out the chosen activity. I believe I owe the very low levels of resistance that I have experienced in programs designed according to this template to the artful use of commit pits.

The first commit pit in the design given in Table 5.2 occurred when we asked participants to *choose* the individuals from whom they collected responses to the Influence Style Questionnaire. We encouraged participants to choose describers (work associates or family members) whose feedback about the participant's use of the four influence styles would be personally significant. We then asked participants to score their own questionnaires, and we gave them written material they could use to interpret their own scores. In this way, before they ever came to the program, participants carried out a research project on their use of the influence styles. Usually, they were hooked into wanting to learn more.

The next choice leading to a commit pit took place on day two when we asked participants to select two style tracks, each one of which required them to use behaviors they normally avoided using. In each of those two style tracks, they participated in a series of intensely involving role-plays in which the given style was used to the hilt. We did not say, "You need to work on your weaker styles." We said, "Over time, you have acquired strength in those styles you habitually use. Now we would like you to *experience* styles that are less familiar to you, so that during the self-directed portion of the program, you can make an informed choice as to whether to develop additional skill in those styles."

Later, as participants entered the self-directed portion of the program, we invited them to "choose whether to work on further honing those styles that already represent strengths for you, or perhaps to work on acquiring skill in a style or styles that are newer to you."

Again, the principle behind the commit pits is that people will learn with enthusiasm and will display little resistance if they are given lots of attractive choices. It is so simple, and it results in such satisfying learning experiences for participants, that it is hard for me to understand why the principle has not been widely applied in the design of training programs. I suppose one reason may be that it requires more creative work to design programs that are full of choice; for example, in day two of the Positive Power & Influence Program, when people explore their underused styles, each of the four style tracks contained about ten role-playing exercises from which participants could make their choices. Had we been willing to give participants no choice of activities, we could have cut the number of exercises by half or more.

With the creation of the Positive Power & Influence Program, I now had all the pieces in place for designing an experience-based process that would help participants to learn almost anything that required change in all of what I called the Big Three: knowing (changing and building conceptual structures), doing (acquiring new behavioral skills), and feeling (shifting attitudes and emotions that block learning). It had been a long road. I began traveling it in my classroom at Yale when I first learned to use social architecture. I learned the uses of authority and of structures (design) to fence or corral the energy of students into the area defined by the subject matter of a course. Once they were in that area, I could give them a great deal of freedom as to how to go about their learning because I had ensured that whatever they did would be relevant to my educational purposes. Because they were free to make choices, they were motivated to give energy to the work; because all the choices led to worthwhile learning about organizational psychology, the learning was focused and efficient. During this period, I also learned to use the motivational power of students' relationships with one another to support the learning process, rather than allowing the social system to remain either irrelevant or detrimental to classroom learning, as it normally is.

In the early seventies, I continued to develop the power and generality of my designs with the Autonomy Lab, in which I learned to trust the power of choice even further, moving from giving choices about how to learn, to offering choices about what to learn. I learned to use the power of *open space*, and to ameliorate the anxiety caused by lack of structure by providing rich resources for participants to connect with (including one another) and by offering assistance in accessing those resources. By observing learners' behavior, I gained new insights about the cyclical ebb and flow of energy in learning and about its *pacing* and *punctuation*. (These latter learnings have yet to be fully exploited. For me, they have deep relevance to the question of how to manage the traumatic aspects of organizational change.)

Finally, in the Positive Power & Influence Program, I and my colleagues learned how to inform choice with information by having participants collect feedback on their skills and knowledge through instruments and videotaped exercises. We learned to orchestrate the process of choice by providing graduated information and experience and by asking participants to take ever more responsibility for making choices as they became more knowledgeable and confident. We also learned to use the power of commit pits to capture the excitement and interest of learners.

Do You Sincerely Want to Be Rich?

It took Dave Berlew and me quite a while to articulate and then to solve our basic design issues in the Positive Power & Influence Program, and it was a year or more before we were ready for a pilot effort, given that we only worked together on the program during my infrequent trips to the United States. We conducted the first Positive Power & Influence Program in Britain for Imperial Chemical Industries in 1973, and soon afterwards, we ran an open program in Dublin for the Irish Management Institute. We had a great deal of fun running these programs. At the time, our design was pretty sketchy: we knew what we wanted to have in the program and where the parts should go, but we had not designed the activities to fill the slots; we used some of the structured exercises published by University Associates (Pfeiffer and Jones, 1969–1971) for the diagnostic parts, and we ran only two style tracks: one hard and one soft. Each of us facilitated one track, and we selected and modified a lot of the exercises as we went along. These early events depended on our skill as trainers, honed by years of ad hoc T-group lab design. We were continually experimenting; we felt we were always on the edge between flaming success and spectacular disaster, and each delivery of the program demanded all the skill and creativity we could muster.

On the closing day of our Dublin session, over several large Irish whiskeys, Dave and I took part in an animated conversation about the Positive Power & Influence Program with Liam Gorman of the Irish Management Institute. It was one of those moments that change lives and fortunes. Liam was very high on the Positive Power & Influence Program, and he convinced us that the program we had developed primarily for fun and only secondarily for profit might be the foundation of a business. His idea was for us to develop the program into a form that could be run by others and then license it to companies for their internal use. I was intrigued with the idea, and at the time, I was negotiating with a client who was interested in using the program to train project managers in influencing without formal authority. The management development manager with whom I was working was under a lot of pressure to bring a program in quickly. Emboldened by Liam's vision of the commercial possibilities of our program, I took advantage of this manager's urgent need and successfully demanded $12,000 to license the manager's company to use the Positive Power & Influence Program, acquiring at the same time a contract to train internal trainers and to develop written materials to which I would keep the copyright.

The Easy Money Trap

In 1973, $12,000 was more money than I had ever taken at one time for anything; Dave and I felt we had stumbled into a diamond mine, one where the jewels were just lying on the ground to be picked up. We were on a tremendous high: we had a good program and we felt proud of it, it seemed to give enormous value to the participants, and it was great fun to run because it gave us opportunities to play games ourselves. Added to that, I had the contract to develop structured training materials for the program, and I could improve our design as I trained the client's internal trainers. I felt incredibly empowered, and my motivation to sell and to develop the program rose to a new high.

As it turned out, it was three years before the next such sale, but in the interim I did quite well by offering the program myself and by licensing it to training firms in Holland and Denmark, whose staff I trained to conduct the program. Both the Autonomy Lab and the Positive Power & Influence Program were well suited to use in Scandinavia and the Netherlands, where most managers read and speak English but do not like to use it constantly. Thus, it was not necessary to translate all the materials in order to use them, yet the experiential work could be done in the participants' own language, as long as there was a native-speaking facilitator present.

I made great friends through my marketing of the Positive Power & Influence Program in other countries. I think particularly of Hans Zuidema in Holland and Hans Harboe in Denmark. They were kind enough to put up with my thinking of myself as a hotshot negotiator and my feeling that my honor was served only by getting the best deal for myself that I could. From them and others, I learned that friendship and loyalty are worth more than commercial advantage, but it took a while for their patience and goodwill to come through to me.

What Do People Really Learn?

I was never quite sure how much skill people took away from the programs, although participants liked them a lot and clearly learned to think about power and influence in new ways. The impact of training on work behavior is highly sensitive to the work situation and context, and the personal risks are too high for most people to adopt in the workplace styles of influence with which they are not comfortable to begin with. After we developed practice sessions on the last day that focused participants on a specific, unresolved back-home problem, we began to get positive reports that participants had gone away from our program and brought their individual problems to a successful conclusion. Some of their stories were quite dramatic, involving tens or hundreds of thousands of dollars, and it was encouraging to hear them. On the negative side, the internal staff of one client I worked with over some years on the Positive Power & Influence Program attempted to organize follow-up practice clinics for participants; these were mostly badly attended and lacking in energy.

When it was possible to take an intact work group off-site and use the Positive Power & Influence Program to bring participants to the point of working some of their real issues in the context of the program, I am sure that significant changes did take place. One client group with which I did this volunteered examples five years later about what group members had learned and how it had changed their working relationships. Such cases were the exception; however, I am sure we expanded people's consciousness about their styles of influencing others and gave them a language for thinking and talking about personal power and influence. In instances where people were ready for a jump forward in their own growth, I am also sure we provided the support they needed and a conceptual framework to help them decide where they wanted to jump.

Playing with Personal Power

I am quite sure that in addition to the money that we and many others made from the Positive Power & Influence Program and its successors, we created a tremendously powerful personal development experience for those who trained the program. During the first three years of working with the program, I used it to broaden my own repertoire of influence behaviors to include all the behaviors in our model. In order to conduct the style tracks, one has to be able to model each style and use it in a way that demonstrates to skeptical participants that each style is powerful and can be used positively and nondestructively. Therefore, each time I conducted the program, I was also stretching and honing my ability to use the styles precisely, appropriately, and with finesse. It took a while for me to feel comfortable using the Rewards and Punishments, and a much longer time to use Common Vision effectively. It was immensely satisfying to me to acquire a sense of comfort in using these styles at last. I discovered that there were parts of me that could only be released to live and grow once I learned to speak the verbal and body language of the associated influence style. The more fluently I learned to speak that language, the more energy was released to move through that medium.

For a while, I became intoxicated with personal power and influence, particularly their harder aspects. I gloried in acquiring a reputation as a tough negotiator and in driving hard bargains with clients and customers, even with business associates. I felt driven to take every challenge that was offered, using confrontations that arose in shops and restaurants, on airlines and at hotels, as food for my appetite for conquest. The avidity with which I now pursued anything to do with power surprised me since during the early seventies I was also becoming involved in my spiritual search, propelled by my ever-increasing sense of a lack of meaning and satisfaction in my work. I began with transcendental meditation, and then, in 1973, I took part in the Arica Institute's training, which was a forty-day total immersion experience providing many techniques for achieving higher states of consciousness. Even though most of the time I experienced myself as the slowest member of the class, I did expect that after the training I would find myself in a pretty high place spiritually. As it turned out, I did develop a fairly clear sense of when I was moving in the right direction, although I did not find my "True Path." So I was unprepared for the drive for personal power and influence that welled up in me as I pursued my work with the Positive Power & Influence Program.

Looking back, I now feel that what the Arica training did for me was to liberate me to work through my latent passion for power. Part of the law of karma, as I understand it, can be expressed as "every desire must be fulfilled." My experience of those years in the mid seventies was that the Positive Power & Influence Program was the perfect place for me to express myself and to play with power: to learn to be tough, to learn to be empathetic, to learn to flex my style to meet changing situations, to get what I wanted in negotiations; in short, to have fun getting other people to do what I wanted them to do.

That kept me immensely entertained for three or four years, and then, quite suddenly, it lost its savor. I began to feel inauthentic and unreal, to feel that I was spending a lot of time and energy manipulating myself in order to play this power game. The cost in energy of winning at everything began to seem too high, and I found myself avoiding confrontations and challenges in favor of conserving my energy and preserving peace and harmony in my environment. Perhaps my desires for power and influence had been sated at last. I know for sure that I became bored with the game.

One of my desires for influence did not abate, though it was destined to be frustrated. I still wanted very much to infuse my enthusiasm for self-directed learning into other professionals, and I hoped the Positive Power & Influence Program would be a way to do this. Hundreds of people have now been trained to conduct the Positive Power & Influence Program and its successors, yet I could number on my fingers the trainers I have met here in the United States who have seen the power of the self-directed aspects of the design or shared my passion for it.

I have pondered why, and the most plausible explanation I can find is that educators do not design choice into their programs because they wish to be in control. I have clearly not let go of this issue, and I shall now take one more shot at convincing my readers of the power that flows from empowering others!

Those of us who live in Western industrial societies have succeeded in bringing nature, including human nature, under control. Now our civilization is sickening, perhaps unto death, because we have overreached ourselves in this. We have built deeply into our culture strong, perhaps addictive needs for control, and educators participate in this general addiction. Because our attachment to control is either unexamined or addictive, we do not understand that by relinquishing control and providing choice, we increase our *influence* and *impact* many times over. If power is defined as the ability to achieve desired results, then my and other trainers' experiences with the Positive Power & Influence Program show that providing autonomy and choice increases the *power* of the educator. Paradoxically, that power is gained by letting go of control.

Of course, the principle applies to managers and leaders as well as to educators. Providing choices, even very limited and simple ones, enlists the will and energy of the chooser. If the choices provided all have positive outcomes for the organization and for the individual, then everybody wins. The social architecture of designing work and learning situations so that people can choose among a variety of positive ways of meeting organizational goals and requirements is a discipline that OD consultants could reap great benefits from if they cultivated it for themselves and their clients.

Buccaneer's Return: The Longing for Belonging

Diana, Susan Jane, and I moved to Berkeley, California, in 1976. For me, the return was motivated by a complex set of internal and external forces. Dominant among them was the alienation and loneliness I was experiencing in England. I admired British culture and ways very much, and I longed to belong, but after a few years in Britain, I realized I could never achieve the degree of integration I wanted, that I would always be an alien, in my eyes and in theirs. When a man I knew as a close friend said warmly, "Roger, I never really think of you as an American," I thought I experienced something of what women and minorities feel when others accept their persons but not their differences. In trying to fit in, I had submerged a number of American qualities I believed were disliked by the British. I had paid what I hoped was the price of membership, and I had been granted guest privileges; it was not enough. That was the moment in which I became serious about going home.

I later came to understand that if I had wanted to stay in England, I could have reclaimed my American ways within my own social and professional circle without great social penalty. As I have suggested, there is a process immigrants and minorities may go through in which the price of acceptance is their willingness to conform. Once that price is seen to have been paid, it is acceptable for them to display, even to flaunt, their ethnic differences. Once they have passed the point at which basic trust has been established, living out their differences confers a certain charisma on them without threatening members of the host culture. What I wanted, however, was unattainable—to be one of *us* rather than one of *them*.

Just a Guy Who Can't Say No—And Who Won't Say Yes

When I returned to the United States and the Bay Area in 1976, I believed, correctly, that getting started as a consultant and management educator in a competitive market like California would prove to be much more difficult than it had been on the East Coast or, indeed, in Europe. Dave Berlew very much wanted me to join with him and a colleague of his, Earl Rose, in a company they were founding to market the Positive Power & Influence Program. Although I was reluctant to constrain myself with organizational forms, I felt the need for collegiality and support as I once again undertook to build my practice from nothing. It felt good to be wanted, and three felt safer than one. I searched my soul and also asked for and received assurances from my colleagues that all decisions would be made by consensus, no matter what our legal documents said. Then I joined Earl and Dave, and signed away my rights in the Positive Power & Influence Program materials in return for stock in Situation Management Systems, Inc. It was a mistake, brought about by my lack of confidence in my ability to survive and thrive on my own and by my wanting to do what others whom I care about want me to do.

During my love affair with personal power, I learned that no matter how tough I was in ordinary life or how resistant to overt pressure, the people with whom I had a heart connection could easily influence me just by articulating a need or want that I could fill. Most people never discovered my secret because I presented myself as someone who knew what he wanted and was determined to get it. But I knew that to those for whom I cared, my defenses were soft as butter. I might put up a credible resistance, but my heart was not in it—what I *really* wanted was to be loved, not to win.

I believe the pattern is common in the OD profession. Owing to an inability to say no, nearly every successful consultant I know finds it hard to limit his or her practice. The French call such a pattern a *déformation professionnel,* an apt name that translates itself. It is a character flaw that makes for success in one's chosen work and, thus, becomes accentuated, even valued. In myself, it is probably an expression of a fairly deep fear of rejection and abandonment. I have worked the issue in part by choosing a lifework in which my acceptance by others as a professional is hardly distinguishable from my acceptance as a person. As a consultant, I risk using fairly deep parts of myself in the service of my work, so I often feel that my *self* is on the line. When people say, "Come work with us, Roger," that inner child who so wants to be wanted jumps for joy. Even after the many years of therapy and personal growth work I have done, my first impulse when someone expresses a need for help or wants to include me in his or her plans is to say yes!

During the decade just past, I have finally learned that if I can check that impulse to say yes and avoid an immediate reply, my intuition will generally tell me swiftly and accurately whether or not that affirmative impulse is in my own best interests. However, in 1976, that awareness was still in my future. My intuitive sense of right and wrong manifests itself in my abdomen, and that part of me was screaming "No!" as I signed on the dotted line. But at that time, I only knew how to honor the messages from my head and my heart, and they told me signing was the sensible thing to do, as well as being pleasing to my friend Dave.

A Formula for Success—Everyone an Entrepreneur

Over the years, I have seen friends and colleagues develop excellent training programs, instruments, and structured games and exercises that they hoped might provide them with every working consultant's dream, non–labor intensive (passive) income. Some of these ventures succeed; many do not, for reasons that have to do more with the attitudes of the developers than the quality of the products. From my own experience, here are some factors that make for success.

- A sincere intention to do whatever it takes to turn one's work into a successful business venture.
- A willingness to share a large portion of the fruits of one's creativity with people who are genuinely interested in and talented at business and making money, and/or a willingness to devote a great deal of personal time and energy to selling one's products.
- An ability to position one's pet ideas and passionate obsessions so that they have mass appeal, and a willingness to refine one's work in response to the market, so that the work has high appeal to those who may use it.
- An ability and willingness to develop materials and manuals that make one's work accessible to people who do not share one's own experience and intuitive grasp of the concepts; in other words, an ability and willingness to find a lower common denominator.

One idea I hold to strongly is that the partnership between the people who design training materials and those who sell and market the materials is an equal one. Many people who have invested their time and creativity in producing materials feel they should receive the lion's share of the returns when the materials are sold and used, and these people are willing to offer only modest (stingy?) commissions to others who sell their programs. Then, for lack of someone to sell and market them, many fine materials, including some of my own best ones, languish on the shelf, where they do no one any good at all.

When Dave Berlew and I were first selling the Positive Power & Influence Program, we conceived the idea of developing a network of agents who would sell and deliver the program to their clients, returning to us a proportion of their sales of the materials. In selecting and contracting with agents, we followed a set of principles, arrived at more or less intuitively, that for me have stood the test of time. First, as agents we wanted skilled management trainers with entrepreneurial talents. We were looking for people whose interests were more service-oriented and commercial than creative, who did not see the programs they conducted as expressions of their own personalities but rather as useful tools by which they could better serve their clients and increase their own income. We wanted to work with people who would be empowered by being able to use our programs.

Second, we did not want to receive commissions on our agents' training fees. We were not normally going to provide clients for our agents, and we felt that as independent professionals they were worthy of their fees.

Third, from our own experiences in selling the Positive Power & Influence Program, we believed that selling training materials is highly skilled work that is different from that of designing the materials but close to equal in importance. We learned that when people are dividing something, the proportion least likely to cause later resentment and feelings of unfairness is fifty-fifty. We offered to give our agents 50 percent of the sales price of the materials they sold, after production expenses were deducted. Indeed, probably my most significant learning about negotiating divisions of work or reward has been that idea that fifty-fifty is the most stable and workable division there is, and even if I think the real contribution is not quite equal, I will always strive to find a way to justify an even split.

Fourth, we did not hold the program as written to be sacrosanct. We saw our work as always incomplete. We were continually revising the materials ourselves, and we welcomed revisions and additions from others. We had no rules about maintaining the integrity of the program by running it always in the same way. While we wanted other trainers to work closely with us in learning the program, we did not have a formal certification program for internal trainers, reasoning that, within fairly broad limits, once they bought materials, they bought the right to use them in their own way.

Lastly, we saw the income from selling our training materials as a return on the time and energy required to develop them that was to be invested in supporting further developmental projects. We felt that if we could create a non–labor intensive income stream from the sale of materials, it would free our time and energy for the creative play which we loved.

While I was still living in Europe, Dave and I had put together several deals with agents based on these principles. We had our share of disagreements and difficulties with these agents, often because of my desire to experience myself as a sharp and sophisticated business negotiator. But the relationships were based on professional respect and mutual profit, which in some instances ripened into love. Our principles worked, most of the time. Later, as the business of selling the Positive Power & Influence Program and its successor programs developed, many different sorts of people and organizations became involved in it, and most of our original principles were abandoned in the press of running the business and making profits. I still believe the power programs are good for most of the participants who attend them, but I am quite sure the power training business is not good for some of those who make their living from it. It has become too hard-hearted; there is too much emphasis on who gets what from whom, and not quite enough on creativity and contribution. I say this as one who got caught up in focusing more on the money than on the art. There is sadness but no pride in my critique.

If I were to start again, I would apply the same principles. I do not believe this is naïve. From the start, I made a good living operating on these principles; by the time I left Europe, Dave and I were well positioned to make some non–labor intensive income. We had fun, we made wonderful friends, and we learned a lot. The Positive Power & Influence Program and its successor programs were designed to liberate and empower individuals, and I still believe that the business arrangements around such programs should reflect those ideals.

How to Turn a Business Success into a Personal Mess

There were severe personal disappointments involved in my time with Situation Management Systems and great pain for me and others in my departure from the company, which took place in 1981 after much struggle. Many consultants consider forming a business with colleagues, and I hope my experience may be cautionary for others. I focus here only on what I learned about myself from the Situation Management Systems experience. I am not wise or objective enough to know what my colleagues needed to learn from the experience.

People who make good colleagues do not necessarily make good business associates. Those who are well adapted to the lonely life of the independent consultant may long for collegiality and support, but they are often unwilling to pay the price. Like a long-term bachelor, I had become set in my ways, used to controlling my own time, unused to sharing, and careless about consulting others when making decisions. I was simply not ready to be a loyal member of an organization. I have never taken well to being an employee. As a member of Situation Management Systems, I continually negotiated exceptions to the rules others were making for themselves as my price for staying in the organization. What I actually wanted was to run my own consulting and training business while remaining nominally a member of Situation Management Systems. That would have worked, I think, except that as an owner and director, I felt a need to second-guess every important executive decision that was taken, even though I lived 2,500 miles away from the Situation Management Systems office in Massachusetts. I have never felt more keenly the tyranny of my own high needs for influence and autonomy than when I tried to fit in with my business associates.

Mostly, they met my every demand and would probably have been willing to continue to tolerate me for quite a while longer had I been willing to choose *either* autonomy or influence, but I wanted both. No matter what we did, I found myself increasingly restive and dissatisfied, and in 1981, I announced that I wanted to negotiate a formal separation from the organization. My associates were furious that after they had tied themselves in knots to keep me happy I wanted to leave anyway—they fired me. They invoked the legal buy-out agreement we had all willingly signed at the outset of our adventure together, and that was that.

More accurately, that was that except for the feelings, and they would not go away. The death of a business association can be excruciatingly painful, especially if it involves a rift in a valued friendship. For me, this separation was probably more painful than my divorce thirteen years earlier. I felt I had lost not only my partner but also custody of our offspring, the training materials we had designed together. I told myself that I had freely entered into the contract we signed, that I had been a consenting adult. I told myself it was ridiculous that I should regard these training programs as equivalent in any way to human children, but my heart would not listen. I had done a lot of work of which I was very proud during the years I had been working with the Positive Power & Influence Program, but I had written little that was not now subject to the Situation Management Systems copyright. Now, I had to give it all up for money. I was paid as we had agreed would be done if one of us left the company. Of course, it seemed too little because the loss I felt so keenly was to my heart, not my pocketbook. Under my contract, I was allowed to continue to offer the Situation Management Systems programs as an agent, but I soon found out that it was quite painful for me to do that work. My wife, Diana, who is a talented trainer, continued to work with the Positive Power & Influence Program, but I needed something different.

As I relate in the next chapter, I did for a while undertake the design of new training programs. However, an inner navigator was directing my energies, little by little, into new channels.

CHAPTER SIX

COMING OUT OF THE CLOSET
AS A NEW AGE THINKER

This chapter covers part of the same period as the previous chapter in order to look back to the point shortly after I arrived in Berkeley in 1976 and began searching for a way to integrate my personal and spiritual process into my work. At the center of my process was my search for a way to work and to relate to others that was more from the heart and less from the will and intellect. In terms of the model put forward in Chapter Two (Figure 2.1), I was cycling away from the pole of *difference,* or separateness, and moving toward *unity,* or being in relationship. I wanted to come home to some form of community. I was consciously looking to emphasize partnership, cooperation and co-creativity, and love in all areas of my life.

A part of me knew long before I left Situation Management Systems that it was past time to move along. Although my office was just across the hall from my bedroom, it was increasingly hard to get up and go to work in the morning! I longed to be back in consulting, but somehow, for every problem my prospective clients came up with, I had a training solution in my hip pocket.

The issue of power was losing its savor for me, partly because it had become mainstream. On our return from England, Diana and I needed to go no further than the airport bookstands to see that we had stepped into a power-oriented culture. We were struck by books with titles like *Looking Out for Number One* (Ringer, 1977), *Winning Through Intimidation* (Ringer, 1974), and *Power! How to Get It, How to Use It* (Korda, 1975).

I lose interest in an established trend. The trends I like are the ones that have not happened yet but that I believe will, or should, come about in time. It is not just that I like to think of myself as being on the leading edge. Deep in my being there is a craving for balance, for redressing excess. I can embrace wholeheartedly that which is moving from beneath or behind and bringing balance into the world. Then, when it looks like being in the ascendant, I see its dark side, and I begin to look for a countervailing force or principle. A trivial example is that I usually root for the underdog when I am watching a sporting match, and if the weaker team forges ahead, I find myself shifting my allegiance. I am comfortable with tension between opposing forces, but I am wary of dominance, of winning and losing. It was my concern for the underdog that had fueled my championing of individual empowerment. Now, seeing so many organizations where all look out for themselves and no one cares for the whole, I was concerned about damage to the ties that bind people together.

I find redirecting the central thrust of my personal energy like changing the course of a large ship. First, I become increasingly dissatisfied with the direction in which I am going. Then, after some inner and outer search and exploration, I decide on a change. I throw the helm hard over to proceed on the new course and—nothing happens! The ship of my life continues to glide through the water as though nothing had occurred on the bridge. Although there is continuing consternation and frantic activity on deck, only slowly is the moment of decision translated into a discernible outward change of course. So it was in my finding a path with heart. I was able to change my behavior in new relationships, especially those in which there was not too much at stake. But in more important areas, I tended to continue my old patterns of behavior. My relationship with my colleagues in Situation Management Systems was just such a continuation of an old pattern, and although I could hear the waves crashing on the shoals ahead, I had neither the skill nor will to turn my ship away from disaster.

Indeed, even after leaving Situation Management Systems, I continued in the same course if at less speed. Together with Diana and psychotherapist Ginger Blume, I designed an excellent program in managing conflict. Continuing to design training programs was a denial of my losses. For years before and during my time with Situation Management Systems, I had honed my skills in educational design. While I readily accept that there are better consultants than I am, I believe myself to be among the best in the design of learning events and processes. I am proud of the work I have produced, and I greatly enjoy the creative design process. In leaving Situation Management Systems, I had not merely lost the existing products of my creativity—they could be replaced. More importantly, I had lost a setting and context that supported my art. The realization slowly sank in that unless I was prepared to involve myself once more in the *business* of training, I could see no real outlet for my creations. Yet this was a business for which I now had little taste. I now had a deep commitment to the transformation of the workplace into a more humane setting through releasing the power of love, and I could not yet see a connection between my new mission and my craft as a designer of educational processes. And so I grieved my way through the early eighties, unable to find real energy for my work, blown along by the same old trade winds, but still slowly turning my thinking in new directions.

Maybe Love's the Answer

When I moved to Berkeley, I found I was able to change my personal style significantly, perhaps even radically. In my new relationships, I felt myself to be more open, empathetic, and a better listener. The response I received from others was much softer, my relationships were easier and more trusting, and this experience was immensely rewarding. In my inner dialogue, I began to draw a parallel between my own process and what needed to happen in the world. I thought there must be many others who felt trapped in assertive, competitive modes that brought excitement and challenge but no peace and contentment. I wondered if the energy for the next wave of change might in fact be in those weary warriors. Perhaps, as people felt more and more isolated and threatened, they would become at least a little ready to explore the nurturing power of love.

Conceptualizing Balance—Alignment and Attunement

Building warmer relationships was only one of several threads I began to pull together in my personal development. I also continued my search for a spiritual path, attending courses and events conducted by various groups and teachers. I did not find the teacher I was looking for, but I did find other seekers, some of whom were in organization development. After a time, I began to meet once or twice a month with a group of organization development consultants interested in translating their personal spiritual interests into their work. The group met at the Institute for Conscious Evolution (ICE) in San Francisco. The ICE was a small organization established by Barry McWaters and Susan Campbell to discuss and publicize the ideas of Barbara Marx Hubbard and others who hold that at this stage in humankind's development as a species, instead of unconsciously going through evolution, we can choose what is going to be our next evolutionary stage, and we can make it happen.

In the ICE, I found a group of kindred spirits; all of us were experiencing a painful gap between our interest in higher states of consciousness for ourselves and the fairly mundane and instrumental issues we were working on for clients. I met with this group of OD consultants for about three years. The meetings were rather frustrating because none of us really knew how to get clients to take big jumps in their personal and organizational consciousness. Thus, we spent our time talking about what we were doing and what we would like to be doing and the big gap between the two that did not seem to get smaller with time.

Often, it seems as though just remaining in contact with an unresolved issue over time leads to a breakthrough. Certainly that had been true in my therapy, where simply staying with the frustration of my inability to move beyond a block once I had identified it seemed to be a significant factor in my healing. In the ICE, we certainly immersed ourselves in our frustrations, but at the same time, we furnished one another with a lot of emotional and intellectual support. A small core of us did not give up but kept wrestling with the issues, and eventually, my own thinking about the problem of inspiriting business organizations began to assume coherent form. As has often been the case, my sense of a lack of balance in a current management fad served as the irritant that provoked my creative juices to flow at last. What I produced was, in my own view, something not unlike the pearl that also encapsulates an irritant. It was my concept of the need for balance between alignment and attunement in organizations.

By organizational *alignment,* I mean a condition in which the members of an organization voluntarily line up or enlist themselves in the pursuit of organizational goals and purposes. By *attunement,* I mean a condition in which an individual, group, or organization is aware of and responds cooperatively to its *relationships* with other entities in its environment or with the total system of which it is a part.

Around this time, the concept of organizational alignment alone was coming into the thinking of other OD consultants and forward-thinking managers, and the work of Peters and Waterman on excellent companies was the subject of intense management interest. I listened to Tom Peters describe his vision of the "hands-on, vision-driven organization," which he later wrote about in *A Passion for Excellence* (1985) and it disturbed me. During my work with new plant start-ups, I had experienced organizations that sounded a lot like those Tom described: they were full of energy and excitement, they had a shared purpose to which people were strongly committed, they were focused on a mission, and they shared some values. In terms of the style tracks of the Positive Power & Influence Program, they had a lot of Common Vision (inspiration and common goals) and a lot of Assertive Persuasion (rational argument and problem solving). These organizations did not run on Reward and Punishment (use of authority to compel compliance), but neither was there much Participation and Trust (openness and caring). During the eighties, I consulted to two of the foremost research and development organizations in the free world, and they certainly did manifest the qualities that Peters and Waterman attributed to high-performing organizations. They regularly produced breakthroughs, and their technical people at all levels were self-motivated and passionate about their work. These organizations were also egalitarian almost to a fault. There was a sense of energy and high excitement about these places, and among their people, there was high morale, camaraderie, and a sense of being among an elite.

At this time, consultants were also beginning to work with organizations to develop corporate visions of the future around which organizational members were supposed to become aligned. Charles Kiefer and Peter Senge and their colleagues were offering Leadership and Mastery, a popular and impactful program that, among other things, taught managers how to promote organizational alignment through developing a personal vision and enrolling others in it. However, I saw something lacking.

Naming the Shadow Side of High-Performing Organizations

What concerned me was that few people in my field were saying much about the dark side of these high-performing systems. I had some good discussions with Jerry Harvey and Peter Vaill, but most of what was in print extolled the virtues of alignment. (Peter later wrote about the dark side in *Managing as a Performing Art*, 1989.) For most employees, these new systems were certainly an improvement on the traditional organization, dominated by authority and bureaucracy, that most people have worked in during much of this century.

Nevertheless, as I have experienced them, high-performing organizations seem flawed as places for people to live and work over the long haul. They demand that members sacrifice their time, energy, social and family lives, and even health to advance the task. The extraordinary personal effort that other organizations expect on an emergency basis becomes an everyday pattern in these high-performing organizations. Over time, people burn out. Such an organization may overrely upon its vision to organize the work and may have inadequate and underutilized systems. It may develop an elitist faith in its own dream and become unresponsive to disconfirming information from the wider environment. (This behavior may be illustrated, for example, by the Bay of Pigs groupthink episode during the Kennedy Administration. In this episode, members of the president's inner circle were so caught up in their sense of mission that they suppressed dissenting opinions and ignored adverse intelligence. Consequently, they sent many men to certain death in an abortive invasion of Cuba.) In this organization, valued ends may come to justify tawdry or even evil means. After all, the passion for excellence is essentially amoral. When one reads Albert Speer's (1981) account of the heady days of the Nazi industrial war effort, for example, it sounds very much like current descriptions of high-performing organizations.

It seemed to me that aligned organizations were often *daimonic*, a word I borrowed from Rollo May (1969) that means the unbalanced or perverted form of a virtuous quality. In the enthusiasm for vision and alignment in these organizations, I thought I could see the workings of the same passion for individualism that I had identified as tearing rents in the social fabric of organizations and the wider society and also destroying the environment. To me, that individualism was (and is) the fundamental daimonism of our society. I could see it in my own determination to succeed at any cost to myself and my relationships; I could see it in the increasing instrumentalism in organizations, according to which people were valued according to their contribution to the task; I could see it in the single-minded focus on economic performance that resulted in formerly valued employees suddenly becoming human garbage that was put out on the street without concern for the social consequences of unemployment. In the pursuit of the liberation and empowerment of the individual, people had created a world in which the relatedness of things and people was ignored. In that world, the single-minded pursuit of organizational goals could be applauded without concern for its impact on the larger systems of which the organization was a part.

As a former freedom fighter for the individual in organizations, I could not but applaud the movement away from managing workers by rewards and punishments, and rules and regulations, toward endeavoring to enlist the voluntary motivation of a workforce that was growing more internally motivated and autonomous. I certainly did not want to reverse that direction. Rather, I wanted to find ways for all individuals to balance the aligned pursuit of their private visions with an *attunement* to the *context* in which that pursuit took place. I wanted to find ways to develop their appreciation of connections, relationships, and their place in a larger whole, whether that whole was made up of an organization's immediate stakeholders (customers, suppliers, investors) or the entire planet. I saw organizational alignment as an expression of human *will* through intellect and activity. I saw attunement as an expression of human *love* through appreciation and cooperation with those organizations, entities, and systems to which we are connected. I believed that if organizations could appreciate and nurture those connections, those "ties that bind," we could achieve balanced and harmonious internal environments—and I believed that developing people's ability to appreciate their connections with larger wholes just might develop the understanding necessary to save our planet from destruction by humankind's economic activities.

Is Problem Solving Hazardous to Organizational Health?

A related theme for me was what I have since come to think of as the iatrogenic qualities of the problem-solving process in most organizations. *Iatrogenic* describes a disease produced by a cure or attempted cure for, usually, another disease, and I was beginning to believe that a lot of problem-solving activities in organizations created more problems than they solved. The following passage from my paper "Strategies for A New Age" (1983, 1984 [†"Leadership and Strategy for a New Age"]) expresses my concern as well as I could today:

> During the last few of my twenty-five years as a management consultant, I have been impressed with the seeming intractability of organization problems. I ask myself why it is that so many of our attempted solutions seem either to produce no effect, or else appear to exacerbate the problems they were designed to solve.
>
> For example, why is it that decades of human relations training for supervisors and managers have not produced committed and happy workers? Is it only a coincidence that as information systems make more information available to managers, it becomes more difficult to make decisions? Why have incentive systems so often failed to keep productivity high, and why have more psychologi-

cally "sound" attempts to motivate workers had similarly ambiguous outcomes? Is there any connection between the development of sophisticated planning systems and the increasingly unpredictable fluctuations in the environment? How is it that organizations seem so unmanageable just at the point when we have learned so much about the arts and sciences of management? [1983, p. 209; 1984, p. 97]

At the time I wrote those words, I had no real answer to the questions I posed. I knew only that most of my clients preferred action to reflection, and I suspected them of going off half-cocked, implementing solutions before they understood the wider and deeper implications of the problems they were trying to solve. It seemed to me that the aligned organization's single-pointed focus on moving through or around any barrier to its goals was part of the difficulty and that the sensitivity to context, relationships, and timing typical of the attunement orientation would be healing and balancing in most aligned organizations. I thought, too, that there was a need for aligned organizations and individuals to redirect some of their energy for action into learning, especially learning that focused on understanding the *system* of which their organizations or units or selves were a part.

In Search of Wholeness in Organizations

In developing my ideas, I was greatly helped by some of the thinkers who visited the ICE during those years, particularly Willis Harman and François Duquesne. At the time I met him, François was Focalizer of the New Age community at Findhorn, Scotland. When he presented his thinking about spirit in organizations, one of his key concepts led directly to my understanding of how vital the balance between alignment and attunement is to organizational performance and health.

François Duquesne said that every organism, to be whole, must be connected to the Highest and also to the planet. When it is connected to the Highest, it is inspired by spirit. When it is connected to the planet, it is nourished by the Earth.

When an organism or organization loses its harmony with the Highest, it becomes dispirited; it loses inspiration and creativity; it lacks the energy and vitality of its members' high values and ideals; it is starved of love and becomes an abrasive, soul-deadening environment in which to live and work. When an organism or organization lacks a grounding and harmonious connection to the Earth, it loses physical and emotional vitality and strength.

When, as is true in many large organizations, the connections to spirit and to the Earth are both damaged or cut off, the organization receives neither spiritual nor material nourishment. It runs only on its accumulated energy, its stored wealth serving to buy the motivation of its members to perform their tasks. Eventually, it will sicken or die. But when organizations are aligned in the pursuit of high purposes and are also grounded in an appreciation of their connection with the many manifestations of nature, they tend to thrive and prosper. They are enlivened and energized by spirit from above, and they are attuned to their environment, their technologies, their customers and suppliers, and to events in the wider worldly environment.

The connection between this kind of attunement and love may not be immediately obvious. Yet it has seemed to me from the start that attunement to connections and relationships requires the action of love. It is love in its various forms that creates the ties that bind, that causes people to enjoy connection and cooperation. Were it not for love, we would not be drawn to connect. We might connect for momentary advantage, but there would be nothing of our hearts in our alliances.

Going Public with Attunement and Love

While I was still playing with the ideas of alignment and attunement, I was given an opportunity to go public with them. In 1982, the ICE was commissioned to produce a report on the emerging paradigm in organizations for the Values and Lifestyles Project of SRI International, and Barry McWaters asked me to write it. I was not sure what the new paradigm was, but I wrote a report called "Leadership and Strategy for a New Age." It was later substantially revised and published, first, as "Strategies for a New Age" (Harrison, 1983) and, second, as "Leadership and Strategy for a New Age" (Harrison, 1984 [†]). The later publication is actually the original version.

In the ensuing years, I have returned again and again to the issues I raised in that paper. It was seminal for me; the roots of everything I have thought and written since then can be found there. I suspect that may be true until I die.

Even thirteen years later, it is not hard for me to summon up the combination of excitement and fear with which I approached the task of coming out of the closet with my assertions about the importance of releasing the power of love in the workplace. I had gone to a country cabin where I often retire to think and write, and I can remember pacing the floor on a cold and rainy afternoon, asking myself (and Diana) if I really dared do it. I saw myself as a person with a reputation for rationality and hard-headedness and clarity of thought. I felt that I was about to cross into a country from which there would be no returning. Once I identified myself as a New Age thinker, there would be no easy way I could lose that identity, and that felt like a huge risk. Yet it also felt like a risk I had to take, because it was the next step in linking my work to my personal evolution, and I knew that unless I could make such links I would lose the energy I always bring to my work when I am on my growing edge.

My own ambivalence was reflected in responses I received when I circulated the report to colleagues asking for comments preparatory to revising it for publication. The responses divided into two camps. At the extreme of one camp were a couple of letters that said something like this: "I read your paper with tears rolling down my cheeks. It is so good to feel that I am not alone. You have put into words what I have been feeling, and it gives me the confidence to go on." The other set of responses came from people who, because they cared about me and about my reputation, wanted me to find other words to use in place of "love." One said, "I really like the ideas in your draft, but I can't show this to my Managing Director as long as you use the word 'love' in the paper. Could you use caring, or nurturing, or something less stark?"

My inner response to that was, "No, I do not think I can use another word. It is the right and true word and the word that carries the power of the process that it represents." I had found in myself a strong intuition to the effect that there is power in using the true name of love, and I have since been grateful to myself for trusting that intuition. In 1968, Ursula LeGuin wrote a wonderful book called *A Wizard of Earthsea,* in which she wove a myth around the idea of the power one evokes when using the true names of things. In her story, wizards learn the true names of things from the ancient language of dragons; knowing the true names enables them to summon, but not always to control, the power contained in the things they name. I believe LeGuin's myth to contain a kernel of great truth, and thus I believe that if I were to use a euphemism for love, I would not be able to evoke either the longings or the resistance that people have for love in organizations or for love in their lives. I would not be able to provoke people to confront the issue of love strongly and take a stand on it, for or against. People had been talking about "caring" in organizations forever, and I had not noticed that that word provoked much more than a big yawn when it was used. I wanted to evoke the power of love in a powerful way. However, I also wanted to do so without completely losing credibility with and access to the high-level organizational leaders with whom I wanted to work.

One event that pushed me to trust my judgment and intuition about how to talk about love was the experience Dave Berlew and I had earlier with bringing personal power out of the closet and into the open in some of the organizations in which we had worked with the Positive Power & Influence Program. We had introduced the program at a time when speaking openly about power in many organizations was like telling a risqué story in mixed company. Part of the attraction the program had for people back then was the feeling that they were about to be initiated into something forbidden and secret—and somewhat disreputable. For example, we had some clients who said, "We like your program, but we'd like to take the word 'power' out of it. It's too strong a word to use in our organization." We always gave them permission, but in the end, they almost always left the word in!

My intuition and hope as I sought a way to release the power of love in organizations was that the need for my work would develop in organizations over time. I took a calculated risk that felt much greater than the risk Dave and I had taken with our work on power. Indeed, love is always riskier than power, which I suppose is why so many people use power instead of love. So, although I did not have a vehicle for working with issues of love in organizations and had no clue as to what such a vehicle would be, I did feel I had a task worthy of my talents and worthy of all my accumulated experience.

It took several years for me to come to grips with the question of how to work with, or even simply talk with, leaders and managers on releasing love in organizations. I found myself taking long periods of time off from work, spending endless hours playing with my computer, joining a local hospice program as a volunteer, and building a rather eclectic consulting and management training practice. I was still driven by a deep insecurity about money that frequently led me to orient my practice toward maximizing my income rather than my enjoyment or the quality of my relationships. Indeed, I have often wondered why someone so insecure about money should have chosen to live by his wits as an independent consultant rather than taking a safer position in the academic or business world. All I am sure about is that I have always felt more constrained by routine, bureaucracy, and authority than I have been frightened by uncertainty. That has led me to choose to live on the edge and to deal with my feelings of insecurity by working harder and, sometimes, by choosing money over what I love.

Healing the Trauma of Change

It took me until the mid eighties to decide that I would be better off avoiding management training and focusing instead on consulting to high-level executives. While I was casting about for ways to bring love into the workplace and also looking for heartful ways to use my expertise in training design, I developed some programs directed toward organizational healing. One that was particularly successful was designed for Transamerica Relocation Services. The company offered a third-party relocation service, buying the homes of clients' employees who were being transferred to other locations. However, in the early eighties, housing prices had begun trending down, and what had started out as a benefit for transferred employees often turned into a nightmare for all concerned. First, in that time of recession and organizational restructuring, many employees were being offered the choice of losing their jobs or moving somewhere they did not want to be. And second, when their houses were appraised, the houses were sometimes found to be worth less than the original cost, resulting in disastrous losses for the affected employees. Some unfortunate souls lost their entire equity, which was often their only real savings. When a Transamerica account executive phoned to let a client's employee know the appraised fair market value of his or her home, disbelief, turning to rage, was a frequent response.

What was needed was a program that would train and coach account executives to deal with angry and traumatized people in a way that was humane and healing rather than adversarial. I designed and conducted such a program together with two talented women: my wife, Diana, and psychotherapist Ginger Blume, both of whom went on to use various versions of it with their own clients. In our workshop, the account executives were introduced to Elizabeth Kubler-Ross's model (1969) of the psychological stages that people go through over time when they approach their own deaths from an incurable disease such as cancer. We reinterpreted the "irrational" behavior of the employees as a natural response to unacceptable loss, and defined the account executives' role as that of facilitating the healing process. Helpful and unhelpful behaviors at each of Kubler-Ross's stages of recovery from loss were identified, and the account executives role-played, recorded, and analyzed samples of their own behavior in dealing with angry, emotional clients. They coached one another in using the behaviors most likely to move a person's healing along and to get the person through the procedures that were needed for his or her house to be purchased. The program ended with some work on managing one's own stress.

The Trauma Program was healing for the account executives. They, like many others in customer service work, tended to be warm, friendly, helpful people. They hated being the source of bad news, and they often became defensive and unhelpful under the pressure of hostility and abuse from their clients. It helped them to step back and see themselves as not the real target and to learn the skills with which they could facilitate the healing process. The skills enabled them to be of real help even though the interactions still did not feel good. Transamerica not only used the program internally, but took it on the road as a service and public relations offering for relocation officers of clients and prospective clients. I felt the program was a milestone in my work with business, in that, for the first time, I had a vehicle that tapped into and amplified the natural desire people have to help one another when they are in trouble. At the best, we enabled our workshop participants to transform a conflict into a moment of healing. At the least, they usually were able to avoid a vicious spiral of escalating conflict and to make space for time to play its healing role.

The Trauma Program also served as a platform for a more general program on managing conflict in organizations. Diana, Ginger Blume, and I developed a training program that integrated powerful ideas from a number of sources, notably Neil Rackham's groundbreaking work on negotiation and Fisher, Ury, and Patton's book *Getting to Yes* (1981). I had worked with Neil some years before in England, and I still believe him to be one of the most creative applied behavioral scientists on either side of the Atlantic. When Fisher, Ury, and Patton's book came out, I saw the possibility of a winning creative synthesis among their ideas. I saw these ideas as leading to healing: establishing a frame of principle rather than one of power, being creative in finding alternative currencies by means of which both parties can be satisfied, distinguishing between needs and wants or demands, and using questioning techniques to determine the other party's needs.

In working on conflict management, I also formed an idea that has since become a cornerstone of my thought on healing in organizations. I came to understand the central role of fear as a barrier to conflict resolution, problem solving, and even learning in organizations. Therefore, an important part of our program was its focus on reducing one's own and the other's *fear of loss*. The idea is simple, yet the implications are huge. When people are operating at high levels of fear, they are not very good problem solvers. Fear narrows the range of alternatives people can consider. Fear reduces their ability to take in and process information, especially if it is complex. Fear predisposes them to premature closure and precipitate reactions. High fear leads people to persevere in tactics and strategies that are not working.

The results of fear are precisely the perceptual and behavioral processes that keep conflicts going. It seemed elegantly simple to me that by reducing their fear (and increasing their trust), both parties to a conflict could have access to higher levels of their creativity and intelligence and then use that creativity and intelligence to find a way through to agreement. Nowadays, when downsizing, reorganizations, and changes in roles and responsibilities are an everyday fact of many individuals' work lives, it is critically important to find ways to reduce the level of fear in most organizations. The search for those means is now a central part of my thought and practice.

Lots of Ammunition But No Shooters

The programs on trauma and conflict were both solid products, well received by clients and participants alike. I had high hopes for them, partly because the United States was entering a period when many people were to experience disappointments in their careers and financial expectations. In the Trauma Program, I felt we had a helpful offering for those whose task it was to carry the bad news. The program on conflict management also addressed a growing need. As organizations become more flat and fluid, it becomes less viable for individuals to rely upon role specifications and authority figures to mediate their differences. They need to acquire skills to resolve disputes without the use of authority.

I was clear, however, that I did not want to place myself in the role of selling and conducting a training program once again, if only because it seemed a diversion from my work on releasing love in the workplace. As a result, the two programs remain unexploited to this day, except for a book written in Dutch by my friend and colleague Hans Zuidema, based on the concepts in the trauma program. In divorcing from Situation Management Systems, I had ended some serious conflicts, but I had also lost the creative give-and-take between commercial and creative interests that had given my training designs to the world.

Training Does Not Lead to Organizational Change

Although I felt good about the products we had developed, in that each of them had a heart and appealed to participants' higher values and feelings, I knew that no training program ever changed an organization's culture; in every case I have seen or known about, a strategy of leading organizational change with training has been a prescription for disappointment.

Change is led by *people* using a combination of power, structural and process redesign, and personal charisma, not by training programs. This is not to say that training has no significant role to play in organizational change, but its value depends upon timing, motivation, and opportunity for application. Training is most effective when it is offered to (not imposed upon) organizational members at a time when they see change happening or about to happen around them, and some of them become concerned enough to prepare themselves to cope with or take advantage of the change. They are then internally motivated to learn, and the organization is sufficiently into the process of change that it offers opportunities to apply new learning on the job. If change is not seen as imminent, training for it is often seen as an irrelevant burden by already busy people, and when they return from that training, the organization offers few incentives or opportunities to apply what they have learned. In such situations, training usually adds to the already heavy weight of cynicism and mistrust that the change managers must endeavor to overcome.

A New Support Group

A major influence on me as I brought my new work forward was, once again, a personal/professional support group. One of the peculiarities of my mind is that most of the time I literally do not know what I think until I hear myself say it or I see it as text. Therefore, it has always been vital to my creativity to have colleagues, wives, or lovers with whom I can talk about the issues in my life and work, and who participate as coparents or midwives in bringing my, or our, dreams into form. My life has been incredibly rich with such persons, who always seem to appear when I need them most and who, through their listening and active participation, love the ideas into reality.

The group I was involved in during these years evolved out of a series of afternoon meetings I had with Juanita Brown as we endeavored to support one another in coping with that perennial dilemma of the successful consultant, saying no. At the time, each of us was wanting to create more time in his or her life for play, rest, and creative work, and from that fairly narrow focus, our discussions came to cover the entire range of our hopes and dreams for ourselves, our work, and our profession. After a while we included others in our group, meeting every three weeks or so in the late afternoon at Juanita's house in San Francisco and continuing through dinner and into the early evening. The group consisted of Emmett and Sandy Miller, Sharon Lehrer, Juanita, and myself. Our pattern was for each of us to "check in" first with what was happening in his or her life and work; we would then eat, and afterwards we would spend the remaining time working with one or two members of the group who had issues that were "hot." The meetings were often intense and deeply personal and were characterized by a blend of high trust and high confrontation.

I spent a lot of my time with the group agonizing over my inability to find a way of packaging the deep convictions I had set forth in "Leadership and Strategy for a New Age" (Harrison, 1984) in a form that high-level managers would be able to hear. I wanted to speak publicly about problem solving as injurious to organizational health and about releasing the power of love in the workplace. But I did not want my ideas to be dismissed as California psychobabble. I believed I needed to anchor my ideas in a rational framework that spoke to the realities with which leaders and managers must cope. I wanted to establish myself as credible, to fit within my audience's framework of ideas in good currency, and from that credible position, to challenge the framework in some fairly outrageous ways.

A real breakthrough for me came when our group spent a weekend at my family's summer cabin, and the others all helped me work out a framework for talking about my ideas. The people in the group were particularly good with graphic symbols and diagrams for getting ideas across visually and they encouraged me to try hard at using icons and symbols. I came away with much greater confidence, based partly on the work we did on organizing the material for presentation and partly on the feeling that if these people, whom I loved and respected so much, were willing to spend so much time helping me with my project, there must be something of value in it!

Next, Juanita and I jointly proposed a presentation on our ideas for the Organization Development Network Conference to be held in October 1985 in San Francisco. In preparation for that presentation, I used a Macintosh computer to make a set of overhead transparencies with icons and diagrams to illustrate my words, something I had never previously done. I was to find subsequently that making overheads for presentations was a powerful way of organizing my thoughts simply and succinctly, much more powerful than writing sentences and paragraphs.

The conference was a watershed for me. Juanita and I were well received, and I felt I now had a framework that, while it was far from elegant, would work and could be improved upon with each subsequent presentation. We had gone public with our colleagues, and it felt as though there was an answering resonance, a sense of many others groping and moving in the same general direction. Since my belief is that consultants generally precede (but, alas, do not necessarily lead) their clients in new thought, I felt the reaction was an auspicious omen. I was encouraged to seek audiences further afield, and during the next year or so, I gave more presentations in the United States and also in Britain, Scandinavia, and the Netherlands.

Along with the boost given to the development of my ideas by the group, these upbeat events were facilitated by an intense reorientation in my personal life that brought me out of my depression and gave me renewed energy for my work. The key event in that reorientation occurred in 1984. Until that time, my life had been divided roughly into three spheres: work, family, and spirituality. After that time, my life became more integrated and less compartmentalized, increasingly flowing together in ways that are sometimes harmonious, sometimes chaotic. This change is discussed in the next chapter.

I have organized the following chapters more by issues and concerns than by chronology. Each deals with much the same period in my life. Chapter Seven deals with my work, Chapter Eight with my personal and spiritual development, Chapter Nine with my deeper learnings about OD, and Chapter Ten with the issue of surrender, which I believe has important implications for our work with organizations. Table 6.1 provides an overview of the interplay of time and issues in my life from 1980 to the present.

TABLE 6.1. PROGRESSION OF MY CONCEPTS AND SPIRITUAL JOURNEY.

Year	Concept	Writing	Events/Projects/ Relationships	Personality and Journey	Spirituality
1980	Alignment versus attune-ment shows need for love in organizations.	"Leadership and Strategy for a New Age" (Harrison, 1984 [†])			Focus on basics: "being a good person"
1981	Problem solving is injurious to organizational health.		Leave Situation Management Systems	Depressed, dispirited (to 1983)	
1982			Healing the Trauma of Relocation program		Volunteer at a hospice
1983	A culture model can be used to talk about love in organizations.	*Diagnosing Organization Culture* (Harrison and Stokes, 1992)	Conflict management program	Reorientation from work to relationships	
1984	Appreciation and inclusive-ness are organi-zational strengths.	*Organization Culture and Quality of Service* (Harrison, 1987b [†])	Zen community project (to 1985)		

TABLE 6.1. (CONTINUED)

Year	Concept	Writing	Events/Projects Relationships	Personality and Journey	Spirituality
1985		"Serving the Customer: Managing Transition to a More Responsive Organization" (now Chapter 8 in Harrison, 1995)	New Age presentations to OD Network and in Britain, Holland, Sweden; electric utility project (to 1986)		Encounter psychics; begin to develop own psychic abilities
1986	Alignment and attunement come together via the alchemical crucible of mission workshops.	"Harnessing Personal Energy: How Companies Can Inspire Employees" (Harrison, 1987a [† "How to Focus Personal Energy with Organizational Mission Statements"])	Mission Development Workshop		
1987	Models of organizational consciousness can be created.	Building an Organization Vision and Mission Statement (Harrison, 1988)	Findhorn Community study; culture change in R&D company (to 1990)	Divorce; relationship with Celest (to 1990)	Open to subtle energies: Reiki; harmonic convergence
1988		"On Community" (now Chapters 15–17 in Harrison, 1995)			
1989			Organization Culture Workshop	Retreat center board (to 1991)	Visit to Sai Baba ashram in India
1990	Organization change is a function of organizational consciousness.	"Culture and Levels of Consciousness in Organizations" (Harrison, 1990 [†])	Culture workshops in India, Britain; talk on organizational consciousness in Britain	Living alone but in community at Ananda	Revisit India; join Ananda Community

1991	Healing the trauma of organization change; mutuality is the organization culture of the future.	*Humanizing Change—Matching Interventions to Organizational Realities* (Harrison, Cooper, and Dawes, 1991)		Healing and letting go; death of my father
1992	Fear and bias for action are barriers to organizational learning.	*Towards the Learning Organization—Promises and Pitfalls* (Harrison, 1992)	Workshops and first project on organizational healing	Begin relationship with Margaret Deabill · Work with devas (nature spirits)
1993		Collected papers and professional autobiography		Take responsibility for own spiritual path
1994				Understand mutuality as the basis for relationship with spirit

CHAPTER SEVEN

SEARCHING FOR A PATH WITH HEART

I began 1984 still depressed and dispirited, struggling to understand why I could not bring energy to my work. During the last few years, I had entertained a host of schemes for enlivening my work. I had thought seriously about starting a small business based on the principles I had been espousing for so long. Maybe, I thought, I should put my time, energy, and money where my mouth is. I had entered therapy again, in an attempt to find a deeper cause for my lack of spirit, and after a while, I was encouraged both by close friends and the therapist to consult a Chilean psychic who was said to give very accurate readings leading to major changes in his clients' lives. At that time I felt really blocked and I figured it would not hurt to try something new. The psychic told me there was nothing wrong with my work and that I was lucky to have found so easily the right work for me but that I did not approach it properly. He said part of the source of my malaise was that I did not know how to rest, and he prescribed short rests at intervals during the day. As for the rest, he told me I was dissatisfied in my marriage and was trying to make up for it through work.

The forty-five minutes I spent with "David" changed my state of mind profoundly. I felt *seen*. His positive observations about my work and life felt both true and liberating. They were also scary, threatening the stability of my pattern of doing and being. However, I was ready for change because my life was not working. I walked out of the session with the feeling that I had a new lease on life, a path ahead that was risky, but one I could follow toward the light.

I visited several psychics during this period, and I have done so on occasion since then. My early experiences suggested to me that it might be possible to develop a sensitivity to subtle energies and so receive intuitive information that could guide and heal. I have always taken some pride in my willingness to follow my curiosity wherever it leads and, after exercising a little prudence, to put all claims to the test of personal experience. I have also tended to assume that if others could do a thing, I could, too, although perhaps not as well as someone with a very special gift. Therefore, I have experimented with a variety of ways to enhance my own intuitive abilities, with some success. In Chapter Ten I discuss my explorations in greater depth. Of course, I am aware that my experiences will not weigh very heavily with those who are already convinced that there is nothing of value to be discovered in exploring extrasensory ways of knowing, and that discussing these matters may, for them, cast doubts on my credibility in other areas. However, it feels important to me to be open about what I have learned, and to treat the unseen as a domain we can explore empirically just like any other domain. I try to draw my conclusions from personal experience and to avoid ideological disputes and leaps of faith.

Looking for a Model for Love in Organizations

Until 1986 or so, I continued the training work I had started in conflict management, but what increasingly captured my attention was the search for ways to talk to leaders and managers about love while both holding their attention and maintaining my credibility. At first, my efforts were in the mental and rational domains. I wanted to touch people's hearts in organizations, but I relied primarily on my mind to carry the work forward. I was cautious about letting my passion be seen lest I lose credibility. My underlying but not entirely conscious belief was that I could persuade leaders and managers to explore ways to release the power of love in organizations if I could also show them how it could be good for business and good for them and their people.

My first need was for a simple model to which others could relate. When I was casting about for one, I had one of those serendipitous experiences that remind me I do not have to do everything for myself. I had been asked to appear on a panel at the annual meeting of the Academy of Management, and I arrived at the meeting room a few minutes early, just as Tom Janz of the University of Calgary was finishing a talk on his development of a questionnaire designed to measure organization culture. The dimensions he had discovered through careful statistical work were congruent with those Charles Handy and I had come up with intuitively in 1970 (Handy, 1985; Harrison, 1972c [†]). During the question period, someone pointed out the similarity and asked Tom if he was familiar with my work. When Tom said he was not, the questioner remarked that I was in the audience and it might be worthwhile for us to get together.

I am always excited when I find someone else going in a direction congruent with mine, and Tom Janz rekindled my interest in organization culture. I decided it was time to dust that interest off and take advantage of what was rapidly becoming a management fad for books and articles on the topic. I reworked my model and redid from scratch the quick-and-dirty culture questionnaire I had dashed off in the seventies. Tom and I collaborated on statistical studies, which supported the construct validity of both our questionnaires, and I collected normative data so that people using the questionnaires could compare their scores with those of a reference group. Later, I was joined by Herb Stokes, who found the questionnaire helpful in his High Performing Systems workshops for work redesign teams. Herb found that the cultures I had called achievement and support expressed the values that self-managing teams wanted to move toward, while the power culture and, less strongly, the role culture represented what the teams wanted to move away from. Herb did a fine job of rewriting questions to be unambiguous to shop-floor personnel, and for six years I distributed our joint version of the questionnaire, *Diagnosing Organization Culture,* by mail order. Now Pfeiffer & Company distributes it, having published it in 1992 (Harrison and Stokes).

Talking About Love in Organizations

I spent a lot of time on the road with the culture model and my new questionnaire, talking to any group that would listen. I described the four cultures—power, role, achievement, and support—and I showed how power and role were typical of traditional organizations, and how Tom Peters's work implied the need for organization cultures that were low on power and role and high on achievement and support. I would then describe the dark side of the achievement culture, showing how its addictive, exploitative tendencies needed to be balanced with the nurturing and healing qualities of the support culture. I was aided in my exposition by questionnaire scores collected from the participants. The scores usually showed that the participants saw their organizations as quite high on power and role but preferred an organization that was high on achievement and support.

As I continued to talk with leaders and managers about love, I experienced a subtle but real shift in the response of my audiences. From an initial attitude of skepticism and indifference, I began to sense a hunger on the part of members of organizations for a softer, more cooperative ambiance, although individuals were (and still are) uncertain how to move their organizations in that direction. It became easy for me to speak openly of the power of love, partly because I was becoming more clear and centered in myself but also because the concept was seeping into the conversations of people in business. I well remember my excitement when the CEO of Wells Fargo Bank used the L-word in a speech to employees, and before long, other leaders were using it occasionally. By the end of the eighties, while I could not say that love was an idea in good currency in organizations, it had become fairly easy to engage leaders and managers in dialogue about it. I could even begin to imagine a day when people would offer training courses in "Loving Leadership," perhaps trivializing the concept in the process!

Can We Make Love Happen in Organizations?

During the eighties, I gave many talks in Europe and the United States. For whatever reason, I often find it easier to risk my new ideas in front of European audiences. I have been fortunate in my European friends, who have provided me in recent years with many opportunities to share my work: Ian Cunningham, formerly of the Roffey Park Management Institute, Edward Posey of The Business Network, Jean Lawrence with the Association for Management Education and Development, Ian Hall of Salford University, Jo Cumming of the Kiel Management Centre, Ruth Handy of the Irish Management Institute, Roger Benson from Findhorn, and Pieter Kruijt and Pieter ter Haar of the Netherlands.

I found European audiences more open than their U.S. counterparts to my ideas about love in organizations, and therefore, it was all the more distressing that I could not meet their need for guidance in carrying my ideas forward into practice. I remember a poignant episode in Holland on a night on which Pieter ter Haar and his wife hosted a gathering for me that included some high-level managers. I was in good form that evening. The atmosphere was electric, and the response to my talk was warmly appreciative. Afterward, two key executives came up to say how moved they were by my presentation and to ask if I could tell them how to begin to implement my ideas. I told them I had not gotten very far with that, and they warned me with great sincerity and tact that if I could not provide guidance for implementation, my efforts would not soon see fruit.

I took such criticisms seriously and set to work. My paper "Organization Culture and Quality of Service: A Strategy for Releasing Love in the Workplace" (Harrison, 1987b [†"Organization Culture and Quality of Service"]) was written to persuade managers of the practical value of the support culture. Service quality was becoming a management fad, and the issue provided an opportunity to awaken leaders to the benefits of releasing the power of love in the organization. I told leaders that people who deal with an organization's environment will act out of the basic cultural assumptions of the organization and will thus deal with customers, suppliers, and the public very much the way they are treated by the organization—as within, so without. I identified four styles of service, one for each of the four organization cultures, and the paper illustrates how the internal culture of the organization affects the quality of service given. For example, highly bureaucratic (role-oriented) organizations can excel at systems that provide fast, efficient service for well-defined customer needs; they do badly, however, at matching service to *individual* customer needs or to special situations, and they tend to be more machine-like than caring and concerned. The support-oriented culture, on the other hand, is well suited to providing individual attention and heartful service but may be inefficient and poorly organized.

An Endeavor to Implement Quality of Service

I made a strategic error in publishing the paper on culture and quality in Britain; it never became well known in the United States. However, my work since "Leadership and Strategy for a New Age" (Harrison, 1984 [†]) has been much circulated from hand to hand, and a copy of "Organization Culture and Quality of Service" did find its way to an internal consultant in an electric utility company. I was given a chance to show what I could do to improve the quality of customer service there, and although the project was not a success, it led to more understanding (a great learning experience!) and two more papers: "Managing Transition to a More Responsive Organization" (see Harrison, 1995), and "Harnessing Personal Energy: How Companies Can Inspire Employees" (Harrison, 1987a [†"How to Focus Personal Energy with Organizational Mission Statements"]).

The first paper was originally written as a competitive proposal to the utility company. (In writing it, I was greatly helped by the counsel of Flo Hoylman, a senior consultant at Pacific Gas & Electric Company, who really came through for me when I was struggling.) But the actual course of events did not greatly resemble the proposal, as is often the case with OD projects. Although I pride myself on my ability to be adaptive and innovative and to spot opportunities when they arise, I should dearly have loved to stick with this proposal, had circumstances permitted. I still like the piece as a blueprint for major organization change, and I would alter little of it now. While, as I said, I learned important things during this consulting assignment, I did not learn as much about improving service as I had hoped. At the heart of my vision of the project, and the basis on which I had sold myself as consultant, was the idea of changing the culture of the organization to one that supported initiative and caring responsiveness on the part of service providers. However, like many other consultants, I had woefully underestimated the magnitude of the task of culture change, especially in traditional businesses. As regulated enterprises, utilities have had good reason to be among the most bureaucratic businesses there are. The idea of empowering service providers to bend the rules and solve customers' problems on the spot was attractive to people in the organization—in theory. However, the organization was a quagmire of antiquated rules. There was also almost no organizational precedent for risk taking and initiative, and few role models.

My strategy was to set up a pilot district and to experiment with changing work systems and procedures to empower the service providers. Concurrently, we on the change team would coach work teams to adopt behaviors congruent with the new vision. We set up a design team of line managers who were also engineers and who, together with the internal consultant, were assigned full-time to implement the change plan. The site was difficult to get to, and the budget did not support my being there often enough to stay on top of the project, so I came in once or twice a month to coach and consult with the team. Given the ambitious scope of the project, the lack of change experience on the part of the design team, and the nature of the utility's culture, I simply was not there enough to make a real difference.

Early in the project, we had convened a group of customer service supervisors and asked them to tell us what prevented them from giving the quality of service they wanted to give. It quickly became clear that these people were motivated to give much more responsive service than they felt empowered to provide, and this is not unusual. I have consistently found that people in bureaucratic organizations want to give better service than they are permitted to give. When these people become cynical and unresponsive with time, that is usually a function of their frustration with the systems rather than an inherent quality of the people themselves. In this case, we soon discovered that the utility's rules were a great inhibitor of responsive service. Within a few minutes, the group of supervisors had identified more than fifty blocks and barriers to service, and most of these had to do with constraining rules and regulations that had been created to prevent some extremely unlikely occurrence either from occurring or recurring. For example, there was a rule that prevented hooking up the electricity in a new house until after the county building inspector had checked the wiring. Because it was difficult to coordinate with the inspectors, this rule often resulted in endless delays in finishing construction. The rule was in place to prevent the utility's liability exposure in case bad wiring were to lead to a fire, or some similar hazard, but as far as anyone knew, this had never happened.

To change the rules and then to change the field practices required that the work systems be understood in depth and that a process be planned and implemented for obtaining support and agreement from those functional managers who had a stake in the current rules and might experience themselves at risk when the rules were changed. It meant taking lots of initiatives both upward and laterally in the organization in order to enroll the guardians of the bureaucracy in a vision of improved service and to obtain their support for specific changes. However, the engineers on the design team tended to see their jobs in terms of implementing projects to conform to a set of specifications within a context of standard rules and procedures. They were not used to making rules or changing them, especially when that action might require that they take risks in communicating upward and influencing people. It proved quite difficult for the members of the design team to take the roles of change agents after years during which their only relationship with the rules and systems was to obey them! In this company, even the idea of a task force that would take responsibility for planning, organizing, and implementing a major change was quite without precedent. The team spent a lot of time waiting for direction, because I was only there once or twice a month, and the vice president to whom the team reported was supportive but terribly busy. Part of his inaccessibility to the team members was also created by their lack of comfort in asking him for the help they needed. This company offered security, a sense of stability and family, and a work life that was not too demanding and stressful. In this, it was similar to utility companies around the United States, but it may have possessed these qualities even more strongly than other utilities because of its location in a predominately rural and chronically economically depressed area. The company was old and traditional, and it was typical for two or three generations of a family to be employed by the company at the same time. Comfort, safety, obedience, and loyalty were strong values, and my vision had the design team transgressing every one of them!

One of my strengths as a consultant is inspiring others to go beyond the limits of what they believe is possible. When a client and I achieve a common vision, I excel in working out with that client a practical strategy for bringing that vision into being. In this case, my vision of the project was clear and maybe even do-able, but it was so far beyond the bounds of the design team's imagined limits that it never became real for the team members. My visits became occasions for me to exhort the team members to go beyond their limits, so there was always a quality in our interactions of their not living up to my expectations. They were somewhat in awe of me, and when I endeavored to get a dialogue going about our differences over the project, they tended to withdraw rather than confront. I had been selected by their vice president, not by them, and they may have felt it was politically unwise to dispute with me. After a while, I found myself feeling very frustrated and isolated, and I stopped looking forward to my visits.

I felt a strong sense of urgency and responsibility for the project, but the way it was set up, I could only affect its course by working through the team. I was being paid a lot of money for my work, and I felt I was not producing results, so I also experienced some shame and guilt. I passed those feelings along to the team by pushing members to take more initiative, with the result, as I have just described, that I became increasingly out of relationship with them.

I continued, however, to search for new ways to make a breakthrough, right up to the end of my contract. And as I describe in the next section, it was exploring one of these new avenues that led to my writing the client communication that later became the article, "Harnessing Personal Energy: How Companies Can Inspire Employees" (Harrison, 1987a).

Exploring the Power of Mission and Vision

At the 1986 annual conference of the Association for Humanistic Psychology, I met a consultant named Bill Kutz who was passionately convinced that the process of creating a mission statement could bring a high degree of alignment to an organization. Bill was very persuasive, and I was looking for ideas for energizing my project. I interviewed him at length and took copious notes, with an eye to using his process to achieve a common vision with my utility project team. Then I persuaded the design team to set aside a day to work on a mission statement for themselves, and several days before that event, I began to prepare myself for the session.

One of my peculiarities is that while I borrow ideas right and left—I have had few original ideas in my life—I have to put them into a form of my own before I can feel comfortable using them. That seems to be how I learn the deeper structure of the ideas and shape them to my own way of working and talking. In putting Bill Kutz's ideas into a form I could use with the utility project team, I found myself weaving in ideas from my work on organizational alignment, and in three days of concentrated work, I found myself with a publishable paper on the subject.

David Berlew was fond of an old Romanian curse that has sometimes described my situation on a project: "May you have a brilliant idea and be unable to get anyone to listen to it." My gift is to see very clearly how things *could be*, and to have a strong intuitive sense of being right. I can cope when others have a different vision; then there is something to talk about and learn from. But it is acutely frustrating when, as in this project, the others appear to have no vision of their own and also do not respond to mine!

In this case, the idea that I had as I wrote was about what happens when bureaucracy and authority are relaxed in a traditional organization. On the one hand, without external control and direction, the other-directed people are left in an aimless, unmotivated state. On the other hand, the inner-directed people will pursue their private, self-oriented goals with little regard to the needs of the organization. If there is a charismatic leader about, then his or her vision can replace coercion with a common vision that provides a focus for integration and coordinated effort. Better still is a vision that emerges from the organization itself and is owned by all who have had a part in its creation. Having failed to inspire the utility company design team with my vision, and sensing that my time was running out, I hoped I could facilitate them in crafting a vision of their own that would sustain them in their further efforts, since I believed they would receive little help from the bureaucracy. I also found that my frustration with the design team paralleled what I had felt with the internal consulting team in Britain that I had once "fired." As on that occasion, I turned to writing to assuage my sense of failure. There was small hope that my intervention would make a real difference, yet I wanted to preserve the insights I had achieved and send them where they might do more good.

The session itself went well enough. The team did come up with a fine mission statement, but the team members and I did not put enough time into the process to craft a vision that would empower the team. Soon, my initial contract ran out, and as I expected, it was not renewed. I felt let down, but I was also relieved that I would no longer have to beat my head against that particular stone wall.

Although I did not gain the knowledge about improving service quality that I had anticipated, I did gain a bone-deep understanding of the power of organization culture to block change. To change an organization culture requires more time than most leaders believe they have, plus a critical mass of dedicated champions and supporters, plus "optimum pain," plus a strong sense of urgency within the organization (see Harrison, Cooper, and Dawes, 1991, p. 69). We did not have any of these elements, and at the time the project ended, I felt they were critical success factors. Now I am not so sure.

It took me a decade to achieve my current level of insight into what was really at the heart of our failure to improve service quality in a meaningful and measurable way. I now believe that to change a whole system, we have to get a representation of the whole system in the room. When we limit ourselves to working separately with the parts, we can very rarely change the system. Each time we work with a part, we leave out everyone in the other parts, and their agreement is needed if real change is to occur. At the time I was involved in this project, I knew, sort of, that we should work with the entire system at the same time, so I tried to plan the work to deal with the relevant parts in an appropriate and orderly sequence. In making decisions with my clients, I focused in this project as in many others on whether to go top-down, bottom-up, inside-out, or outside-in. Usually, my rule of thumb was, "Work where the energy is, and leave for later those who are not ready to work." We never seriously considered putting all the parts in one room and working our way through the chaos that might ensue. If we had considered it, I would not have known how to make such a process work. Later, in the early nineties, when I discovered future search and other approaches to working on whole systems, I could see a way forward. By that time, I had had another shot at changing an organization's culture, and I was about out of ideas.

Reflections on Learning from Failure

Because I did not fully understand the power that organization cultures have to maintain themselves, and because I did not yet have an adequate concept of how one might work on a whole system at once, my attempts to learn from the electric company project focused on what I personally did wrong. Self-examination has always produced learning for me, and this time was no exception. I am not sure I had the balance right between my contribution to the outcome and the contribution of the systemic factors, but at least I was working on something that I might be able to change. Here is what I learned about myself in this project—and also in the next one, because I did not quickly find a more effective way of managing myself. I was dealing with my fairly entrenched pattern for coping with situations that go awry.

There is a certain set of circumstances that has led me on occasion to try to manage a project from my role as a consultant, and as a manager, I am quite demanding. I first encountered the pattern in myself during the 1967 Peace Corps project that led to my leaving National Training Laboratories (NTL). I went to Toluca, Mexico with a team of returned Peace Corps volunteers. When we met setbacks in working with local authorities, I pushed hard on my team to be more assertive. Eventually, they rebelled, and after an emotional confrontation, I was relieved of my authority by the project director. The event was a big professional failure, and it led to my departure from NTL.

Structurally, the utility project was similar to the Peace Corps project in these ways:

- I had a strong intuitive knowing about what was true and what was the best way to go.
- I was unable to persuade others of the validity or the importance of what I believed I knew.
- I had a sense that I was highly responsible or even solely responsible for the outcome.
- I was with others who were unable or unwilling to engage in passionate debate on the merits of the issues—perhaps because they disliked conflict of any kind, perhaps because they felt themselves at risk of losing the debate or appearing inadequate.

When any one of these conditions does not obtain, I get on fine, and I go for years without activating my management pattern. Early in a project, when I am collecting, sorting, and sifting information, I am open to many different ideas and interpretations, and I actively seek help from others. I am very receptive and collaborative when I do not *know*. At a certain point, however, the pieces fall into place, and I have a sense of possessing a perfect "thought crystal" that includes all the data I have. When that happens, suddenly, I am no longer very open to alternative interpretations. Out of politeness, I try to listen, but I am not really present to others' ideas. My convictions may later have to change in order to include disconfirming data that come in, but until then, my mind is pretty firmly made up. Most of the time, others find my mental models useful and plausible. When they do not, I wait for more data to turn up, telling myself, "If the model is true, it will come around again."

I like negotiating and joint problem solving, and I have great patience when there is sufficient time. But when time is short, and when I cannot get others to understand, the intensity of our discussions will escalate. When others are unwilling to engage in such passionate give-and-take, I find it frustrating, because it becomes very important to me to *get the solution right*. Although I like to have my own way, that is not what I get passionate about. What I get passionate about is being heard and understood. I try hard to speak what seems to me to be the truth. Once I have had my say, I can usually go on as a member of the team, feeling that my integrity has been served by my having spoken. That is not the case, however, when I have allowed myself to assume explicit or implicit responsibility for the outcome. Then I become managerial.

According to most models of proper OD work, we OD consultants are never supposed to believe that we are primarily responsible for outcomes. Yet when I have a strong personal investment in the work and time is short, I can change quite quickly from a collaborative colleague, understanding listener, or thoughtful advisor to a heavy-handed authoritarian manager. Thus, under pressure, I behave the way I saw my father act when he was under pressure. I know better, but it happens. Managing is definitely not my best thing. My best thing is seeing and knowing. I am probably worst at managing. A psychic once told me, "You are an architect, not a builder." I like to think of myself that way. It reminds me to focus on what I do best and to forgive myself for my inadequacies. Like many others, when I do not have someone to do the job that complements mine, I do it myself as best I can.

I have often said that there should be a section set aside in professional education programs and conferences in which practitioners can share the projects that did not work, the ill-conceived interventions, the failed strategies, and the like. Knowing that I have learned deep lessons from my failures and supposing that I should learn from others' as well, it has seemed to me that confining professional meetings to presentations of what works gives participants only half a loaf—and the smaller half at that. I, for one, am usually willing to share my not-so-successful experiences, and I tend to give myself a pat on the back for my willingness to be open and vulnerable when I do so. However, it is another matter when the cause of failure seems partially embedded in my character, in those parts of my personality that most of the time I succeed in ignoring or minimizing. When I share these failures, it feels as though I am publicizing myself as unsuited to the work of a consultant if not also somewhat inadequate as a person. Yet there is something that urges me to continue, a voice that says I am not completely different from everyone else, that I am not the only one who has made these mistakes, and that my own shadow side may be echoed in the collective shadow of our profession. To face the darker side of myself in my professional life is painful, but it offers the possibility of growing beyond my current state of competence. If we consultants can together face the dark side of our profession, we can perhaps heal our work in the world and do both ourselves and our clients a service.

Are Organizations Conscious?

In addition to my work with the electric utility, during the seventies and eighties I worked with two large and very successful freestanding research and development organizations. At this same time, my search for ways to release love in the workplace was beginning to lead me to a theory about the *consciousness* of organizations. I had come a long way from believing that organizations were unreal abstractions and that only the people in them were "real"!

In the organizations I was working with, I was beginning to notice that the cultural preferences of organizational members formed a pattern that depended on what cultural mix was currently dominant. Most people who filled out my organization culture questionnaire preferred higher levels of the achievement and support cultures and lower levels of the power culture than they currently had in their organization. And members of organizations that had strongly traditional power and role cultures expressed the strongest preference for more of the achievement orientation; however, it seemed as though members of these organizations could not conceive of the fourth culture, the support orientation, as a real alternative. It was the members of organizations that were already somewhat established in the achievement orientation who tended to want a better balance between achievement and support. It seemed to me, both in looking at these score patterns and in reflecting on my consulting work, that in business it is rare for organizations to release the power of love until after they empower their members to create and contribute to a shared purpose. In business, then, alignment seems to be prior to attunement.

I finally came to see that organizations, like people, are faced with a series of evolutionary challenges throughout their lifetimes. The classic progression is that the (usually) autocratic entrepreneurial startup organization (power culture) has to become more bureaucratic (role culture) as it grows, in order to cope with complexity and size. Then, as pressures of rapid change eventually render the cumbersome structures and systems of the traditional role organization ineffective, top management attempts to make the organization faster on its feet, more innovative and productive, by flattening the organization structure and squeezing out middle managers. Decision-making powers are devolved to lower levels of the organization. Now, the organization begins to look and feel like an achievement culture.

Most organizations have not yet reached this point, and few seem to have gone beyond it. Therefore, I cannot demonstrate the likelihood of further evolution to a culture more balanced between achievement and support. However, a likely direction for further evolution is pointed to by the way many members of well-established achievement cultures express a desire on my questionnaire for a warmer, more personal and humane support culture. In conversation, too, they often refer to the dark side of the achievement culture, manifested, for example, in burnout, workaholism, cutthroat competition, loneliness, and impoverished personal and family lives.

In time, I came to see that undertaking major culture change, or *organization transformation* (OT) as it is sometimes called, can often be grandiose and somewhat dangerous. I began to counsel consultants and managers to undertake such change rarely. I now believe that culture change projects are responsible only where the things the organization has to know and be able to do to succeed in a business sense are seriously blocked by the current cultural orientation. Otherwise, the changes are too costly, take too long, and cause too much disruption and impaired functioning while they are going on. I deal with this subject in more depth in *Humanizing Change: Matching Interventions to Organizational Realities* (Harrison, Cooper, and Dawes, 1991). At the time of which I am writing, however, these thoughts were taking shape but were not fully formed. The next project I undertook brought my thinking along in this direction.

Undertaking Large-Scale Systems Change

My next chance to work on a major change process in an organization came from a manager in the research and development (R&D) subsidiary of a major oil company. I had known and liked him for some time, having done training and team development for him in the early eighties, and we had stayed in touch, getting together occasionally for lunch. At one such meeting in late 1986, he told me he had unexpectedly been promoted to president and CEO of his subsidiary. He had a vision for transforming his company from a rather traditional bureaucratic organization into one that was fast on its feet, receptive to new technology from the outside, and responsive to its internal customers within the larger organization.

After my experience with the electric utility, I was wary of taking on culture change, but this project had a lot going for it. The CEO was willing to bet his career on success, and he seemed to have both the resources and the autonomy to make it happen. I had seen him work with people, and he was charismatic in a sincere, low-key way. I knew his previous subordinates were devoted to him, because they readily volunteered that information. I knew the petroleum and chemical industries better than any others; I knew R&D organizations, having, as I mentioned, worked with two of the top R&D organizations in the free world during the eighties; and I understood and liked the engineers and scientists who worked in such organizations. Finally, I was very excited about the prospect of working to change a whole organization in fundamental ways. I undertook the project willingly and thus began three intense and involving years, full of emotional highs and depths, achievements and frustrations, clarity and confusion. It was a project in which I learned much, and contributed much. It ended in some sadness and more than a little ambiguity.

My client, whom I shall call "Neil," believed his immediate problem was to enroll his immediate subordinates, the department heads, as willing supporters of his vision. I had not long since written "Harnessing Personal Energy" (Harrison, 1987a), and this seemed an ideal situation in which to conduct a mission development workshop.

The workshop I designed for the management team formed by the CEO's subordinates was unusual in that it was based on the self-directed principle of *maximum feasible choice,* a style I had first experimented with in the Autonomy Labs. First, I created a workbook that contained a collection of exercises divided into three phases:

- "Exploring Individual Visions of Life and Work": individual needs, personal work histories, individual strength assessments
- "Organizational Diagnosis": organizational history, myth, and legend; organization culture; stakeholder analysis; organizational strengths and weaknesses
- "Creating a Vision and Mission": how to move from individual visions to group consensus

The workbook, which I published as *Building an Organization Vision and Mission Statement* (Harrison, 1988), contained twice as much as could be done by a group in three days. This gave participants a range of choice, from left-brain processes to more intuitive, holistic sensory processes. A subset of the management team picked from the workbook the exercises that would be done and worked out a time schedule for them.

The workshop was a great success, and I now make it a practice to design events collaboratively with a client team. By testing a design with people who will take part, I avoid errors and misunderstandings, and my events have higher credibility and relevance than if I design them myself. When a collaboratively designed event is in progress, the people on the team work to make it a success. Beyond these considerations, it just feels better to me to share the work with my clients. When we work together on a design, our connection becomes one of the heart, rather than just the head, and we forge stronger personal bonds.

After this successful start, I worked on the culture change project at this R&D subsidiary for about three years, usually spending two days a week on the project. It was the most satisfying work I have ever done and, in some ways, the most impactful. Yet I learned more about how difficult it is to change organization culture than I learned about how to change it. Part of what was satisfying was my personal and working relationship with the internal consultant who partnered me. From the outset, we had established the kind of collaboration and collegiality that a loner like myself dreams about. We complemented each other in classic style.

I have always deeply valued an internal-external team approach to organization change. When I was an internal consultant at Procter & Gamble, I valued bringing outsiders in, and I received good counsel and support from those I worked with. When I began to work as an external consultant, it was natural for me to seek and use the special knowledge and access of internal colleagues. Almost all of those relationships have been very positive for me, leading to deep and lasting friendships in some cases. Internal consultants know the organization, its people and its politics, and they are always there, sensing the organization from moment to moment. They can keep a project going on a continuing basis. In contrast, the external consultant often has a wider experience with a variety of organizations, is given more credibility by top management, and is able to confront that management more strongly when necessary.

In addition, I enjoy the mentoring relationships that sometimes develop with internal consultants. I am as passionate and indefatigable a teacher as I am a learner, and the process of exchanging insights and useful information is endlessly satisfying and enriching for me as long as it takes place within a relationship that affirms each party and builds mutual respect. I have always learned greatly from the people I have mentored, partly, I think, because I have picked capable and creative people to mentor. To drop a name or two, in the sixties I had the pleasure of helping Tony Petrella and Peter Block, two soon-to-be giants in the field of OD, move from personnel to consulting roles.

In the R&D subsidiary project, it was also satisfying that I was involved and on-site at the R&D company often enough and long enough to have a sense that I had joined the organization. I became aware of how much I have longed for lasting work relationships, and I realized what I have missed by being a loner so long and so totally. I was better known and more highly valued in this project than I had been for a long time, and that satisfied a deep part of me that wanted to belong, to love and to be loved in a much broader sense than we usually use that term. It takes me a long time to feel that I belong anywhere, because I am both shy and introverted, and I was there long enough to establish meaningful bonds, both with the organization as an entity and, to a lesser extent, with individuals. I developed a lot of love for the collective that was the organization. When it came time to leave, and that under not-so-pleasant circumstances, it was heartbreaking to the same degree that it had been heartwarming to be there. However, I never regretted having given myself in that way. I would like to love both well and wisely, but if I cannot do both, then I prefer to love well.

During most of this project, I was able to hold a fair degree of detachment from the outcomes of my work and just keep on doing my best from day to day. However, there came a time when, under stress, I pushed too hard on some key players and came to be seen by them as working my own agenda rather than helping them with theirs. At that point, those affected withdrew their trust from me, and it became clear to me that I could no longer be effective.

Factors Affecting the Outcomes of the R&D Company Project

As the implementation of change developed, these were some of the factors I faced together with Neil and the internal consultant.

• Neil had a strong sense of his own vision for the company, a vision shared by few in the organization. Indeed, with one or two exceptions, Neil's immediate subordinates tended to mistrust his vision; some viewed it as impractical and out of step with the traditional culture of the organization. Most gave lip service to the vision but adopted a passive, rather political, wait-and-see attitude. They were seen by the remainder of the organization as not buying in.

• The greatest support for the vision was among middle managers one level removed from Neil. Those who had personally worked for him were particularly supportive. However, few were prepared to take personal risks in support of the change in the absence of a strong lead from their immediate superiors.

• Neil was a genuine visionary. He inspired others with his sincerity and commitment to the vision, and by his willingness to show an extraordinary degree of vulnerability. He is the only client I have ever had who regularly cried in public when strongly moved, and as nearly as I could tell, it increased his credibility more than a strongly assertive style would have.

• Although able to inspire others in public, Neil was an introvert and rather shy. He did not readily seek others out, press the flesh, or manage by walking about, and so he readily became somewhat isolated from the rest of the organization.

• There was a general view among individual contributors, the scientists and engineers who made up the bulk of the professional staff, that the company was doing well, that it was producing good R&D products for its customers and that not much needed to be changed. The company had not yet had large layoffs that would frighten and shake up the managers and employees, and a false sense of security pervaded the organization. The word was, "Where's the train wreck?" meaning, "Why worry?"

• Neil took the line that the strategy and tactics for implementing change should be congruent with the vision. Since empowerment, initiative, and upward influence were significant parts of his vision, he felt it would not be walking his talk to be assertive and impose the changes he sought. Instead, his strategy was to encourage initiative by communicating and inviting, by relaxing bureaucratic and authoritarian barriers, and by rewarding initiative when it appeared.

• From that first off-site workshop to develop a vision and mission statement, the objectives of the change were defined in process terms. Such phrases as "being fast on our feet and close to the customer," "eliminating 'not invented here,'" and "being vision driven" tended to describe the objectives of the project. When I asked the clients to specify the desired outcomes in measurable or even in observable terms, the result always turned out to be disappointingly vague. There was a reluctance at all levels, including Neil's, to be specific. I am not quite sure why, but I think that phenomenon was part of the general reluctance to commit to dates and performance targets that is fairly common in R&D organizations. Long-term research projects have uncertain schedules and outcomes. There is also often an attitude of not letting R&D clients know too much about the details of projects, for fear they will interfere. This reclusive and timid attitude toward deadlines and public commitments carried over, perhaps, into the change project.

• I was seen as Neil's consultant. I was perceived to have access to him and influence with him. I acquired some secondhand power and influence because of this relationship, but I had to work hard to build trust and confidence with the rest of the organization. The people I had the least rapport with were Neil's direct reports, who were also the people with whom he had the least trust and open communication. After getting off to a very good start in the vision and mission workshop, my relationship with several members of this group soon became somewhat distant and uncomfortable. It was a classic case of the top endeavoring to make an end run around the next level down, and I found myself carrying the ball a lot of the time. In contrast, I had good relationships with people below this level.

• The vast majority of people in the organization were intelligent, hard working, loyal to the company, and dedicated to doing good work. The company was well resourced for change in terms of people and funds, and it had a history of reasonably good industrial relations.

As I look back on the project, given all these issues, I did a lot of things right in communicating the vision, providing opportunities for middle management to contribute to it, and stimulating and encouraging local initiatives lower down in the organization. What was lacking was follow-through, a willingness on the part of management to ask lower levels to set measurable goals, make concrete plans for implementation, and commit to their achievement. The behavior of the people in the organization reminded me of the traits exhibited by my students at Yale when I had first freed them from the normal constraints of assignments, deadlines, and grading. They had used their freedom to devote more time to working on the assignments of other teachers who were more demanding. Similarly, the managers in this project tended to spend their time and energy and that of their people on work that had deadlines, where the outcomes were measured in numbers and where customers were waiting for the output. The lesson I learned is that there is a kind of Gresham's law in goal setting and goal achievement. Gresham's law applies in economics and proposes that soft money, for example, paper money unbacked by gold and silver, drives hard money out of circulation because people hoard coinage that has intrinsic value. The analogy in corporate goal setting is that hard (measurable and observable) goals draw more energy than soft goals. Organizational members will work on goals that have a clear relationship to business objectives in preference to working on those directed at improvement of such organizational processes as communication, quality of work life, organization culture, and the like. In the R&D project, because the goals of the culture change were never made a part of the deliverables of work units, these goals competed at a disadvantage with the daily routine of getting the wash out.

Moreover, my close connection with Neil was a mixed blessing without which I might have done better at building trust and rapport with the department heads. Because most of them did not identify their own interests with the change project, they were careful what they said when we met, and I was curiously disempowered. Because I knew it would be easy to make them feel threatened and thus drive them deeper into denial, I was reluctant to confront them about their disaffection. As I look back, I think I was somewhat ashamed of my borrowed power, and my creativity in using my skills was impaired by that shame. It is not likely I could have turned their attitudes around in any event, but I was not at my best in that situation.

Together with my internal colleague, I spent a lot of time trying to find ways to hook the culture change to some harder, more business-relevant activity. Eventually, we found two promising areas: a previously mandated reorganization and the growing interest in the organization in quality. A number of the organization's clients were working on Total Quality Management (TQM), and they were putting some pressure on the R&D company, as a supplier, to follow along. At first, there was great skepticism, which I shared, that methods for improving quality in manufacturing and petroleum processing could offer much that would improve knowledge work such as research and development. However, one department had begun quality training as a way of building a closer relationship with its main client, and the others were under some pressure to follow suit.

I now see the TQM movement as one of the most favorable forces in business today in the direction of transformation because it has the potential to move an organization toward both the achievement and support orientations and away from the grosser forms of power orientation. Once an organization has done all it can to automate production and design systems and procedures that will prevent workers from making mistakes, the only competitive edge that is left to achieve is enlisting the hearts and minds of the workers in improving work processes and devoting their will, mind, and love to making these processes work. This last competitive edge can only be accomplished by an organization that reduces fear, shares power with employees, and learns to work in teams to solve problems and improve operations.

Most organizations initially go about installing TQM in a way that is consistent with their current culture, not the culture toward which they want to move. They begin with training in one of the various approaches to quality, and unfortunately, that training is also often the end of their quality program. My orientation to quality is that it begins with understanding what is happening where the work is being done, studying work processes for improvement, and particularly, involving the stakeholders of the organization in deliberations about quality. Training can then be made available to quality teams on an as-needed basis when they run up against situations in which they need additional skills and knowledge to move ahead. This seems eminently sensible to me in view of the fact that lack of knowledge is seldom as much of a barrier as lack of empowerment. That was especially true in the R&D company, where professional staff and technicians alike were unusually intelligent and highly educated, and proud of doing a good job.

At the time I left that project, the various departments were proceeding in somewhat different ways, but I felt that my point of view had been received and, to some extent, appreciated. The quality effort was not yet sufficiently advanced to know whether it would produce what Neil, the internal consultant, and I had hoped from it in cultural transformation, but it was attracting more energy and enthusiasm than the idea of culture change had.

The main thrust of the efforts the internal consultant and I made to hook the organization transformation to some concrete business activity took place around the previously mandated reorganization of the subsidiary. The parent company required subsidiaries to conduct a thorough organizational study at regular intervals, and the R&D company was overdue, Neil having asked for the study to be postponed until after his culture change effort was well launched. I worked closely with a subgroup of department managers, hoping to plan the study in such a way that the reorganization would not just be moving boxes around on the organization chart. My intent was to base the reorganization on a thorough study of the way the work was done and the ways different parts of the company needed to relate to other stakeholders, such as customers and clients, corporate headquarters, and so on. Together with one of the department managers, I attended a fine workshop by my old friend Tony Petrella on organizational restructuring, and we came back enthused about creating a team of respected middle managers to lead a study of the organization and propose structural changes. The department managers seemed surprisingly willing to delegate this responsible task, and in due course, a design team of six of their most respected immediate subordinates was selected and instructed to give full time to the work.

I was very happy with this turn of events. The six team members were all at least moderate supporters of the culture change and, like me, saw the restructuring as an opportunity to make meaningful changes in the way the company did its work and related to its customers. I saw the design team adding the weight and energy needed to make the transition a reality. I began immediately to involve the team members in an educational process designed to acquaint them with various approaches to large-systems change and, in particular, sociotechnical systems (STS) redesign. Together, the team members and I attended seminars and conferences on STS. We invited a consultant specializing in STS to come and conduct a "system scan," first with the design team and later with Neil and his direct reports. I asked a colleague to join me in working with the design team, because she had participated in a similar project with one of the Big Three auto manufacturers. Those days were the high point of my work with the company. I felt that I and the others working on change had a vehicle for making a positive difference in the way people lived and worked in the organization, that we had been given the green light to do so, and that all that remained was to carry out our work with creativity, dedication, and intelligence.

As it turned out, that was a slight oversimplification. What really happened was that things went along nicely until just before the first major checkpoint, when the design team was due to report to the top management of the R&D company on the team's plan to study the organization. My colleague and I met with the team at a two-day off-site to prepare the plan and the presentation, and about halfway through the first morning the group suddenly went dead. One minute group members were working through my colleague's proposals for a highly interactive and participative study process, and the next minute the energy had dropped, people were tense and uncommunicative, and it seemed impossible to come to agreement on any aspect of the plan.

During a break, my colleague and I conferred. My hypothesis was that there was something the group feared that they were not comfortable discussing. My colleague favored continuing with the planned schedule for the day while I felt a compelling intuition to go after the underlying fear. We could not agree during our short break, and I decided unilaterally to suspend our work until we could deal with the process. It did not take long to learn what the problem was (but it did take a long time to repair the relationship with my colleague).

It came out that the design team members had been conferring privately about different ways of configuring the company. They were not nearly as wedded to my idea of a study-based reorganization as I was, figuring that, collectively, they knew the work of the organization well enough to come up with at least an approximation of the right structure. What they discovered was that there was no way any of them could see to restructure the organization that did not involve eliminating half the jobs at their own level and at the level above them, that is, Neil's immediate subordinates. They now believed they had been set up to do the dirty work that their superiors did not have the courage to undertake and that their serving on the team that reduced the ranks of their own level by half would deal both their future careers and their present relationships a grievous blow. They felt powerless to resign their assignment, but they had completely lost their stomach for it. They were deeply resentful of what they believed was a trap, and they felt that Neil should have taken on the task of reducing the size of the organization before asking them to change its shape.

This was one time in the project when my close relationship with Neil paid off for everyone concerned. I was able to convince the group that they would have a fair hearing if they told Neil they wanted him to do his job before they did theirs, and with some trepidation, they phoned him on the spot and set up an appointment. When presented with the group's concerns, Neil willingly agreed to take charge of the sizing question, which he said he would discuss with his corporate vice president. At that point, I relaxed, believing that the crisis was over and that we could now get on with our study.

It was not to be. Now the design team members felt their task was over, that they should return to their normal duties, and that there was nothing they could do until the sizing issue was resolved. Moreover, my colleague, with whom I had formerly enjoyed a cordial and cooperative relationship, told me she was not happy to continue working with me because she had felt disregarded and run over when I had decided to intervene in the process during the critical off-site meeting. I was dismayed because I valued my colleague as a friend as well as a professional and also because a similar issue had recently come up in my primary relationship. It was one of those times when I looked at myself in the mirror of others' eyes and saw my darker tendencies arising to destroy things I greatly valued in life: love, friendship, trust, and closeness. I also knew that if a like issue were to arise again, I might well decide it the same way, choosing what felt to me to be right action over what seemed to be the right way of being in relationship. We talked at length and achieved a degree of reconciliation, but uneasiness remained on both sides.

Meanwhile, I was greatly disturbed by what I saw as the design team's defection. I saw the one best chance we had to make a difference in the working life of the organization fading into the never-never. I pointed out that now that it was relieved of the most onerous and risky part of the task, the team was free to continue with the study of work processes, especially in the lower reaches of the organization, since work at that level was expected to be undisturbed by the middle management reorganization. The design team was deaf to my counsel, but as my exhortations to action became louder and more desperate, the members heard my urgency, and it was at this point that they began to believe that I had turned from being a helpful facilitator into a powerful and threatening outsider working my own agenda. Unfortunately, because of my relationship with Neil, they did not share their change of heart with me. Instead, they discussed it with my colleague, who respected their confidence and did not warn me that anything was amiss until later, when the situation had become irretrievable.

Once the reorganization of the R&D company was seen by corporate management as requiring the transfer or severance of high-level managers, the process disappeared into the stratosphere, where such matters are deliberated at great length and with little regard for the effects of delay on the organization. I continued to lobby for the importance of continuing with the organizational study, both with design team and with the department managers and CEO. I knew I was risking my credibility, but I saw the issue as critical and worthy of my "falling on my sword," if necessary. Then my colleague informed me of my loss of credibility with the design team, and I realized my suicide might already have taken place. I checked with other friends and colleagues to learn whether my usefulness was indeed at an end. They told me, regretfully, that it was. It was hard to believe that in less than four years I had alienated key members of two different client systems by pushing them too hard, but there it was. Never was I more poignantly aware of the truth of the saying that warns that we get to repeat each of life's lessons until we learn it!

Meanwhile, the power to determine its own shape had passed out of the hands of the R&D leadership. Neil committed his own version of hara-kiri when he agreed, out of principle and conviction, that the R&D and engineering subsidiaries ought to be merged, after having been separated for some years. It was unclear who would be CEO of the combined organization. It seemed likely that much that had been achieved toward a cultural transition would be swept away or overtaken by the merger.

There was one thing more I thought of to do that might preserve our work. I proposed a survey designed to assess the current organization culture, compare it with the pretransition culture, and record the attitudes and opinions toward the transition of people at all levels. The survey provided me with modest satisfaction. Using the culture assessment instrument that Herb Stokes and I had developed (Harrison and Stokes, 1992) and comparing the current results with data collected at the beginning of the project, I found statistically significant shifts in the directions toward which we had been working. People perceived more achievement and support and less power orientation than they had three years previously. I do not believe that the survey itself had much, if any, impact on the continuing efforts of the company to transform its way of working, but it satisfied me that our three years of effort were not in vain. The colleague with whom I had such a painful falling-out inherited my role, and she and her partner continued the process of work study and redesign that we had begun together.

It was not the first time that I had invited someone to join me on a project and ended by losing the client to him or her. It was the most painful time, however, because I had come to feel so attached to and identified with the organization. There is always a risk of losing a client to one's colleague. Perhaps that is one reason so many of us work alone much of the time. To me, the risk is justified by the additional power a team approach brings to a project and by the enjoyment of working together with others whom one respects and trusts. In the case of the R&D company, it was a benefit to the client to have my colleague in place once I left.

Although all of us who worked on this project achieved less than we had hoped, I do not see this project as a failure. The survey results confirmed our impression that significant shifts in attitudes were taking place. We were all working on the edge of our understanding of how organizations change, and we were faced with difficult dilemmas. The most difficult of these was whether to move the change by power and authority or rely on inspiration and example. Neil was committed to the latter approach, which had worked well in his previous managerial assignments. However, as CEO, he had 1,100 subordinates, whereas before, he had had less than 100. For his approach to work, he needed to inspire his department managers and enroll them in his vision. With one or possibly two exceptions, he failed in this attempt. Whether the others were too old, too tired, too political, or too cynical to buy in, I am not sure. What is clear is that the vision was Neil's, not theirs. Our very powerful visioning exercise at the outset of the project bought Neil some credibility and time. The second round at the next level of management was also a very strong event. After that, we could not keep the momentum going.

In retrospect, it is significant that we felt we were making good progress as long as we were able to get the parts of the system we wanted to impact into the same room, sharing an experience, and working with their own data. The power of our early events was in our ability to lead people to an unaccustomed level of trust and openness, where they could acknowledge what was and was not working and share their differing perspectives on the organization and its environment. As soon as we relied on people who had participated in these high-energy events to tell and sell their insights and visions to their colleagues and subordinates, the process bogged down. The immediacy and excitement of creating the future with one's fellows gave way to the cynicism with which each new management initiative is normally met in large bureaucratic organizations. My colleague and I believed that we needed to translate the vision into two or three well-implemented initiatives that would produce concrete results by which skeptics could measure the intent and the reality of the vision. We believed that for those initiatives to compete for time and resources with the daily round of work, they had to have the urgency of a top-management mandate behind them, and be led hands-on by Neil or one of his lieutenants. We kept agonizing over the choice between vision and inspiration on the one hand and the use of authority and directive leadership on the other. I now believe that we were working the wrong dichotomy. What was missing was an opportunity for the whole organization to engage in examining together the emerging realities faced by the company, and to find not only a common vision but a common willingness to act together to create more of what they all wanted. The tragedy was that there was so much common desire among people at all levels but we were never able to create a way in which they could all discover that truth and separate their differing goals and interests from the core values and goals they shared. In the end, the company divided into those who cared deeply about the "transition," as it was called, because they had found a way to own a piece of it, and a much larger group of those who either did not share the vision or did not trust that it would come to anything. The two groups became somewhat isolated from one another. I believe that our attempts to bring them together (the Transition Support Team that was representative of all levels and departments; two Transition Fairs, from which I still have the T-shirts; informal lunches with Neil; and the like) were seen by the latter group as irrelevant because they did not directly impact the work to be done. And so it stood when I left, just before our effort was overwhelmed by the reorganization.

CHAPTER EIGHT

BECOMING WHOLE ENOUGH TO BE HELPFUL

In the late seventies, I turned in my spiritual life from seeking higher states of consciousness to a more sober process of trying to clean up my act as a human being. After some years of search and endeavors to master meditation and other techniques, I realized one night in 1978, as I left the Nyingma (Tibetan Buddhism) Institute in Berkeley, that I was trying to achieve the spiritual equivalent of a graduate degree without having completed the introductory course. My idea of being on a spiritual path was simply that it would enable me to get into higher states of consciousness, and so I had failed to ground that work adequately in a foundation of truth and goodness. I assessed myself as courageous with the truth in my work with clients, and I felt solid about my willingness to be present for people who needed my help. I had learned to assume responsibility for the results I got in life, pleasant or unpleasant. On the downside, however, I saw that I had cut corners in my personal relationships and in business. I tended to be a taker, out for personal advantage. I was sometimes untruthful, especially when the truth was embarrassing to me or hurtful to another.

After a hard look at myself, I decided I would give up meditation for a time, since it was not working for me anyway, and that I would focus on becoming "a good person." Those words look awkward in print, but they are the words I used in my inner dialogue. I knew I had a long road to travel, but I began working on such things as telling the truth in all situations; taking only what belongs to me and giving others what is due to them; becoming less oriented to making money and more generous and giving; avoiding hurting others through word, thought, or deed; and becoming less addicted in all ways—to work, to material possessions, to relationships, and to food and drink.

Me and My Shadow

A large part of my remedial course in moral development was learning to embrace and integrate my two contradictory shadow parts. There is a part of me that lives for excitement, risk, creativity, and play. That part willingly says, "Yes!" or at least, "Why not!" to each impulse of heart or intuition. It pushed me to partake in the great liberation of the sixties as I adopted the younger generation as my own. It was during that period from 1962 to 1968 that I lost my writing block and found my unique voice. The resulting creativity has served my work and my clients well, and it has also served my self-oriented impulses. It fueled the drive for freedom and autonomy that nudged me to define my own job at NTL in disregard of the work I had been hired to do. It was my main support as I left colleagues, marriage, and country to adventure abroad. It has been in attendance each time I have said, "Yes, I can!" to a project my intuition said I could do but my rational mind did not know how to implement. These projects include most of the worthwhile challenges I have accepted as a consultant and educator, such as creating the Autonomy Lab or releasing the power of love in organizations.

There is another part of me that is most alive when I am loving and being loved but that for many years was unconvinced that I was worthy of love. It is this part that has caused me to hold onto relationships, whether professional or personal, when my more free-spirited part was ready to move on. When the two parts have come into conflict, I have often tried to follow both of them, endeavoring to preserve the relationship and live a free and autonomous life at the same time.

For example, when I agreed to do an administrative job for NTL and then used my position to operate much like an independent consultant, I wanted to belong, to have close personal and working relationships, and I also intensely wanted to continue my exciting work with the Peace Corps and other international agencies. I tried to do both, and ended up with neither. My relationship with Situation Management Systems provides another good example. No one twisted my arm to join the company. I did not like the deal from the beginning, but I wanted the security and benefits of the association. In my heart, I was still a lone entrepreneur, and I acted like one. My agenda was individualistic, and I kept taking more freedom until eventually my colleagues became fed up.

After my separation from Situation Management Systems, I went into a kind of decline for a time, and the years between 1981 and 1984 felt rather dull and lifeless. Then came my meeting with the Chilean psychic that led to my becoming aware of my free-spirited part, experiencing how strong a pull it exerted upon me and how dispirited I could become when it was chronically unsatisfied. David told me, through his translator, "You are very good for working, and sometimes you are an artist of work. . . . There is nothing to fix there. You and your work at moments are the same thing, and you have the enthusiasm of three men. . . . Even when you have done it the worst, you've always done it in a satisfactory way; that is, you go from satisfactory to bright in the activity."

That got my attention, because it affirmed something that in my best moments I believed was true. Then he spoke of frustrations and dissatisfactions in relationships, difficulties I had been ignoring because I did not know what to do about them. Again, I felt really *seen*. He spoke directly to my free part, warning that if I did not follow my impulses, I would remain melancholic and dissatisfied. His advice was frightening to the part of me that wanted stability and safety in my relationships, but the free spirit in me loved it! I experienced an immediate release of energy. I felt alive once more, and in the days that followed, I became determined not to allow my spirit to die, whatever the cost. With great trepidation, I followed David's advice, and in doing so, I created turmoil and pain for myself and others. Among the casualties was my marriage to Diana, which ended in sorrow and remorse in 1987.

Patterns that are life scripts are difficult to change but not impossible. I began to work on my relationship pattern in earnest in 1988, after I damaged another relationship not long after it had started. I began to work to integrate and harmonize the two conflicting parts of myself by visualizing them and entering into dialogue with them. I was greatly aided in this process by Virginia Dickson, a gifted healer and energy worker, with whom I worked intensively for several years. It has been a great blessing to have both parts of myself as functioning members of my personality, contributing their gifts to my life and relationships. I can be both more loving and more authentically myself. I have been free of the destructive pattern I have described since that time, although I remain vigilant for any sign of its return.

The decade following my encounter with David in 1984 was not entirely taken up with my painful struggle to "fix" myself. Following my divorce, I entered into a deeply passionate love relationship to which I committed myself body and soul until it ended in the early nineties. It was a journey filled with love and light, as well as struggle and pain. It was a healing journey and full of growth as well. I learned to open my heart and to experience the joys of living from the softer, more feminine side of myself. Although it ended painfully, I came away from it better integrated and feeling better about myself than I had been at any time in my life. That relationship was also a crucible within which I deepened my spiritual life and began to build a personal relationship with God. I also began to develop my abilities to connect with the unseen, by which I mean sources of healing, knowing, and guidance that are beyond our five physical senses.

Although the mid eighties was a period of renewed interest in spiritual matters for me, I still did not develop a regular spiritual practice for myself. My interest was rather diffuse, but in one way my professional and spiritual interests were coming together. I had long been attracted by the idea of community living, having experienced in two marriages that my needs for intense emotional interaction could overload a pair relationship. I imagined that in community life one might spread the emotional load and so live more harmoniously with all. I also became interested in understanding communities as organizations. I was especially interested in spiritually oriented communities because I felt that I would

probably never develop a disciplined spiritual practice without some external structure that would enforce regular meditation for me.

A Zen Community Project

My initial opportunity to explore community firsthand came when I was asked to
work with a Zen community during a difficult transition in leadership, their former *roshi* (spiritual leader) having been asked by the community to leave because
of an abuse of his position. My work with the community consisted of facilitating a number of long meetings and retreats during which the remaining community leaders endeavored to pick up the pieces, deal with a multitude of financial
and organizational problems, and move on. In many ways these meetings were
a mirror image (that is, a reversal) of typical meetings in business organizations.
The community members were reflective, they avoided premature action, and
they paid careful attention to achieving consensus before going ahead.

I learned a great deal working with the members of the Zen leadership. I was
impatient with their patience with one another and their ability to resist coming
to closure, but they made progress. When they finally made decisions, the choices
were usually sound, and the group was committed. They supported one another
as they grew into their new and rather frightening responsibilities. None of the
people in the leadership group were born leaders, probably because the charismatic former *roshi* had gathered around him people who were loyal followers and
would not challenge his authority. His departure had followed a period of reck-
less expansion into a number of businesses, only some of which were viable. There
were deep divisions around the *roshi*'s exodus, and community membership was
shrinking. In the businesses, the community was having to move from a volunteer
work force to a mixture of paid and unpaid staff. In the midst of this confusion,
the group kept a sense of perspective and good humor that was amazing to me.

In working with the Zen group, I followed a practice I had begun when I was
first in Europe and working in cultures not my own. Rather than trotting out the
gifts I have brought from my background and experience, I encourage my clients
to use their unique traditions and skills to address their issues. In that way, I learn
about the deep structure of their culture, and I communicate respect for it. Later,
I can add what I have brought, couching it in language and metaphor that con-
nects with the group members' shared cultural experience. In the case of the Zen
community, I had faith that its rich spiritual tradition would provide a viable approach to almost anything that might come up. Since I had only a cursory famil-
iarity with that tradition, when my clients found themselves in difficulty, I would
first ask whether there was not some Zen teaching relevant to the dilemma of the
moment. I tried to stretch their understanding and utilization of their spiritual
practice into the worldly concerns they were facing at the time. It was not dramatic
work, but it was quietly satisfying, and it stimulated my hunger for community.

From Organization to Organism at Findhorn

In 1987, together with my new partner, Celest, I began to explore community living. We began with a visit to Findhorn in Scotland, a New Age, spiritually oriented community. Roger Benson, a talented OD consultant and one of the focalizers at Findhorn, asked me to do an organizational diagnosis of the community, which was going through difficult changes. Celest and I interviewed a good-sized sample of old and new residents and guests, and came up with a lot of meaty and interesting but indigestible data. We tried to fit them into the organization culture model we were exploring at the time, and they could be made to fit the model moderately well, but it was unsatisfying to me. When a model really works for me, there is a brilliant clarity to it. It is almost like a crystal in one's mind, and it is a deeply satisfying aesthetic experience. When I do an organizational diagnosis, I generally overwhelm myself with input and let the data churn around in my thoughts; eventually they organize themselves into the crystalline pattern, and I experience an emotional release and a feeling of great satisfaction. At those moments, I feel as though I am doing an important part of what I came into this life to do.

Celest and I had very little time to prepare our presentation to the entire community, and both of us became anxious. With three hours to go, I was still worrying with the data, looking for the pattern, which just would not come, probably because I felt under so much pressure. Finally, we went to the meditation temple in search of inspiration, and I lay down on the floor under the center of its dome and asked the Angel of Findhorn to give me the pattern that would communicate what community members needed to understand about their organization. I was not sure what the Angel of Findhorn was, but most of the community members seemed to feel there was an "overlighting spirit" (guardian, protector, overseer) that looked after Findhorn's well being, and I knew I needed all the help I could get! After a while a pattern came to me, and I share it here because I believe it applies to many voluntary groups and organizations.

There are four forces that are found in different amounts in any community. The first three are alignment, attunement, and individualism, which I define as follows:

- *Alignment:* the workings of *purpose* in a group. A group is aligned when there is a strong sense of a mission and common goals and values to which all the members are committed.
- *Attunement:* the workings of *love* or *heart* in a group. A group is attuned when the members have strong feelings of caring for and connection with one another, when being together is just as important or more important than the task or work they do.
- *Individualism:* the workings of *self* or *ego* in a group. A group is individualistic

when people are primarily there to foster their own growth and to meet their own needs.

It is the balance among these three forces that creates the community's climate or culture (Figure 8.1). When a community is in transition, the balance among the forces is disturbed, and people take sides around the values of each orientation. Then the three forces tend to be centrifugal, pulling community members in differing directions and contributing to disintegration and divisiveness in the group. Many communities fall apart trying to resolve such imbalances.

Every group must find a balance among the three forces and find a way to hold itself together in the face of the tension they exert. In business or government, the tension is managed by the application of power and structure: the control of monetary resources and the power to make and enforce policies and procedures. In intentional communities like Findhorn, there has to be some more intangible unifying force. It may be the charisma and personal power of a leader, or it may be what I call *spirit*, the fourth force shown in Figure 8.1.

Spirit is that sense of *unity* or *oneness* that is beyond our egos, our emotional entanglements with one another, and even our passions for doing good. In a community like Findhorn, spirit is experienced through meditating together and through tuning in to higher guidance. When we join together in asking to know what is for the highest good, and we open ourselves to receiving that knowledge, we are invoking spirit. The guidance arrives as intuitive knowing, freed from the influence of our hopes and fears. Spirit, in a group that knows how to access it, can be a powerful unifying force against the opposing pull of the other three forces. I put it in the center of the model in Figure 8.1 because, unlike the other forces, it is not divisive, but integrating and healing.

I find this model to be useful and easy for community members to understand. It offers a way of understanding the reasons why communities disintegrate so readily, and why those that do not so often have a shared spiritual practice and commitment. We North Americans tend especially to individualism, and we experience the isolation, loneliness, and stress that are the costs of living in a society where people are primarily oriented to looking after themselves. We want the benefits of community: we want to be attuned, to be in relationship. But that attunement requires a degree of trust and a willingness to surrender our autonomy that most of us cannot bring ourselves to do in relationship to others. Surrender is never easy for highly individuated people, and some degree of it is necessary for any community, group, or organization to work well. It can be made easier by a shared spiritual commitment to which all can dedicate themselves.

In Search of Co-Creative Relationships

My experience with developing the model at Findhorn was bittersweet. It was the first time I had asked the unseen for help with my work, and the immediacy and

FIGURE 8.1. A MODEL OF COMMUNITY CULTURE.

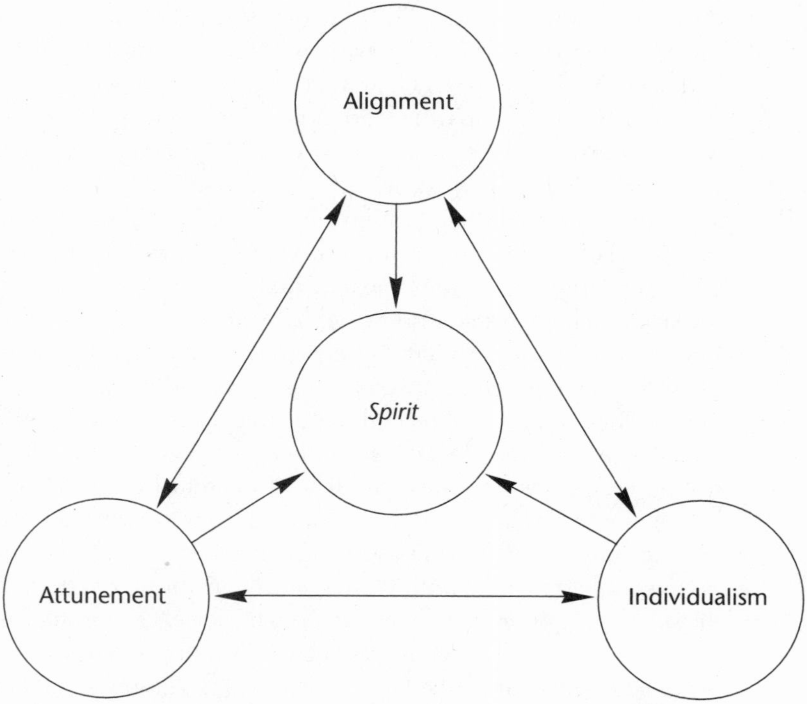

elegance of the response was a wonderful encouragement. I began to ask for help whenever I was stuck. Now my practice has evolved to where I always ask for help and guidance in my professional and creative work. It is always given when I ask for what will bring the highest good. I feel myself not so much an independent contributor as the embodied member of a team, the local agent. I suppose that what I do is not much different in essence from any other kind of prayer.

However, the experience at Findhorn also contained a serious interpersonal failure. I received my gift of insight with only three hours to go before Celest and I were to make our presentation, and our preparation for it was hurried and ragged. Celest was upset by my having ignored her wish to prepare well in advance, a reaction presaging that of my colleague in the R&D company project a couple of years later. Celest, too, decided she wanted no further professional association with me. This was particularly poignant to me because we were sharing our lives at that time, not only our work. From our early work together, I felt I had found someone with whom I could have a true co-creative partnership. In our scheduled presentation to the Findhorn conference only two days before, Celest and I had presented "From Organization to Organism" together. I had described our new model of the evolution of consciousness in organizations, and Celest then talked about how people might apply it and led the community through a visualization process.

As Celest spoke, she had seemed surrounded by light and love, bringing into the group's space a transcendent quality of feminine wisdom that had little to do with her actual words. The audience was deeply moved by the feelings she brought into the hall. Many people came to us afterwards to say how inspired they had been by what we gave. I knew in that moment, watching and listening to Celest, that this was true partnership. It had something to do with each of us doing what he or she did best, and together creating something whole that was beyond what each of us brought as an individual. I knew that I had been searching for that experience of diversity within wholeness all my life, finding it in my best moments in NTL and in my work with David Berlew. Now it seemed once again within my grasp, but within a space of days, it was lost again. I bitterly regretted my lack of sensitivity and respect, but I also knew that under similar circumstances, it would occur again. So it did in the R&D company project.

The search for co-creative partnership has been, for me, another side of my longing for community. I recently came to a deeper understanding of its essence in dialogue with Carl Peters, a gifted therapist. A co-creative partnership includes two processes: one is the give-and-take of building on one another's ideas and selecting the best of those ideas to produce a joint product. Attitudes and skills of *cooperation* are essential to this aspect of the co-creative process. It requires the willingness to listen and genuine interest in one another's ideas that comes from mutual respect. It requires an openness to having each person's ideas modified and sometimes discarded, an openness fostered by a shared purpose that is experienced by each person as larger than that individual's ego gratification. I have experienced such a dance many times with colleagues, most recently in the work on organization renewal I have been doing with Sandra Florstedt, an OD consultant in Palo Alto, California.

The second process is more mysterious. It is each partner's being present for the other in support of the other's creative moments. For me, the birth of my daughter, Susan Jane, was such an event. The joy of it was in surrendering all my will and ego and devoting all my love to Diana's birthing of new life. It was perhaps the peak experience of our marriage; we were high on it for days or weeks thereafter, and I still feel love and joy when I think on it. Yet I had not *done* anything. My contribution was simply to *be there*, a present participant in the mystery of my partner's creation. Before that experience, I would not have believed that devotion to another's creative process could have been so full of magical joy.

The patriarchal culture from which society is just beginning to emerge provides many examples of women who devote themselves to supporting a male partner's creativity; now there are couples here and there in which a man supports a woman's creative process. I had a moment of that with Celest at Findhorn. I do not know any couples in which *each* partner supports the other in this way, and it is this mutual support, each being totally for the other's creative process, that is the holy grail for which I look and long. It may not be achievable at this stage in this society's emancipation from the patriarchy, partly because so few men are willing to devote themselves to supporting a woman's creativity and partly because so few women are willing to let them. To allow oneself to be supported in this way requires an acceptance of the mystery and power of one's own creative process such that one surrenders to it completely, follows it wherever it leads, and accepts the devotion and surrender of another who places himself or herself in service to it.

To support another in this way requires going beyond the ego investment that many of us in this society have in the products of our own creative processes, so that we do not feel diminished by the power of another's creativity. It requires that we accept our differences in partnership and do not compete to be good at the same things. We need to know that what we offer in our devotion to supporting the other's creativity is good and that it is *enough*. The task demands much more than most of us can manage to sustain, but each opportunity to practice it offers the chance to know for a moment what it is like to walk the earth in partnership as gods. We should not let our periodic and inevitable descents from grace prevent us from partaking in that joy.

Experiencing the Shadow Side of Community

Our disappointments in one another aside, Celest and I were inspired by what we experienced at Findhorn. It is a place where people devote themselves to bringing light and spirit into the world and provide their visitors and guests with an experience of what it is like to live in that light and spirit on a nonsectarian path. On our return to Berkeley, Celest and I initiated several attempts to bring people together to explore community, and we soon became associated with a Findhorn-inspired retreat center in California. That association provided us with an initial lift and then a difficult descent into the dark side of community. The retreat center provided the most intense experience I have had of conflict between speaking my truth and being accepted by a group of people I cared for.

The retreat center was founded by former Findhorn community members who wanted to create a "center of light" that would carry on the Findhorn traditions of reverence for all life, spiritually oriented cooperation with nature, and consensus-based governance and decision making. The founders located a magnificent piece of land combining hilly redwood forest, rich bottom farmland, and a river. It was equipped with a fine lodge and about thirty cabins in various states of repair. The founders fell in love with it, and so did others interested in the community. They raised enough money to purchase a lease with an option to buy the property. When the option came due, they would have to come up with around $250,000 for the down payment.

The retreat center was led by a charismatic former real-estate developer with a gift for creative financing and visionary communication. It attracted a mixed group of New Age people, mostly professional and managerial, who were invited to purchase limited partnerships in order to raise the down payment. The community was organized as a retreat center, providing housing and meeting facilities for workshops, training, and the like. Unfortunately, the income did not equal expenses, and during the first years, much of the money collected from the limited partners went to operating expenses. The down payment remained a dream.

Celest and I became limited partners shortly after learning about the retreat center, and we took a keen interest in the financial affairs of the organization. We were seen as supportive and helpful, and in due course, we were invited to join the board of directors. By that time, we were both convinced that the retreat center was in serious financial trouble, was running the risk of failing to keep its commitments to investors, and would only survive by some miraculous process that combined divine intervention with human grit and determination.

I almost did not make it onto the board because, under questioning, I so offended the board members by my remarks about how I saw them handling the organization's finances. I said I saw the community as being in deep financial trouble and unlikely to meet its commitments to investors. I suggested that if we as board members could not turn things around, we should go to the investors, open our books, and ask them whether we should continue, or close down the operation, sell the option, and use the proceeds to pay the investors back as much as we could of their original investment. In saying this, I was being deliberately provocative, sending a wake-up call to the board members, whom I regarded as having their heads in the sand and engaging in New Age wishful thinking. Some of the board members saw me as a negative thinker and lacking in faith. Their article of faith was that by holding fast to its positive intention and by affirming prosperity, the board would be able to "manifest" the money in some miraculous way. I believe board members only voted me in because, at some level, they knew they needed someone to represent the shadow and speak the unspeakable. It is a role I have taken since childhood.

There is no one, I think, who has more faith than I in the power of thought and intention to manifest miraculous results and enlist unknown and unseen forces on one's behalf. I believe that my good fortune in life has been beyond luck, and I feel guided and protected at every turn. Changes in my personal and professional life and in my prosperity have often had the quality of an affirmation in which my desire and will are responded to by the universe, and miraculously, my intentions bear fruit.

There are natural laws that govern the making of miracles, just as there are for other phenomena. I do not know all of them, but some of those I believe I know were being violated by the board members. They had plenty of faith and good intentions, but they were out of tune with current reality. They were engaging in groupthink, convincing one another that the financial picture was better than it was. And because of their mutual self-deception, they were complacent. Thus, they were in nonconformance with laws I believe we must respect in working with unseen worlds.

One of these laws is to hold a high vision and to be determinedly honest about current reality. All of us exert maximum power through our thoughts when we hold both our vision of the future and an accurate view of how current reality differs from it. This is also the view espoused by Charles Kiefer and Peter Senge in their Leadership and Mastery course, which I attended in the early 1980s. According to this "rubber band" theory of manifestation, it is essential to affirm the vision and also to be scrupulously honest about current reality (see Figure 8.2).

When we hold a vision and at the same time allow ourselves to be fully aware of current reality, we set up and maintain a continuous tension between the vision and reality. It is as though there were a rubber band connecting the vision to reality. The distance between the two stretches the rubber band. By holding our vision firmly, we fix one end of the rubber band. Only reality is movable in a system that includes both reality and a resolutely held vision. Our minds do not like an unresolved tension, and neither, it seems, does the universe. The fixed vision exerts an attraction on reality, and the latter begins to move toward the vision, reducing the tension.

I and many other people have experienced this phenomenon. When our intention is firmly fixed on our vision, and we are honest with ourselves about how far we are from the realization of that vision, we find we are then programmed to observe and take advantage of every event that impacts our project. We begin to see opportunities where before we saw barriers. Our creativity is enhanced, and we receive inspiration. Heaven begins to move in mysterious ways, and large and small miracles occur.

The retreat center board members exhibited an error that I have also seen committed in business groups that use visioning: most of their time and attention was put into articulating a vision, and much less was given to diagnosing current reality and comparing it with the vision. Groupthink and selective perception were

FIGURE 8.2.   KIEFER AND SENGE'S RUBBER BAND THEORY.

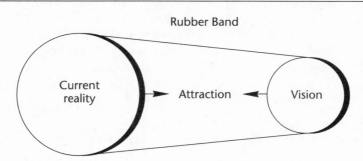

Source: Fritz, R. *The Path of Least Resistance*. New York: Ballentine Books, 1989, p. 114. Used with permission.

used to reduce the tension between the vision and reality, in the interests of comfort. When there is little tension between our perception of current reality and our vision, there is little energy for change. This might be called a type one visioning error. (The type two visioning error is to be unable to lift our heads from the ground in front of us and gaze into the future long enough to articulate our hearts' desires. Type two errors are common in organizations that are good at tracking their performance but that lack vision. They remain mired in physical reality, and again the tension that makes for change is lacking.)

The board members' second error was not to understand or practice *true faith*. To me, true faith stems from intuition, an inner knowing that is uninfluenced by the twin sirens of wish and fear. Intuition's powerful searchlight is dimmed and deflected from the truth by either of these emotions. The board's hope for a miracle went under the name of faith, but it was nearly pure wish. One way to tell the difference between wish and true faith is to examine whether the profession of faith is used to deny or distort what we normally think of as reality. By the time Celest and I joined the board, it was clear to us that wish was masquerading as faith, and truth was suffering thereby.

The story has a happy sequel, although it was bittersweet for me personally. The board was able in due course to acknowledge financial reality, and to take creative steps to resolve its contradictions. Board members raised the down payment on the property by selling individuals the right to use parts of the land to construct vacation housing for themselves. Celest and I were eventually honored as performing a useful, legitimate role. The board had lost its innocence, and it was far from the cozy, happy group it had been before we came, but it was wiser and more effective. However, after that, I never felt quite accepted or trusted by some of the members nor by the staff, some of whom had seen our willingness to contemplate shutting down the operation as a betrayal and an assault upon their livelihood.

At the time, I said to myself, as I have so often in similar situations, "Somebody has to do it. I guess I'm elected." But the positive outcomes in this situation cost me too much pain, and I ended by asking, "Why me? Why do I have such a passion for carrying the shadow for everyone else?" I am no longer so willing to make such sacrifices to help others understand their dark sides. I suppose I shall always have a keen eye for the shadow, but I have become more discerning and reticent about putting my comfort and membership on the line in support of my view of truth.

Passages to India

My next experience of spiritual community was in the ashram of Sai Baba in India. It came about because, in 1989, I was offered a trip to India. In return for giving seminars in Indian companies, my fare would be paid to a conference, "Business as a Learning Community," in Goa, that Harrison Owen and I had initiated. Since contracting a serious case of bacillary dysentery in Mexico in 1967, I had been avoiding travel to any area where I might repeat such an experience. Now, weighing my wish to participate in the conference with my reluctance to expose myself to disease and depressing conditions in India, I phoned Jack Hawley, a fellow consultant who had spent a lot of time in India, for advice. I also asked him where I might go in India in search of spiritual experience. He told me that he and his wife, Louise, were devotees of Sai Baba, an Indian saint and avatar. They now spent about half their time at his ashram in the little village of Puttaparti, near Bangalore, where Jack was working on a book on the application of spiritual principles to management (for the fruits of Jack's labors, see Hawley, 1993). Jack and Louise warmly invited me to come there. In the mid eighties, I had once before briefly entertained the idea of visiting Sai Baba, drawn by my aunt's firsthand stories of his spiritual powers. When I decided not to go, put off by my health concerns, I mused to myself that I was perhaps in the situation of a Roman at the dawn of our Christian era who heard of Jesus Christ and believed what he had heard but neglected to go and sit at His feet out of concern with the difficulty of the journey.

Now I felt that perhaps I was being given a second chance for enlightenment, and with some trepidation I agreed to attend the conference. My mood was low as I boarded the plane. My relationship with Celest was nearing a breaking point. I was losing my R&D client to my colleague. My daughter had recently decided that she wanted to live full time with her mother. I felt lonely and rejected, and my self-esteem was badly bruised. But when I arrived at Bombay in the middle of the night, all that changed. I stepped out of the plane into the warm night, and as soon as my feet touched the ground, I felt a warm, comforting peace descend upon me, as though the Divine Mother had wrapped her arms around me. I gave a great sigh and said to myself, "It's going to be all right; you're being taken care of."

I had some adventures getting to the ashram. The airport taxi driver took me to the wrong hotel. A man I was supposed to meet in Bangalore was away, and his assistant did not know what to do with me. Toward evening, he put me on a ramshackle bus for Puttaparti, where I finally arrived four and a half bone-rattling hours later. The town square was deserted, not a rickshaw or taxi to be seen, so I followed some others who were headed to the ashram on foot, dragging my heavy suitcase behind me. The ashram was shut, but a guard let me in, and miraculously, the housing office was still open. When I arrived at my assigned lodging, the building was locked. A guard appeared and let me in. When I knocked on the door of my room and identified myself, I was ordered to "go away and come back in the morning." However, other voices invited me in, and I was given a thin pad to put between me and the concrete floor and a space in which to lay my body down. Throughout these events, which ordinarily would have caused me uncertainty and anxiety, the feeling persisted that I was under the protection of some loving power; it was a uniquely comforting feeling and unique in my life experience.

The second morning I was there, I began my spiritual practice by getting up at 4 A.M. and going to the temple for daybreak ceremonies. It was pouring down rain, a torrential tropical storm, when I ventured out in the pitch black that morning. I almost did not go on, but something impelled me to wade through the ankle-deep water rushing through the streets. Once seated in the temple and beginning to chant "om," I was saturated with the most intense feeling of love I have ever experienced. It was not a feeling either of loving or being loved, but of being love, of existing as love and in love. It was so sweet and wonderful that I could not stop sobbing with joy. I knew I was experiencing the presence of God, and I felt that Sai Baba was making it possible for me to have this experience. I knew at that moment what grace is; never in my wildest dreams had I expected such an experience, and it was nothing I had to deserve or do anything to receive. My heart opened, and a great gratitude to God for this love and grace poured out from me.

Along with my joy, there was a fear that the experience would end, and I would once again be alone. I kept praying silently, "Please don't leave me now that I have found you." Of course, the bliss diminished, but it returned, more or less strongly, from time to time. It was my sign, my talisman, my welcoming to the knowledge that God is and that God is love.

Confrontation with My Own Harmfulness

Most of individuals' time is open at the ashram, and I spent a great deal of that time reviewing my life in its new frame—myself as a child of God. One powerful experience occurred when I read a "Thought for the Day" from Sai Baba. These thoughts were always posted in the main street across from the dining hall. The words were something like, "If you step on a man's foot and break a bone, it will heal. If you hurt another with your words, the wound will never heal." Those words, which rang utterly and completely true, struck me like a thunderbolt. I had always thought the opposite: "Sticks and stones may break my bones, but words will never hurt me." Of course, my own experience was that words did hurt and that I could take a long time to recover from them, but I thought that was just because I was overly sensitive.

I returned to my room and lay down on my cot, thinking of all the hurtful things I had said to people in my life whom I loved: my wives, my lovers, my daughter, my parents, and on and on. I must have cried for hours. Perhaps I was wallowing in self-blame, but I felt I had been given the gift of a chance to live differently, without harm to others. I resolved never to harm another soul with unkind or angry words. I have not succeeded in this endeavor, but it remains a constant ideal, and it is satisfying to me to experience myself moving toward it.

After twelve days at the ashram, I went on to the conference, "Business as a Learning Community." My initial contact with the other conferees was a major culture shock, not because they were Indian, but because I felt plunged back into a world of illusion. Somehow, I got through the first evening's cocktails and appetizers and introductions, but I was barely present. My altered state made it difficult for me to function intellectually, and the consequence was that I connected with other participants at the level of heart or not at all. Indian businesspeople are no more overtly spiritual than Westerners, but I was, even for me, unusually willing to be the first to share. I moved to quite a deep level of rapport at the spiritual level with some of the people in the conference, and this rapport delighted me.

Giving Organization Culture Workshops

After the conference, I went to Delhi and paid for my air fare by giving a new workshop, "Working with Organization Culture," to top managers of the Birla Group, a family-owned conglomerate that manufactures, among other things, most of the cars sold in India. My experiences in the R&D company project had taught me that culture change is difficult, painful, and expensive. I was coming to think that it is more useful to think of culture as a limiting factor in a change, and to work more with the culture rather than against it. In this workshop, I introduced for the first time the concept that has since become a hallmark of my work on the management of change: that change strategies and tactics be matched to the culture of the organization.

The workshop was well received, and I left with invitations to return to India, which I did together with Celest, four months later. By that time, Celest and I knew we would separate on our return, and the trip was both sad and sweet for each of us. We went first to Sai Baba at Puttaparti, then visited another great saint, the Mata Amritanandamayi on the south coast, did some sightseeing, and together conducted the workshop Organization Culture and Total Quality Management in Delhi. We were treated with great kindness and hospitality by our hosts, and we made more good friends.

More Reflections on Community

On my first trip to Puttaparti, I was so self-involved that I paid little attention to the organization and functioning of the community. This second time, I saw it through Celest's eyes, and I took more distance from it. To an American, there is a strong feeling in the community of order, discipline, obedience, and control. There appears to be a tight hierarchy, blessed by Sai Baba. However, Sai Baba takes no overtly visible part in the operation of the ashram, which is the size of a small town, including schools, a college, and a hospital, and which I believe has facilities to house and feed upwards of 20,000 people during the great religious holidays (including Christmas!).

There are strict rules of behavior, especially between the sexes. Men and women are discouraged from having any contact unless they are husband and wife. There are guards, called *sevas* (*seva* means "service"), everywhere to enforce this and other rules. One learns the rules and procedures through doing the wrong thing and being corrected by one of the *sevas*. There are almost no requirements made on those who are in residence. It is not necessary to attend any function. Neither is it normally possible to influence the establishment in any way. One is not even allowed to contribute money without special permission from Sai Baba himself, and permission is refused if the gift is not offered from the heart. Room and meals are provided to all at the same absurdly cheap prices; the rooms for Westerners have toilets and cold running water and are unfurnished, with three to four persons assigned to a room. Indian accommodations are much more spartan and crowded, in accordance with Indian custom.

Access to Sai Baba is limited to those he chooses during his twice daily appearances at *darshan*. During *darshan*, the people sit in rows around the temple courtyard, after having waited outside for some time. The order of admission is determined by lottery. Everyone has an equal chance to be in one of the front rows, from which it is possible to call out to Sai Baba as he passes or offer him a letter.

From the community organization and operation, one gets the impression of Sai Baba as a stern but compassionate father. After leaving Puttaparti, Celest and I went to the ashram of the Mother, Mata Amritanandamayi, where the energy was very different. The community was smaller and newer. The Mother receives her devotees during *darshan*, often holding them in her arms. People are orderly and well behaved, though there are few signs of authority or control. The atmosphere of the community and of the temple are suffused with love and the presence of the nurturing feminine. Yet it is clear that the Mother is in charge of and takes care of all who are present in the ashram and that she decides what will and will not be done.

Both these communities were different from anything I had experienced at home. In both, individuality was honored only at the highest level, that of the soul, in a deep respect for the unique qualities of each person's spiritual path and journey. At the level of daily life, things were ordered by authority in such a way as to leave the individual free to seek God without having to make mundane choices. Obedience and conformity were seen as liberating to the spirit rather than constraining. When I was able to adopt that mindset, it worked for me. When I became preoccupied with concerns about whether I was being treated with the dignity and respect due me as an individual, I became agitated and unhappy because there was little for my ego and worldly self-esteem to feed upon in those settings.

A Miracle of Healing

A lovely miracle occurred for me at the Mother's ashram. Celest and I went for *darshan*, and the Mother held us both while one of her devotees translated some questions I wanted answered. The answers were disappointing, and I left puzzled and frustrated. Then, when I returned to our room, I was amazed to find I had been completely freed from all grief and anger around my impending separation from Celest. Nothing was left in me but sweet and undemanding love and forgiveness and compassion for Celest and for myself. I remained almost continuously in that state during the remaining two weeks of our trip. On our return to the United States, the state dissipated as I returned to more familiar surroundings and concerns. However, I carry with me now the certain knowledge that forgiveness and allowing are the ultimate state of health and well-being. Forgiveness is a blessing and a release that we owe ourselves rather than something we owe others. It is a gift rather than a duty. This understanding has become a part of the deep structure underlying my current thought and writing about the healing of organizations. Needless to say, it is rather a hard sell in the current business climate!

I enjoyed working with Indian managers on organization culture, because it gave me an opportunity to test the relevance of my model in another culture. It was particularly exciting to encounter examples of ethical power cultures, in which values like loyalty, obedience, compassion, and responsibility for the welfare of employees were strongly articulated.

I came away with a respect and liking for the Indian managers I met and a wish to return. For one like myself who is interested in understanding the power of love in organizations and in society, India provides incredible riches. The Indian culture is charged with the feminine and with love. There is a softness to the atmosphere of the cities of southern India, with all their dirt and human misery, that is missing in Western urban scenes. For example, I found the streets frightening at first, clogged with traffic of all descriptions, horns blaring, all the people going as fast as they could. Then I began to discern a quality of *dance* in the way the vehicles and their drivers relate to one another. Brightly painted signs on the rear of huge lorries invite passing cars to sound their horns, and when they do, a languid hand appears from the cab, waving the passing vehicle by. Drivers jockey for position at intersections, but the feeling is good natured. All seem to intend that everyone get where he or she is going as fast as possible and without an accident. Contrast the feeling in a city like Boston, where almost every interaction with another driver is a challenge to a duel, and people see themselves as warriors of the road.

I have not yet been able to integrate the strong sense I feel in India of love and softness, with the murderous communal and domestic violence that seems so common there. It remains a contradiction, inviting me to go deeper for understanding. Regardless of contradictions, I continue to carry within me a strong heart connection to Mother India, her life, her spirit, and her people.

CHAPTER NINE

FOSTERING HEALING AND LEARNING IN ORGANIZATIONS

O n our return from India, Celest and I separated as planned. As I considered where to live and what to do with my life, I was once again drawn to the idea of living in community. I was feeling fragile, even shattered, and I felt it would be good for me to have other people around me during my healing. There were groups of Sai Baba devotees in the Bay Area, but so far as I knew, no community, and my experience of their group meetings had left me feeling pretty much the way I felt at Puttaparti—on my own. In the research I had done about intentional communities, one that kept coming up was Ananda, founded by a disciple of Paramhansa Yogananda and located near Nevada City, California. It seemed a place to start looking. After I phoned and learned that a one-week course in meditation was beginning in a day or so, I packed and left so quickly that I forgot to cancel my business appointments for the following week.

My week at Ananda was healing for me. I was touched by the music, a combination of traditional Hindu chants and other chants composed by Yogananda and by J. Donald Walters (Kriyananda), Ananda's founder. The chanting opened my heart and let God's healing love in. For years, I have chosen to pursue spiritual practices that evoke love and compassion in me. I have passed by other paths I deeply respect, such as Zen, because they do not open my heart. Ananda, with its focus on chanting and devotion and awakening the love of God, felt like a place I needed to be, and I was delighted to hear that they were opening a satellite community in Mountain View, about thirty-five miles south of Berkeley in the Silicon Valley area. I visited the new facility, a cluster of apartment buildings with mostly one-bedroom apartments and space for perhaps 120 persons, and instantly decided to move there. It was an uncharacteristically impulsive decision for one who normally weighs all the factors. As I write this, I have been in this community for four and a half years.

Kriyananda founded Ananda to carry out an intention of his guru, Yogananda, to establish "world brotherhood communities" where people who were not ready to become monks or renunciates could live in an atmosphere of peace and harmony, with structures that would support their spiritual practice. Here, there are few rules (no alcohol, no drugs, and a vegetarian diet). We can join others for weekday evening meals, for which we pay and, optionally, work. Each person is responsible for his or her own finances. In the apartment complex where I live, we pay market rents.

Adherence to a spiritual path is expected but not enforced: we are expected to meditate regularly and to join with the community in worship and prayer. There are morning group meditations, group classes, and Sunday services, and spiritual counseling is available from the community's ministers. People vary greatly in the extent to which they avail themselves of these resources, and there seem to be no penalties for failure to conform. For example, during a period of six months or so, while reevaluating my commitment to this path, I participated in none of the community worship and classes.

The best thing about Ananda is that it is a *sane* and a loving place, and at the level of daily life, it works very well. It is easy here for me to practice my intention to avoid hurtful speech. Our implicit norm of nonviolence in word and deed creates an atmosphere in which people show their best side most of the time. My aggressiveness and competitiveness are not normally evoked by the behavior of others here, and so I can live from my loving and light-seeking side. My darker self has not departed, but there is little for it to feed upon. When I leave to work or play with others outside the community, I can usually carry on those positive patterns until I return for a "recharge." The result is that I am a sweeter person than I was before I came here. I like that a lot!

My life here is not without inner struggle. I am as individualistic as anyone I know and as committed to values of empowerment and participation. I have found it a real stretch to live in this "dharmocracy." Decisions for the community are made by the spiritual leaders, who are believed to know best by virtue of their progress along our spiritual path. Criticism of those decisions is gently discouraged. At first, I was just glad to be living in a community that worked, where people treated one another with kindness, and where my practice of meditation and prayer was supported. My primary concerns were healing from the loss of my partner and finding a place in this new and unfamiliar social structure. I am older, more affluent, and perhaps more involved in the outside world than the majority of the others. Although my soul settled in quite quickly, it took a long while for my personality to feel at home.

For example, I soon found myself irked by community meetings in which communication was one way. I did not accept that those who are most spiritually advanced and closest to Kriyananda are also wisest and most competent in leading all aspects of community life. I was concerned by what I felt was a tendency on the part of some community members to venerate Kriyananda as more than mortal. I think I was also put out at being nobody special in the community and at not being sought out for my organizational expertise. I am used to being noticed, not only because of whatever personal magnetism I have acquired but also because doing the work of a consultant makes me stand out as different or special in whatever organization I enter. Consultants are not always liked or accepted, but they are almost always noticed! At Ananda, although kindness and a sort of impersonal acceptance are available to all, I have experienced an unaccustomed invisibility. Distinction is earned through service to the community and devoted participation in spiritual instruction. Access to the councils of the community is offered to those who have shown their dedication in these ways.

Dropping the Burden of the Shadow

I know from observation and study that a leadership group whose spiritual development falls short of sainthood makes a mistake if it cuts itself off from the wisdom and the feedback from the rank and file. Cults begin when inquiry stops. I thought the Ananda leaders were encapsulated in a social matrix made up of people like themselves. I felt they were losing touch with the rest of us (meaning me!) and that the community was losing energy and vitality as a result. I went through an acutely uncomfortable period during which I felt myself to be the only one who saw that the emperor was not fully dressed. I felt inner pressure to speak my truth, but I feared to become even more isolated if I spoke. In the past when I had such feelings, I felt it my responsibility to uncover what I believed to be the truth—wherever I saw it, whatever the cost. That was the role I took at the retreat center. I paid for it by losing my comfort and sense of membership in the community. This time, however, I was silent while I wrestled with my issues. I was bone-tired of carrying the dark side of every group I joined. The part of me that wants peace and harmony was questioning my compulsion to speak the unacknowledged, and I doubted that my compulsion was truly in service to me or to the community.

I have tended to relate to every group, beginning with my family, as an outsider. Thus, I have often chosen to take the role of change agent, whether my choice was mutually agreed or not. My self-assigned function includes telling or uncovering the truth, and when I do not speak out, I feel that I no longer possess integrity. I also tend not to experience the feelings of loyalty that motivate others in groups because I do not consider myself to be *a part* of groups or organizations. I remember getting a look at my personnel file when I was at Procter & Gamble.

The plant manager under whom I first worked described me as intelligent and competent but seemed puzzled by my lack of any demonstrated sense of loyalty to the company. I was puzzled that he should have expected it. It was an indication that something was missing in me that was highly valued in the corporate world of that time (although not now).

For a long time, I felt that at Ananda I did not want to live out the outsider's script that I have followed all my life, yet I had no well-articulated alternative. I felt that to give in and go with the flow was weak and lacked integrity. So I lived in an uncomfortable condition of indecision. Eventually, I realized that my purpose in being in an organization need not be to change it (a blinding flash of the obvious!). I decided that there is no compromise to my integrity in remaining silent or accepting things as they are as long as others are not being harmed or exploited. This decision gave my heart ease, and I became more comfortable. I knew that if asked I could and would speak my truth although I was quite sure I would not be asked.

Even so, the issue of truly joining in has continued to be a barrier to my participation in the life of my chosen community. I have often absented myself from the community's work, play, and spiritual practice, and I have withheld my time and energy. I am recycling a life pattern of minimizing my participation in situations where I feel I cannot fully be myself. Certainly as a youth and young adult, I tended to withdraw from family and school, and I contributed as little as I could. When I believe I cannot be accepted for who I truly am, I tend to withdraw in this way. Unfortunately, I have only to perceive a little of what seems to be evidence that I am not safe to trigger my withdrawal.

The Ananda Community is founded on the assumptions underlying *discipleship,* rare in our culture but common in the East. One of these assumptions is that one's spiritual teachers are aware of truths that cannot be communicated by the spoken or written word but only through experience. Therefore, in order to have experiences that lead to a higher level of understanding, one must at times place oneself in obedience to the teachers' guidance, on the basis that "they wouldn't be there if they didn't know what they are doing." Sometimes, the guidance will not seem to make rational sense, and then one is expected to put oneself into a state of inquiry, asking, "What may be blocking me from appreciating the wisdom of my teacher's words or actions?" Although I have taken discipleship vows, I find myself holding back from giving that level of trust to the leaders of my community, either in spiritual or in secular matters.

In life and learning, I follow the dialectical pattern I referred to in Chapter Two (see Figure 2.1). Speaking my truth and keeping silent are two poles in my dialectic that I have now explored in my life in community. Withholding my energy versus being obedient is a related issue. Integrating those opposites will require that I shift to a higher level. I feel that there is such a larger shift moving in me, and perhaps in the world as well, and that it has to do with the meaning of *surrender* in the life of the individual and in organizations.

A New Model of Organization Culture

In order to provide a frame for my discussion of surrender, I will first summarize the model of organization culture with which I am currently working. It derives from the work on individual development that I published as "A Practical Model of Motivation and Character Development" (Harrison, 1979), and from my thinking about levels of consciousness (Harrison, 1990 [†]). The dialectic of individual (and also organizational) evolution seems to me to involve tension and movement between poles of relationship and separation. Moving into relationship, whether of dependency or of interdependence (mutuality), always involves some kind of surrender. Refusal or negation of surrender is then required to move to the next stage of growth, one of separation or differentiation. After working for some time with the model I described earlier of the power, role, achievement, and support cultures, I learned ways to revise the model and make it more useful. I am currently working with a model of four archetypal cultures called *transactional, self-expression, alignment,* and *mutuality* (Figure 9.1), and my description here is condensed from the second section of *Humanizing Change: Matching Interventions to Organizational Realities* (Harrison, Cooper, and Dawes, 1991).

The cultures are arranged to reflect successive developmental stages. I call the first and lowest-level culture transactional because it motivates through *exchange.* People get what they want in return for doing what they are told to do. This culture is typical of traditional business organizations, which operate on fear and hope of reward and exercise control through personal power or impersonal bureaucratic roles, structures, and procedures. Another name for the transactional archetype is patriarchy. It fosters dependence, and when one is operating in the transactional mode, the meaning of *surrender* is to give up one's own will in return for protection and sustenance. One gives obedience in order to get tangible and intangible rewards which one is too weak or disadvantaged to obtain for oneself.

The transactional form has been challenged in the recent past by an emergent set of values and organizational arrangements based on individuality and autonomy. I call this more recent form the self-expression culture. Its basic assumption is similar to McGregor's (1960) well-known Theory Y, that people have an internal motivation to produce and create and that they work best when they are given meaningful and intrinsically satisfying work and are trusted to manage themselves. The self-expression culture is found in many high-technology firms, some R&D and consulting organizations, and many associations of individual professionals such as doctors and lawyers. There has been a great increase in the number of organizations with strong self-expression elements in the last decade or two. Individuality and celebration of the self have been developing strength in the larger culture since the sixties. People want and expect to have challenging and meaningful work through which they can learn and grow, and they expect to be given responsibility and autonomy in the doing of that work.

FIGURE 9.1. LEVELS OF CONSCIOUSNESS IN ORGANIZATION CULTURE.

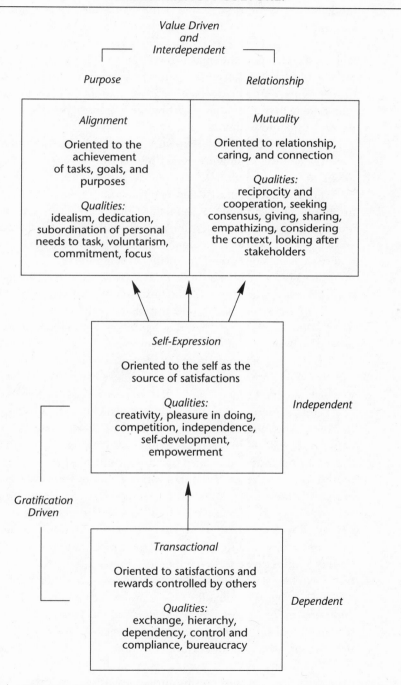

When one is operating in the self-expression mode, *surrender* means the negation of selfhood. It is giving up the ego, as well as the will. The self-expression mode is often a transitional state, similar to adolescence. It involves negating the surrender of the transactional phase, in the service of personal (or organizational) differentiation. In this mode, the ego is not completely secure. Threats to the ego are seen by the individual as reversing the gains made through his or her personal evolution. The struggle against ego death is not carried on solely with authority figures but with peers as well. For example, the difficulties people have in maintaining marital relationships are due in part to their seeing the marriage partner as a threat to selfhood.

The transactional and self-expression cultures are *gratification driven*. In contrast, the cultures of alignment and mutuality are *value driven*, because the motive power in the latter cultures is beyond the satisfaction of some need or lack. The motivation is always more than material, and it may be in part altruistic. Organizations with alignment and mutuality cultures are directed to the pursuit of some ideal, principle, or goal that is intrinsically valued, or they have a strong caring or service orientation. Aligned organizations appeal to the intellect and the will; mutuality organizations are of the heart, evoking the love and compassion of their members. Both involve a movement away from the radical separation of the self-expression mode toward relationship. Both require surrender.

The alignment culture is exemplified by the vision-driven organization in which common effort is achieved by voluntary commitment to an overarching purpose. The basic assumption of alignment is that one finds meaning and personal worth in *surrender* to something bigger than and outside of oneself, whether that something be a leader, a nation, a principle, a cause, or simply a challenging task to which one has become committed. In recent decades, the Peace Corps and the civil rights, antinuclear, right-to-life, and pro-choice movements have each given us examples of alignment, as have religious cults and Islamic and Christian fundamentalist groups. In business organizations, we see alignment in new businesses and plant startups and in such activities as nuclear test shots and intensive care units. However, the aligned organization does not have to be good or noble. Fascism and communism have both created aligned cultures that evoked willing surrender to gods of dubious origin, and a team planning and implementing a new version of the Great Train Robbery could embody the alignment culture. In business, people willingly surrender their personal time, their family and community relationships, and even their health to the achievement of goals that at the time seem larger than the self but that later seem less than world shattering. Tracy Kidder movingly describes the process in his account of the development of a new computer in *The Soul of a New Machine* (Kidder, 1981). In aligned organizations, the individual surrenders to something larger than his or her ego, but the organization often remains out of relationship with its larger environment.

In mutuality cultures, people find meaning in *relationships*. Mutuality cultures exemplify the values of community: cooperation, appreciation, respect for diversity, and caring and looking out for one another. The driving force in such cultures is human love, not in its romantic or erotic sense but in its larger sense of friendship, brotherhood and sisterhood, empathy and compassion. Such cultures operate through networks of mutual caring and reciprocal responsibilities rather than through power hierarchies or formal structures, rules, and procedures.

The mutuality ethic is one of responsibility and caring rather than one of rights and justice. It derives from the feminine side of our nature rather than from our patriarchal archetypes. Its basic assumption is systems oriented and participative: as individuals, and as organizations, we are not independent but exist as parts of ever larger systems that nurture and sustain us; every action we take impacts everything else in the system, so we need to appreciate our connections in order to act responsibly.

My idea of the mutuality culture has much in common with Rhiane Eisler's feminist partnership model (Eisler, 1987; Eisler and Loye, 1990). My transactional culture sounds much like her dominator model. We differ in my including self-expression as an in-between way of managing relationships, and in my interest in nonhierarchical ways in which masculinity can be expressed, such as in stewardship and the aligned culture.

I believe we cannot effectively deal with the major issues organizations face without balancing masculine ways with feminine ways, as exemplified by the mutuality archetype. I have seen mutuality working in balance with alignment in production plants organized around self-managing teams. Such diverse OD tasks as training in managing diversity, systems thinking, and working on whole systems (for example, as in future search conferences) share basic assumptions of the mutuality archetype. Sociotechnical systems (STS) approaches are based on learnings from mutuality cultures evolved by coal miners in Britain.

In the mutuality mode, *surrender* is to the *whole*. There is an appreciation of oneself as a part of something larger which must always be honored in thought and action. In high forms of mutuality, one does not give up one's self or individuality to the larger whole but rather accepts the responsibility of membership in it. That responsibility may be described as the commitment to act in harmony with all that is. Some Native American traditions exemplify mutuality in their respect for all life and their imperative to live in harmony with nature.

Applying the Consciousness Model to Myself: Searching for the Power in Surrender

When I use this cultural framework, or consciousness model, to understand my own issues with organizations, I can say that when I was younger I reacted negatively to the transactional culture I found in my family and in school. I adopted a stance of rebellious self-expression in all sorts of relationships, personal as well as organizational. Acting for myself autonomously and independently was for a long time my growing edge. In my work in NTL, I then discovered the alignment mode. The experience of camaraderie and commitment to a shared goal has always motivated me. It was a major satisfaction in the work I did on plant startups and in collaboration with David Berlew.

When my autonomy is threatened, however, I experience giving in and going along in order to get approval as weakness and as a retreat to an earlier transactional mode. And I still tend to frame surrender in those terms, as do many. That orientation is supported by our highly individualistic North American culture. I have cunningly crafted a life in which my autonomy is rarely constrained, and I have been willing, though not content, to pay for it with loneliness. Now, later in life, my difficulties in living in community revive the issue, and I am looking to grow beyond the dichotomy of dependence versus autonomy.

I do not yet operate reliably at the level of mutuality. I can understand what it is like to operate there, and I have experienced it in some relationships. On the level of mutuality, surrender is a freely given acknowledgment that there is something I value that is greater than my individual wants, needs, and interests. When I place myself in service to that value, I honor it. I do not diminish myself, and I do not give my power to someone or something else. I have lost nothing. I give out of my fullness, and I remain full. There is no way that we can live together in peace and wholeness, whether in our relationships and families, our organizations, or our relationship to nature and the Earth, unless we can learn to surrender to a greater whole from that place of our own wholeness, valuing our surrender as an act of power and love. Paradoxically, we cannot reach that place of surrender without first having empowered ourselves.

From the transactional orientation, surrender is an acknowledgment of dependency; it expresses one's lack of power or emotional neediness. At that level, we do not have anything to give; we surrender in order to get. At the level of self-expression, we view surrender as a retreat from the ego and from our newfound autonomy and self-empowerment. It feels like a backward step in our own evolution, giving up our hard-won gains. But at that level, we have at least acquired something of value that we can give. When we feel strong enough and loving enough, we can experiment with surrender out of our own fullness. We can join others in a shared commitment to a common goal (alignment). We then stand at the doorway to mutuality, and we have within our hands the keys to peace and harmony. Until we learn to surrender, we are doomed to a life of lonely, autonomous striving, with each person acting by and for himself or herself and succeeding or failing on his or her own. Love and the experience of community do not flourish in that stony soil.

As I have experienced surrender from the place of self-expression, it is either a step downwards to dependency or a step upwards to alignment, accepting constraints in the service of a shared higher goal. I have looked for an enduring professional relationship, a life partner, a spiritual teacher, and a community. I have known that each of these relationships would require surrender, and I have held the thought that I could achieve voluntary and willing surrender if only I could find a person or organization worthy enough, something or someone higher with whom I could align my will and energy. But given my acute sensitivity to the darker side of that which is publicly proclaimed to be true and good, it is no surprise that I have always found a flaw, a weakness, some failure of integrity or greatness that rationalizes my holding back and that seems to doom me to lonely autonomy.

When we are small and weak, we surrender because we have to. It is a question of relative power, of the will. When we achieve empowerment, our surrender is volitional and conditional upon the perceived value or goodness of that to which or to whom we surrender. It becomes a question of discernment of relative worth, a function of the mind. At the level of mutuality, surrender becomes an expression of love, of the heart. Love itself is the justification of the act, not the worth of the person or organization or cause to which we surrender. That is what sets it apart from alignment, where surrender is conditional upon the worthiness of the purpose.

In the community of which I am a member, I see surrender going on at all the levels I have described. There is a part in most of us that wants to be taken care of, provided for and directed, given reliable rules to follow in a turbulent and fluid world. We are willing to accept guidance and direction from those we regard as more enlightened to help us achieve goals of security and relief from fear. Other goals provide a sense of alignment to higher purpose and a concrete path to the achievement of that purpose. Examples of such goals are building and maintaining the community, acquiring a church, or attracting more souls to the light. At another level, that of mutuality, surrender is freely given love for God and guru and for the living representatives of our path.

Like so many others who live much of their existence in a self-expression mode, I am drawn toward mutuality by a vision of wholeness and harmony between myself and all that is, and I am held back by transactional fears of being betrayed, dominated, and exploited. I have come to understand that the issue is not the worthiness of my community, the rightness of our path, or the holiness of our guides and teachers. For me, now, the issue is my fear of losing what I have gained. Yet I know that issue is an illusion. When I truly understand that I am more than my ego and that I can if need be survive betrayal, domination, and disillusionment, with pain but without permanent damage, then surrender becomes possible for me. When I fear that my self is something that can be taken from me by others, that it is contingent upon their goodness and trustworthiness, then I hold back.

As it is for individuals, so it is for organizations. In business, we have sacrificed loyalty for self-interest. As an expression of the patriarchy, that loyalty may be something we want to let go of. But there is a higher form of loyalty, surrender out of love, unmotivated by fear, hope of gain, or attachment to outcome. Another word for it is *commitment*. That kind of loyalty is freely given; it cannot be compelled or bought. It is akin to selfless service. It is intrinsically rewarding.

This is a period in which the ties that bind people together in organizations have been weakened, ignored, then rent asunder by acts of self-oriented individualism and exploitation. The individual exploits the organization, and the organization exploits the individual. Each views the other instrumentally, and their relationship continues only while it is mutually advantageous. Abandonment by employees and betrayal by organizations tend to be the norm. In these times of intense global competition and financial pressures, we are experiencing the darker side of the self-expression culture, unrestricted personal competition. Its motto is, "Everyone for himself" and "The Devil take the hindmost."

From my business and personal relationships and my experiences in community, I have come to believe that there can be no final solution to loneliness, alienation, and competitive struggle without freely given loving surrender. Cooperation is another word for it, but I prefer surrender. People can cooperate temporarily for mutual advantage without commitment. Such arrangements are fundamentally transactional. At that level, cooperation does not provide the glue that is needed to hold relationships or organizations together on a continuing basis. Surrender is not the whole solution to alienation and competition, but I believe it is an essential part. As long as we strive for advantage or hold our egos sacrosanct, struggling over who is right or who is best, we shall have no peace. We shall continue to tear our organizations and our society asunder.

The power of love is that it does not have to be convinced, persuaded, negotiated, deserved, compelled, or rewarded. It is a gift that benefits the giver as it does the receiver. It is the ultimate in renewable resources—the more it is given, the more there is to have and give. But how are we to release its power in our organizations that are now riven with power struggle, competition, and mistrust?

When I talk with leaders and managers about how to release love in their organizations, I speak of the power of love in the work itself: the enjoyment of being productive, particularly in a team; the sense of craftsmanship that comes in doing quality work; the joy in creativity and artistry; the importance of beauty in the workplace for evoking feelings of love. I talk, too, about the behaviors that foster love: the power of appreciation, recognition, and acknowledgment; the bonds that are created through mentoring, teaching, and coaching relationships; the value of being present, of listening and responding from the heart. I speak about giving trust to evoke trust and about the healing power of peacemaking and harmonizing.

People listen; often, I believe, with longing. Yet I feel I have been missing something that is necessary to trigger the release of love. We OD consultants do not start on some neutral ground; we start with organizations that are full of hierarchy, fear, mistrust, and competition. We have to work with people who have experienced abuse, abandonment, alienation, and betrayal in their organizational and personal lives, who have learned to close their hearts and button down their feelings in order to keep despair at arm's length.

Patience and healing are two keys to releasing love. Not long ago I heard the moving story of a General Motors plant manager who led the transformation of one of the worst performing assembly plants in GM's system into an organization that set new records in quality and productivity. She did it through participation and through demonstrating trust in employees. Because the employees did not trust, at first they did not keep their end of the bargain. When that happened, she spoke openly about the betrayal, but she continued to trust.

This is a practical instance of surrender. The plant manager gave up control of employees' behavior and surrendered the outcome of her act of *trust*. She remained true to her vision of the inherent goodness and trustworthiness of employees in the face of their initial failure to keep their commitments; she *forgave* their betrayal. She also spoke the *truth* about these betrayals of trust; she did not collude with employees by not mentioning the betrayals aloud. As the employees tested her resolve to trust and experienced her *commitment,* they honored their undertakings more and more, and the transformation gathered momentum and power. The plant's performance improved to the point that a decision to close it down was reversed by higher management.

I like that story because it shows how trust is not enough, just as in manifesting a vision it is necessary to tell the truth about current reality. Figure 9.2 is a model that shows what I believe are the essential steps in the process of creating mutual trust and releasing the power of love in organizations. It begins with my, your, or anyone's willingness to trust, followed by the surrendering of control over the outcome and behaving in a trusting manner. If trust is betrayed, we identify the betrayal and speak the truth about it. In speaking about the betrayal without judgment or blame, we practice forgiveness. We reaffirm our willingness to trust, surrender the outcome once again, and so on, for as many cycles as necessary or as many as we can endure, whichever comes first. I am not advocating blind or stupid trust. With frequent betrayals, our willingness to trust runs dry, and the cycle is terminated.

I cannot talk in great depth about how the model works in the world because I have come to it recently. It works for me, but I have yet to define the boundaries and limiting conditions. This model feels more complete to me than others

FIGURE 9.2. MODEL OF A LOVE-ENHANCING CIRCULAR PROCESS.

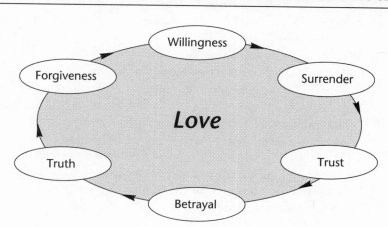

I have played with mentally. I believe that surrender and forgiveness are important elements that are seldom dealt with explicitly.

Accessing the Power of Love and Surrender

How OD consultants are to implement a love-enhancing model in organizations remains murky to me. People are now much more open to the *idea* that organizations need love in order to be effective than when I began to discuss the issue, but they remain dubious about its practicality. In fact, the suggestion of actually practicing love is an uncomfortable one for organizations. It evokes the disorder and the distractions of the erotic. Moreover, everyone knows the pain any kind of love can bring in relationships. Some people even view work as a blessedly impersonal place. If they do not have their hearts warmed at work, at least they are not as likely to be hurt as they are at home. It is also true that people do not know how to use love effectively in the workplace.

I believe, however, that for many leaders and managers the most serious drawback to releasing the power of love in work is not that it is impractical or ineffective to do so but that it cannot be controlled. Many leaders would rather have control than have access to more energy, devotion, and commitment on the part of people in the organization. When leaders and managers have to choose, they choose control.

Love and surrender have their daimonic side (as I defined that term in Chapter Six) as does every other good. The world is full of codependent relationships in which people surrender out of fear and without integrity. Love without truth and loyalty without truth can be as destructive as truth without love, perhaps more so. Loyalty without truth can be seen in organizations where people collude with leaders in the latter's betrayal of their responsibilities and in their illegal and immoral acts. In spiritual communities, followers turn blind eyes and deaf ears to abuses of power, sex, and money by leaders. Where people fear to speak and hear the truth, there can never be freely given loving surrender. Truth, of course, is often feared by leaders for the same reason they fear love; once it is let loose, it tends to spread uncontrollably.

In spite of the many uncertainties around the place and power of love in the workplace, I remain convinced that for me it is the only game worth playing because it is the only one that is sustainable. We have created a world in business where each individual looks out for himself or herself, where each organization looks out for itself, where people are viewed by organizations as supplies to be used and thrown away, and where people view organizations as "deep pockets" to be "ripped off" and exploited. It is a world that is disintegrating through lack of nurturance and maintenance. The advent of the mutuality level of organization culture is not only desirable for the healing of ourselves and our organizations, it is essential to our survival on the Earth.

Toward a Comprehensive Model of Organization Change

In the period since 1990, I have been living a rather private life, doing more writing than in the past but publishing little. However, I crossed a watershed with the monograph *Culture and Levels of Consciousness in Organizations* (Harrison, 1990). I now feel that I can say something worthwhile about organizations on a larger scale. I have been elaborating a comprehensive model of organization change that helps people think their way through a change: place their particular project on a map and plan their change strategy. Before, I thought of myself as something of a miniaturist, developing theory and elaborating models of practice for discrete aspects of the change process. With this new model, I step into a whole new arena, scary but exciting.

In 1990 and 1991, I worked with Jane Cooper and Graham Dawes of the Roffey Park Institute in Britain to expand my work on organization culture into a more comprehensive model for consulting and managing change. It was in the spring of 1991 that we brought forth *Humanizing Change: Matching Interventions to Organizational Realities* (Harrison, Cooper, and Dawes, 1991). Then in April of 1991, I conducted the first of my Humanizing Change workshops, sponsored by Marianne Erdelyi in Cleveland, Ohio. Giving this workshop has been a satisfying part of my current practice, partly because it gives me the satisfaction of giving back to others involved in change work some of the help I have received from mentors and colleagues along the way. It is similar to the satisfactions I receive from shadow consulting, which has also become a focus of my current work.

The workshop is but one part of my efforts to shift the focus of OD consulting from change to healing. I have seen the stress that attempts to change culture put on organizations, and I now advocate leveraging the strengths of the current culture as much as possible. Too often, organizations look outside of themselves when the qualities they need are hidden inside. Leaders try to wrench the organization into an appropriate mode, and in so doing, they create conflict and trauma for themselves and others. If, instead, they take the time to assess the readiness of the organization to change in various ways and to match both intervention and consulting style to the organization's culture, change can be more harmonious.

For example, transactional organizations need heavy support for change from the top, and change needs to be enshrined in new rules, roles, and structures. That is not true for self-expression organizations. As I have learned in my work with R&D organizations, self-expression organizations tend to embrace change as long as it is locally initiated. However, they often show a not-invented-here attitude to good ideas that originate elsewhere. They need to own the change, often by creating an innovative local version of whatever is happening. Mutuality organizations may be more deliberate and thoughtful than other organizations about adopting innovations, going through processes of deep reflection and consensus building before going ahead. That was my experience in the Zen organization I worked with in the eighties. Japanese organizations are also reputed to follow such patterns.

I learned something more about the trauma of mandated change when, in the fall of 1991, I journeyed to Australia and New Zealand to give a series of Humanizing Change workshops under the auspices of Kevin Hardy and Jane Bryson of the Management Consortium. I found these particular workshops difficult. Most of the participants were managers or internal consultants in the public sector who were tired and burned out from successive waves of politically mandated change in their organizations. In both Australia and New Zealand, public services were being pressured to implement leading-edge improvements such as employee involvement and Total Quality Management at the same time as their budgets were being cut and their head counts reduced. I found that quite a bit of what I had to say about matching interventions to organizational culture seemed beside the point. The participants had few degrees of freedom in implementing change. Their organizations were in retreat, their clients and colleagues were in shock, and they were feeling inadequate as they tried to drum up enthusiasm for upbeat, forward-looking programs in organizations reeling from one wave of imposed change after another. My discussions with the participants in these workshops convinced me that it was time to reframe the work of organization development, making a shift from the idea that organizations needed *agents of change* to the idea that they needed *facilitators of healing.*

For a long time, most of my client organizations had been reasonably fat and happy, sure that their way was fundamentally best, or at least good enough, and willing to consider only incremental change. To use the metaphor of the castle and battlefield once again (see Chapter Two), they were firmly in the castle, behind the moat with the drawbridge up and the portcullis down. Now the situation is reversed, if only because so many organizations have been undergoing reductions in force, downsizing not once but many times. It is now documented that the survivors of downsizing are as much or more traumatized than those who have to leave (see Noer, 1993). Those responsible for implementing change are more often than not in denial about the impact of these changes on trust, social cohesion, loyalty, and productivity. Frequently, they endeavor to implement quality and performance improvement programs or even organizational learning while the organization is still in shock following surgery. Even under ordinary circumstances, such programs require extra effort and motivation from organizational members if these individuals are to take personal risks in the service of change and improvement. To expect them to master Total Quality Management while they are healing is like telling someone who has just lost an arm or a leg to start training for the next Olympics. It is small wonder that so much work on quality in organizations that are undergoing downsizing is perfunctory. It is usually limited to training, and it is too seldom taken seriously. Organizations reap pain, not gain, from forced traumatic change. People in such organizations are going through the motions in their work, trying to hold things together, taking whatever personal and political steps they can to protect themselves from the worst, and hoping for an end to changes. Unless the betrayed trust and broken self-confidence can be mended and bonds of cooperation can be restored, such performance improvement programs have little chance of creating anything but more failure and disappointment. At best, they become nonevents; at worst, they are a drain on the organization's energy.

My professional interest in healing was given additional poignancy when my father died in the middle of my trip to Australia and New Zealand. From observing myself and my family in that time, I learned more about what people need and do not need when in grief and loss. People need love and acceptance and downtime. I believe consultants' most important work in this time is not making change happen but healing organizations and individuals who are traumatized by change. Change is coming down on all of us from all sides. There is more change than organizations and their members know what to do with. We consultants can best serve our clients by allying ourselves with the forces of healing.

In 1992, I was motivated to draw together a group of friends and acquaintances, most of them consultants, to pool our experiences and understandings about organizational healing. I was surprised that at the first meeting about thirty people showed up, and I was also amazed by the depth of the process we created. I introduced the meeting by describing my experiences in Australia and New Zealand, saying that I felt we were entering a new phase in the development of our practice and our priorities as OD consultants. Then each person shared what he or she wanted to about what organizational healing meant personally and what he or she was seeing in client organizations. As we went around the circle that afternoon, not one person talked about the ingenious healing interventions he or she was using or put himself or herself forward in an egoistic way. There was a great deal of openness about the pain people were feeling and seeing in organizations and the sense of inadequacy we felt in dealing with it. The meeting had not been designed or intended as a healing experience for us, but it turned out to be one!

During the latter part of 1992, I put together Organizational Healing, a one-day workshop, and delivered the workshop twice during a trip to Britain. The intent of the workshop is to raise people's consciousness about the importance of planning for healing when undertaking organization change and to begin to enlist others in developing the theory and practice we OD consultants so badly need in the area. The workshop was well received, and I have repeated it in Britain and at an Organization Development Network national conference. At present, the main focus of my interest in organizational healing is to understand how some individuals and organizations manage to recover from traumatic change so quickly while others remain in denial, anger, or depression for a long time. I am also looking for those factors that make it possible for some organizations and some organization members to transcend the castle versus battlefield dimension and to learn to thrive on change.

Organizational Learning Revisited

During 1991 and 1992, I once again essayed a business and professional association with an organization. I was much attracted by the people and the values of Innovation Associates, a consulting firm in the Boston area founded by Charlie Kiefer and with which Peter Senge is also affiliated. Peter had just written an enormously popular book, *The Fifth Discipline* (Senge, 1990), and Innovation Associates wanted someone like me to lead some of their newly hired consultants in large-systems change projects. Like most such ideas, it has not worked out as we anticipated. It is difficult to be an effective member of a small consulting organization when one lives 2,500 miles away, but I have been satisfied to see that I have moved some distance beyond my rebellious ways with organizations of which I am a member. The chief outcome of my association with Innovation Associates has been a renewed interest on my part in learning in organizations. At first, I thought perhaps Peter Senge had said it all in his book, but after thinking about the relationship between learning, action, and organizational healing, I decided I could at least provide a copious footnote! As I write this, the monograph *Towards the Learning Organization—Promises and Pitfalls* (Harrison, 1992) is in its third revision. In it, I describe how I apply the principles of self-directed learning to my practice as a consultant, and I explore how the shadow in organizations blocks learning. (Owing to its length, this monograph has not been included in my forthcoming *Collected Papers*. I will probably expand it into a book on organizational learning *and* organizational healing in due course.)

My interests in healing and in learning are now inextricably intertwined. Much of *Towards the Learning Organization* deals with ways of healing the four blocks to learning that are now endemic in many if not most organizations. They are:

1. The inhibition of learning by the presence of fear, anxiety, and other strong negative emotions in the organization.
2. The inability to acknowledge the shadow: aspects of the organization's doing and being that are contrary to the ways organizational leaders and members would like to think about themselves.
3. The unmet needs for healing in organizations that are undergoing major change.
4. The bias for action and competitiveness that is embedded in the character of most leaders and managers and in the culture of their organizations.

As I look at what is happening in organizations right now, I am more than ever impressed by the *iatrogenic* quality of management (and consultant) problem solving in organizations that I described in Chapter Six. We create ever tighter spirals of *local* problem solving, leading to unintended consequences that in turn lead to more local problem solving, more unintended consequences, more problems, and so on. Only by becoming much more conscious of the need for systems thinking and reflective (as opposed to trial-and-error) learning in organizations can we break that spiral.

I have known for a long time that the way we go about problem solving creates big problems, but I was not clear what the alternatives were. I only knew that *reflective learning,* by slowing down the process, at least avoids the harm that our bias for action creates. Recently, I have also become aware of the power of organizational *appreciation,* by which I mean deep understanding of the organization *as a whole* arrived at through communication and reflection. I discovered that innovative consultants had for some years been pioneering large-group approaches to organizational learning, in which the participants all learn together about the organization's current state and plan for its future. These approaches have great promise for healing the ever more frantic addiction to urgency and tunnel vision that afflicts most organizations.

It was not until the nineties that I learned about future search conferences through Marvin Weisbord and Sandra Janoff. They have been integrating early work in Britain and Australia by members of the Tavistock Institute with insights developed by Ron Lippitt and Eva Schindler Rainman from the theories of Kurt Lewin. Shortly after hearing Marvin talk about future search at an internal presentation at Digital Equipment, I met in quick succession several innovators in this new art of "getting the whole system into the room": Kathy Dannemiller, Richard McKnight, and Bill Smith. These others do not call their work "future search," but their approaches seem to share the same values and assumptions about what it takes to facilitate real change in organizations.

Future search is a large-group experience in which members of each of the significant stakeholder groups of an organization are brought together to review the past, understand the present, and envision the future of the organization-in-its-environment, in all its messy complexity and uncertainty. At a future search, shop floor workers participate equally with top management, customers, suppliers, community members, and so on. The idea is to have people there from every group that has a stake in what the organization does, whether they are favorably disposed to the organization or not. They pool their experience, their points of view, their knowledge, and their creativity to find common ground on which they can unite for constructive action toward a jointly desired future for the organization. Because future search brings together people who have a shared interest in the organization but who normally do not interact with one another, the process is characterized by a very rapid expansion of participants' awareness of issues, values, needs, and possibilities for common action.

When I first heard Marvin speak about future search, I had one of those blinding flashes of the obvious that opens new vistas in old landscapes. It suddenly seemed so simple and so clear, that if we want people to work together to change things, we need to get them working from a common appreciation of how things are, how they got that way, and what are the internal and external realities that hold the present situation in place. If we want them to cooperate in planning and action, we have to find common ground between them on how they would like things to be different in the future, and we have to give each of them a stake in a shared vision of that future.

For me, encountering future search was the organizational equivalent of the expanded vision of relationships that I received in my first T-group experience. In fact, the principles behind the new technology are similar enough to the assumptions underlying the T-group that there is clearly some common ancestry. There is the same belief in the contribution that diversity makes to creative problem solving, the same egalitarian values, the same faith in the ability of ordinary people to manage themselves toward win-win outcomes, and the same confidence in the power of participation to ensure commitment to implementation. For me, what was so exciting and empowering about the revisioning of organization development that all these people were doing was that each of their methods offered ways for all the different parts of the organization to acquire a shared understanding of the organization, both internally and in its relationship to its environment. I saw their vision as systems thinking for ordinary people, and I jumped on the bandwagon with them as fast as I could. In rapid succession, I attended a training conducted by Sandra and Marvin, co-led a couple of future searches for nonprofit groups, and even read Sandra and Marvin's very worthwhile books (Weisbord and others, 1993; Weisbord and Janoff, 1995)—a true sign of commitment, from the likes of me.

In the next and final chapter, I sum up my insights and learnings along the road I have traveled in my long journey as a consultant, and I close with a look to the future.

CHAPTER TEN

APPRECIATING DILEMMAS
THAT DON'T GO AWAY

Since the conclusion of the R&D project described earlier, flawed though it was, I have taken considerable pride and satisfaction in the level of art I have attained as a consultant. In that project, I helped a bureaucratically bound organization set itself on the path of transformation to higher levels of consciousness. I learned to work both systems and cultural issues. I touched the hearts and minds of more than a few people. I even managed to leave at the right time, though not as gracefully as I wished!

It delights me to discover how much I know about consulting and planning change. In the work I have done to open myself to my intuition and allow myself to be guided by those flashes of certainty that now come so frequently, I have found new sources of understanding. Frequently, the insights arise unbidden, with no effort from me beyond listening and being present. Sometimes I actively ask for guidance. I like to think that there are guides and guardians who watch over me (and I guess that others do, too, because as I write this the media are full of people's experiences with angels!). It comforts me to experience them on the job, guiding and supporting me. When I am at my best, I am not *doing* so much as I am being open to inner guidance. I will be sitting in a meeting, listening to my clients or colleagues talking about what to do, and I say to myself, "*That* won't work—but *this* will." There is not any sense of probability about it, no doubt or question. It seems hypocritical to introduce what I *know* in a nondirective way, to take the role of facilitator. I speak my truth directly, and others usually pay attention. If they do not, I can let it go, because if I am on to something, another opportunity to test it will come up. Anything that is true is going to come up again and again until people get it.

Dilemmas Along the Way

My friend and early colleague Peter Block (1981) has written a very good book called *Flawless Consulting*. Only the title gives me pause. I have experienced excellence in my practice, and moments of absolute *rightness*, but flaws are still part of the essence of our practice as OD consultants. This is true for our clients as well. They and we face dilemmas for which there are no perfect resolutions, only the necessity of choice. In this section, I discuss dilemmas from my practice that I believe all OD consultants face frequently or continually.

I experience all of them as genuine dilemmas; that is, one must choose where to stand on the dimension defined by each pair of polar opposites. Making the choice does not fully relieve the tension, because each end of each dimension has value and is desirable in part. To fail to choose where one stands on a dimension may mean that one is unaware of the dimension. The result of that unawareness will be a tendency to be inconsistent or hit-or-miss in one's relationship to the issue the dimension represents. One may also become frozen at a single point on a dimension, usually near one of the poles, unaware of the possibility of choice or unwilling to explore the dimension. That often leads to rigidity, masquerading as integrity. Early in my own career, I was often aware of only one pole, which I thought of as a "rule of good consulting." I was unaware of the value inherent in the opposite pole, and I, too, tended to be a bit rigid.

Each of the dilemmas I discuss in the following sections has been important to me, and during my career, I have moved on the dimension that it represents.

Facilitating Versus Participating

The dimension of facilitating versus participating is one of the first dimensions that most consultants encounter. As a psychologist in training, and later as a T-group trainer, I was taught to withhold my participation in order to avoid creating client dependency on me. The dominant value was for the individual client to learn for himself or herself and for the group or organization to learn for itself, and the rationale was that the authority of the professional was so overwhelming to clients that they would have to treat the professional's interventions as directives rather than as points of information. The client was to learn to solve problems rather than to be given problem solutions.

When I was at Yale, Chris Argyris and I discussed the issue of creating dependency, sometimes with great passion. At that time, Chris took the position that in consulting, and in education, too, fostering autonomy was next to godliness. I was not so sure. In my own life, I had been helped most by people who showed or told me a new skill or a new idea and then let me make it my own through use and experiment. I felt there was such a thing as *realistic dependency*, as distinguished from the dependency built into a patriarchal and hierarchical culture. Realistic dependency is temporary, and the person who is currently in charge or currently teaching gives support and direction in order to *empower* others. Both Chris and I felt passionately about this issue, and I doubt if we ever fully understood one another. Of course, I knew that when one is assisting others to learn and grow there comes a time when one must push them out of the nest in order to foster their further growth. I felt strongly, however, that to refuse help when it was wanted and needed could be uncaring; I had even seen it be sadistic. I had also personally experienced being thrown back on my own resources by my father at times, I believe, when some teaching of basic principles would have given me a good start. That issue had been especially acute when I asked for help with my algebra homework! Thus, my own experience had taught me that there are times when a little help empowers people rather than creating their dependency.

I wanted very much to be helpful to my clients. However, I was trained in a nondirective model, both by my experience in personal therapy and my work with T-groups. So I struggled with the dilemma of facilitating versus participating, endeavoring to discover the criteria for when to be helpful and when to hold back.

By the time I went to Europe, I had written my papers "Choosing the Depth of Organizational Intervention" (Harrison, 1970 [†]) and "When Power Conflicts Trigger Team Spirit" (Harrison, 1972e [†"Role Negotiation"]). I had become disaffected with the depth psychology model from which our practice derived, a model in which the "presenting problem" of the client is discounted as a screen for some "real issue" that seems to lie ever deeper. I had learned from my own psychoanalysis that deeper was not necessarily truer and that deeper insight did not always facilitate change. My experiences in the Peace Corps taught me that I was personally at my best in a partnership with my clients in which I provided a conceptual frame and methodology for the enquiry and the clients provided a depth of knowledge and experience in the work to be done.

Then I went to that first startup project in Europe, where my colleagues and I only began to be helpful when we offered quick fixes for day-to-day problems. I learned that an organization in crisis was like the people I and other trainers sometimes saw through near-psychotic crises in T-groups. Before these people could learn much that was new, they needed to be brought back to a level of functioning at which they were not having to use all their resources just to cope. In those situations, being directive and giving answers to problems did not foster dependency; it fostered good functioning.

In addition, I found that clients in Britain were impatient with a nondirective approach. If I was to get beyond the first interview, I had to establish credibility by making programmatic suggestions. Also, the fact that my fees were higher than those of local consultants meant that clients expected a show of expertise. Perhaps I expected it of myself as well. What started as a necessity soon became a source of enjoyment. I found I liked being an expert! It had been much easier to be nondirective when I was relatively inexperienced. Once I was seasoned in practice, I seemed to know things I should not be able to know. Many patterns repeat themselves. The content is different, but the structure is the same.

Today, I listen till I have a few data points, and then I leap to conclusions. More often than not, my clients confirm these intuitive leaps. But I am reporting how I practice, not how I should practice. The dilemma of dependency has not gone away. When we offer clients answers, we do invite dependency or its counterpart, resistance. However, I find dependency is less of a dilemma for me now, for two reasons. One is that clients are both less credulous and less resistant than they used to be. Over the years, there has been a major shift in our society in attitudes toward authority. People have become more self-reliant, both less trusting of authority and less frightened of it. I find fewer clients with whom I have to hold back. Partly that is because I now work at higher levels in organizations, where the people have always been tougher and more self-assured. But I find the new attitudes true at lower levels as well, especially in rapidly changing highly technical organizations, where acquired knowledge gives its possessors only a short-term advantage. I find quite junior managers and professional people ready to step into dialogue, trusting in themselves and testing my contributions against their own intelligence and common sense. That is the kind of dance I like to join!

The second reason why I live more comfortably now with the dependency issue is that, while I am often quite certain I know what is going on, I have much less certainty about what will work. I no longer have faith in interventions or technology or anything that is applied to organizations from the outside. I view organizations as organisms with a life of their own, and I see my work as that of an organic gardener, not a mechanic. I believe my work is to foster healing in organizations that want to become whole. In each of my recent projects, I have endeavored to foster a self-managing change process. So far, my success has been mixed. I have learned that no one has the answer and that everyone's resources are valuable. When I give way to wanting to be a doctor to my clients, I alienate myself from them, and if they go along, they become alienated from their own healing resources. In the deep dialogue which is my preferred approach to healing from within, there is a place for guides and mentors and even seers but not for experts. There are no complete answers. All I can offer is to be a companion along the way, a committed and perceptive companion, I hope, but certainly not a doctor.

Working One's Own Agenda Versus Taking On Clients' Agendas

I have always had my own agendas for the organizations with which I have worked. The idea of value-free consulting has no meaning for me. I endeavor to give clients what they and I contract for, but I have often had a covert agenda as well, and I have not always been open about my larger goals and motives out of fear of losing the work. At times, I have felt some shame over having an agenda different from that of my clients. That was the case when, in the early seventies, I "fired" the clients for whom I wrote "Strategy Guidelines for an Internal Organization Development Unit." (Harrison, 1972c [†"Guidelines for an Internal Organization Development Unit"]). In that case, I did not even tell them they were being fired! Since openness, truth telling, and empowerment have usually been central to my personal agenda, there is real irony there.

The times when my agenda has been most closely aligned with that of an organization's leaders have been in the two startup projects. There I felt I could give myself to the goal of coming on-stream on time and under budget. I could also pursue the human issues with complete congruence. Both startups were situations in which power and authority counted for less than commitment and contribution. I have found myself most at odds with my clients when I see them protecting their power at the expense of both the human spirit and the bottom line. That was what made it difficult for me to work with some of the department managers in the R&D company.

After I began working with my organization culture model (Harrison, 1990 [†]), I became much more congruent. The model helps me commit to work with clients in their move to the next level in the evolution of their organization. If I am to work with an organization, I need to be willing to take its level of consciousness as a given and then work to help it at its growing edge.

For example, many organizations are moving from the traditional organization culture (transactional culture) in the direction of more empowerment, more openness, and more self-reliance (self-expression culture). That was the intention of the CEO in the R&D company, and I could fully support it even though I could see the dark side of the desired change. As authority becomes less heavy-handed and structures less hierarchical, much self-oriented energy is released in an organization. It may become more internally competitive, feeling less like a family and developing a norm of sink or swim. With my strong personal values that favor love, cooperation, and the mutuality culture, it can be bittersweet for me to watch and to help implement these changes, just as it is difficult for parents to see their children as young adults break away in ways that seem rough, uncaring, and selfish. I have to remind myself again and again that people have to be strong and autonomous before they can freely give their cooperation. It has certainly been so in my evolution as a person, but I ask myself if there is not a better and a quicker way, given that the Earth cries out for cooperation and love.

Until I find that better way, my resolution of the dilemma between working my own agenda and that of my clients is to find those situations where I can make common cause with my clients in a movement toward higher levels of consciousness, defining the next step in terms of the readiness of the organization, rather than in terms of my own desires. (See Harrison, Cooper, and Dawes, 1991, for some ways to implement this idea.) This activity is not always as satisfying or fun as it was to see myself as a warrior for the human spirit, but it is a path that has both integrity and heart for me. As I shift the focus of my work from changing organizations to fostering healing and wholeness, it becomes easier to be open and congruent with my personal agendas.

Confronting Differences Versus Maintaining Rapport

Most of my early development as a consultant centered around the dilemma of confronting differences versus maintaining rapport, and that dilemma is one with which I have worked in a variety of ways ever since. It is a fundamental dilemma in work and personal relationships. I feel that I may be finally at peace with it, after all these years.

My initial experiences in T-groups led me to speak my truth indiscriminately and to invite, even demand, that others do likewise. When this generated more heat than light or stopped the conversation, I began to work out a variety of routines for being as open as I could be while still maintaining rapport. My first attempts were mechanical and manipulative. For example, I became very excited when I learned that my senior colleagues at Yale responded more positively when I reframed a piece of feedback to them as a description of something I had learned about myself. For example, I might say, "You wouldn't believe how long it took me to learn that if I stopped talking and waited for a response after making my first point, then when I went on, I had people's full attention. When I used to string my points together one after the other, the others became so full of their unspoken rejoinders that they couldn't hear what I was saying!" In a similar vein, I learned that one of the best ways of fostering openness was to disclose something that made me a little vulnerable, but not too much. For example, "I still get really nervous when I'm lecturing, and there's no response and no questions. How do you cope with those situations?"

My work in groups also taught me not to confront defensiveness too vigorously or press to prove my points. I learned that if an observation I made about the group's process was right, opportunities would come up again and again to come back to it because patterns of behavior are repetitious and cyclical. If a group disagreed with my interpretation, I could afford to let it go and wait until it came around again.

While I was working intensively with the Positive Power & Influence Program, I attended a session by Terry Dobson, an aikido master, on applying Japanese martial art to consulting and training (see Dobson and Miller, 1978). From aikido, I learned to move with the energy of an attack or criticism rather than rebutting or countering it. I made it a matter of personal pride never to defend my points with an argument, and in giving the program, I had lots of chances to practice! Now, when a point I make is criticized, I will often acknowledge that it is merely my opinion or my personal experience and invite critics to share their own thought and experience. Then I invite others to join the dialogue, and we all learn together.

When the energy is dissipated, I acknowledge what I have learned from it and then move on.

From Sue Walden, a teacher of improvisational theater in San Francisco, I learned the principle of "Yes, and. . . ." By using this tool in dialogue, whether on stage or off, each person keeps the energy flowing by picking up the other's train of thought, acknowledging it, and only then redirecting it in the way he or she wants to proceed. It is a simple principle, no big deal, but the effect on the energy flow and harmony in the group is often magical!

The effect on me is magical, too. It expands my thinking, and it opens my heart to the other(s). It is a good example of the principle that individuals can change their feelings by acting "as if." Recently, I was giving a talk to consultants on bringing spirituality into consulting and training work, and in the question period, a member of the audience surprised me by saying, "Roger, I've followed your work for many years, and I've gotten a lot of value from your writings on the importance of evaluating training. Could you tell these people how they can bring better evaluation into their work?" It was a complete non sequitur, and as near to completely untrue as it could be. My first impulse was to say, "You must have me confused with someone else!" but I knew that if I stopped the questioner in his tracks, it would not shut down just him, the energy in the whole room would drop. As I pondered my response, my learnings from Terry and Sue flashed through my mind. I knew that if I was to walk my talk there and then, I had to find some harmonious way of moving with the energy of the question and redirecting it back into the discourse. What I finally said was, "You know, I am now working so far out on the edge of my competence and understanding that nothing I have learned about evaluation seems to apply. These days, I just have to tune into my intuition and whatever guidance I can get and go ahead as best I can." That got a big friendly laugh from the audience. The warmth in the room went up a few degrees, and we carried on with great good feeling.

A really important learning came to me from my work in training negotiators. It is that one of the greatest currencies or bargaining chips in a negotiation is a person's feeling of being acknowledged to be in the right. I became so impressed with this that I used to say, "You can get anything you want in a negotiation as long as you are willing to make the other negotiator right. If you blame, criticize, or attack, you will have to give up some of your 'bottom line' objectives to balance the transaction."

My greatest learning about rapport is a subtle extension of this principle, and I did not discover it until the late eighties. I found that I can say almost anything and remain in rapport as long as I can say it with compassion, without attachment to how it is received, and without an emotional charge: no judgments, no anger, no pulling of guilt or shame. The reason I did not discover this principle sooner is that I do not hide my emotions easily, and I have a strong attachment to having my message heard. I had to acquire some detachment and compassion. I had to learn to do my best and then leave the outcome to God and my clients. Until then, it was not possible for me to keep negative feelings and urgency out of my voice when I spoke about things about which I felt strongly. Thus, I did not experience until quite late that the keys to rapport are compassion, nonattachment, and an open heart, not the content of one's communication. Of course, there are still many times when I fall into judgment and anger or I take on responsibility for the outcome. Then I am likely to evoke defensiveness and lose rapport. However, I find that having the principle of nonattachment to outcomes in mind and having the intent to follow that principle is slowly increasing my ability to benefit from this learning.

My broadest insight has been that trust in relationships includes more than one dimension of behavior. We can trust others to understand, empathize with, and accept us and that leads to comfort and rapport. We can trust others to tell the truth even when it costs them something, and that leads to confidence in the information we receive from them. As a consultant, I want to engender both kinds of trust, and therein lies the rub, because they are partly contradictory. When I confront a client with a hard message to hear, that builds the client's trust in my willingness to speak my truth. But that same communication may damage rapport if the client feels judged, rejected, or misunderstood. I have found no resolution for this dilemma. My only guidance is to make the choice with full awareness.

Working with Structures and Systems Versus Working with Process

When I first began working as a consultant to organizations in the sixties, I learned about the power of groups, but I was naïve about the power of structures and systems. I had the idea that structures and rules were disempowering, because I worked mostly in organizations with strong hierarchical and functional structures that hampered lateral cooperation and all but top-down communication. My innocence disappeared in the first new plant startup I worked with, when I found what it was like to work in an organization where the systems and structures, roles and responsibilities were inadequate and unclear. It was a strong hit, which I never forgot. Hierarchy is disempowering but so is chaos. We needed structures and agreements to enable teamwork and cooperation. But there is a dilemma here, a choice to be made between working with structures and systems versus working with process.

In my second startup project, I learned something about how to design enabling structures and systems collaboratively. My colleagues and I used a variant of role negotiation (see Harrison, 1972e). Each manager came with a list of the tasks and functions he thought he was responsible for, and the group examined these for overlap and gaps. Then group members traded responsibilities and tasks until everything was covered, and everyone had a role specification he could live with and that made sense to the others. I still like that approach. It is a quick and simple version of job redesign, and it can be reiterated as often as necessary.

It has the great advantage that the participants own and understand the process and commit themselves to make the new design work.

I find that clients often collude in focusing on process, rather than structures and systems, as a way of maintaining the status quo. In bureaucratic, hierarchical organizations, the power to control behavior is carried by the structures and systems. Working on teamwork, communication, culture, and other soft processes does not change much of the action unless the work leads to corresponding changes in roles, responsibilities, and systems. The hard and the soft need to change together or in close sequence.

At present, we are exhorted by New Age thinkers to embrace chaos (disorder), which makes sense to me if we see it as a sign that the forms we are endeavoring to maintain are inadequate and that we need to move to a higher order (see Wheatley, 1993). Chaos is necessary to move us through our current contradictions, in the same way that people may sometimes need a nervous breakdown in order to heal and grow. However, I do not personally find chaos desirable or fun, except when I succeed in finding some new order hidden in it. I suspect most of us will have our fill of chaos before very long and will yearn for new order.

Relying on Reason Versus Using Intuition

Along with many managers and consultants, I have moved over the years from relying almost solely on my reason to trusting my intuition. Intuition is faster, and it is more certain than common sense or reason. However, I have also learned to respect significant caveats around relying on intuition. Thus the choice between relying on reason and using intuition presents yet another dilemma, one that leads me to use reason and intuition together and often to use one to check or test the other.

I grew up in a family full of scientists and engineers dedicated to empiricism and rationality. Feelings were often hidden and denied. I learned early to interpret the promptings of my intuitive knowing as irrational nuisance or emotional disturbance, particularly when they concerned my own needs or others' motives, feelings, and intentions. It surprises me now to remember that, for a long time, to say that something was based on intuition was to describe it as a product of sloppy or lazy thinking. If something was worth knowing, it was worth studying and testing empirically!

Yet even when I was unaccepting of my intuitive abilities, I was drawn to explore the realms of the unseen. I have been curious about paranormal psychology (telepathy, clairvoyance, and the like) ever since I first heard of the concept as an undergraduate at Dartmouth College. I wanted to do research in the area for my Ph.D. thesis. The more I read of the scientific establishment's debunking of research in parapsychology, the more I wanted to look into it. I knew, however, that if I seriously pursued my interest, it would cost me endless delays in acquiring my doctorate. The thesis project I finally chose was as close to research on telepathy as I could come and still remain respectable: I designed a little study of the relationship between supervisors' empathy and the job satisfaction of subordinates (Harrison, 1959)!

However, in graduate school I was pretty well brainwashed, and I lost what little interest I had had in things esoteric or spiritual. My growing edge during the sixties was the senses, not things extrasensory! Then, living in England awakened my curiosity about the paranormal once again, when I encountered so many seemingly reasonable and ordinary people who reported having seen ghosts. Belief and disbelief often seem to be more cultural than otherwise, and in England it came to seem quite normal to me that ghosts would turn up here and there. I was only sorry I could not see them myself. I did not attach any practical significance to such phenomena, but they softened me up and gently pried my mind open once again.

In the New Age circles to which I gravitated after my return to the Bay Area, there was some talk about intuition and psychic abilities. By then I had had enough experience with meditation and other mind-altering mental and physical exercises to take seriously the idea that we could know things through other faculties than the five senses. My interest grew, and in the early eighties, I attended a workshop for developing one's psychic abilities given at the Esalen Institute by a well-known psychic, Ann Armstrong. I shall always be grateful to Ann and her husband, Jim, for helping me over the threshold into the realm of the unseen. In the workshop, I experienced my own rather weak ability to see and know beyond the senses, and I saw that everyone there was capable of some level of such seeing and inner knowing. From that point on, I committed myself to developing my intuition to the highest level of which I was capable, and the more effort I put into that endeavor, the better my results became.

I have never had any trouble reconciling my commitment to scientific method with explorations into the unseen. For me, being empirical and scientific means taking seriously all phenomena, all experience. If our current methods do not permit us to study a phenomenon "scientifically," then we need to find other methods, but we should not turn aside from our inquiry. I hold that being empirical means experimenting to find what works, and afterward inquiring how and why it works.

At about this time, I realized that I have always had a strongly active intuition and that most of the ideas I presented with skillfully constructed reasoning had their origins outside my rational mind. During my work with the Positive Power and Influence Program, I began to notice that although I presented my conclusions rationally, I did not often arrive at them by a rational route. One moment I would be wrestling with a problem; the next moment, there would be an answer. Then I would test the answer against the facts as I knew them and begin to construct a rationalization for presentation to others. I had always done that, but I suppressed my awareness that the ideas I labored so long and hard to justify rationally often just popped into my head.

I do not know where ideas come from, but I have found that it works for me to assume that there is consciousness everywhere and to think of my seeking for guidance as a conversation, or as a kind of prayer. When I could accept that my best ideas did not come from my rational mind, I began to work easier and smarter. Instead of presenting my ideas in a rational framework, I could share my hunches and invite my clients to test them against their own experience—and their own intuition. It was scary at first, but I actually found less client resistance to ideas presented as hunches than there had been when I pressed my points with reasons and arguments. By inviting my clients to test my intuitions, I avoided competitive discussions about what was factual or reasonable, and I included the clients in the problem-solving process. Of course, there are still times when I have to do proposals and presentations that are closely reasoned. I do not enjoy doing them, but I do not object on principle. I accept that I have to earn my right to be intuitive by passing rational tests of this sort.

As I became comfortable relying on my own intuition, I noticed that I was not always comfortable when others relied on theirs, and I asked myself what was different about people whose intuitions I seldom trusted. There was one alcoholic friend in particular who was forever justifying some self-destructive course of action in the name of intuition. For me, too, there have been times of strong emotional arousal—wish, fear, or fantasy—when I cannot trust the messages I receive. Especially in relationships, when I have been torn between duty and desire, I have asked for and received guidance that later seemed to have led me astray.

Such exceptions prove (test) the rule, and I had occasion to ponder them long. I came to understand that wish and fear can masquerade as intuition. Intuition is one of those faculties in which we gain the greatest power when we care least about the outcome, and it is subject to serious degradation through attachment.

In the last few years, I have experienced a dramatic increase in the power of my intuition. Partly that is because I have become more detached from the outcomes of my work. When I can accept reality as it is, I can see it more clearly. In addition, intuitive power is a gift that comes into its greatest power in the second half of life, if we can accept it. Anyone can have intuition at any time in life, but the greatest power comes from the partnership of experience and intuition. When I was first working as a consultant, I saw mainly the coarse grain of events in organizations. My mentors trained me to look for certain relationships and processes: for example, "seven types of decision making"; "hidden agendas"; even or uneven distributions of participation, power, and dependency, and so on. There was a lot going on that did not make sense to me because I had no categories to put it in. I learned more categories from dialogue with colleagues, from reading, and from reflecting on and actively conceptualizing my experience. Then I could see more events and observe more connections among them. I moved from coarse-grain to fine-grain discernment.

I have continued to learn to see events in more detail and connections in more variety right up to the present. However, my rational mind does not cope well with multivariate phenomena. I can readily see things that less experienced people scarcely ever notice, and I can see relationships among them, but my intelligence is usually overloaded when I try to understand relationships involving more than two or three variables at a time. When I look at the theories I and others make about organizations, most seem to me to deal only with the most obvious connections. Those coming out of the work of the "systems thinkers" at MIT and elsewhere are more complex, but they are still rather awkward, inadequate representations of the richness of people's experience. They lose most of the minute discriminations and subtle connections that people have observed.

When I visit an organization, I like to overload myself with observations, immersing myself in what, as I remember it, William James called the "blooming, buzzing confusion" of unconceptualized events and processes. My rational mind hates the mess, and it would like to start theorizing right away. My rational mind does not care for *mystery*, for *awe*, or for *reverence* in the face of the unanalyzable. It wants me to get back on stable ground, and I used often to give way to it. Now I am resistant to its siren call. I rather enjoy hanging out in confusion, because experience has taught me to trust that it will not last.

Intuition is the faculty we have for dealing with confusion and mystery. Intuition loves those complex webs of connections, and it can extract truth from them. I have no idea how it does this—it is a mystery! My intuition seems quite formidable now that I have lots of experience. Early on, reason seemed to work for me about as well as intuition. My reason can deal quite adequately with a few bits of information connected in simple ways. But as my experience has grown, reason has increasingly seemed limiting and pedestrian. Once I began deeply to trust and rely upon my intuition, it really began to perform for me. When I am just sitting there, taking in what a client says to me and not actively trying to create meaning from it, magic happens. I listen to the client describe a knotty situation, and if I am "on" that day, deeper structures come into focus. I confirm my insight with the client, if I judge it not too threatening; otherwise, I wait until an appropriate way of framing it comes to mind.

If our ideas about how we know truth prevent us from trusting our intuition, our experience will not help us as much as it could. Our intuition will keep giving us hints and nudges, but if we do not listen, we will miss the message. It is important to realize that intuition *is testable*. We do not have to abandon reason and empirical study when we enter these realms. For example, in her book, *Color and Crystals,* Joy Gardner-Gordon (Gardner, 1988) gives a simple way both to test one's intuition and to strengthen it. When you have a thought or impulse that seems to come out of nowhere, write it down. Then follow it or not but record your choice. Later, record whether the outcome of following or not following your intuition was positive or negative. After you have done this for a while, compare the number of times when you believe the outcome of following your intuition was or would have been positive with the number of times when you believe it was or would have been negative. The results may tell you about the power of your own intuition.

I also learned to expand my intuitive powers from my work with a talented healer, Virginia Dickson, and from the writings of Machaelle Small Wright (1990, 1993, 1994), to which Virginia introduced me. Under Virginia's guidance, I began by using a pendulum (a form of dowsing) to test which vitamins and minerals my body needed each day (see Graves, 1989). At first I felt rather foolish doing this, but my curiosity led me on, and I began to test the usefulness of dowsing for choosing between alternate courses of action. Now I use it to obtain answers to many questions that can be answered with a yes or no.

Through the work of Machaelle Small Wright, I have learned to establish relationships with unseen teams of helpers who not only bring me guidance, but also heal physical ailments and psychological knots (Wright, 1994). It is like having direct action to guardian angels. I have learned to clear negative energy from working and living spaces (Wright, 1990, 1993). I have learned to view my business and my clients' businesses as gardens, overlighted and tended by powerful nature spirits who will provide information on strategy, tactics, and timing on request (Wright, 1990). I do not know how any of this works, but it does work for me, and for others I have introduced to these practices.

My intuition has been aided and enriched by my work with healing energy. In 1988, I first studied *reiki* (Haberly, 1990), a method for bringing healing energy to the body and mind through the hands. With further study and practice, the power of the energy I am able to bring in has increased dramatically. In addition to working with friends and family, I use *reiki* sometimes in my work with groups and teams to bring qualities of harmony and well-being into the spaces where we work. Feeling that healing energy coming through me and having others report that they experience it, too, provides me with additional evidence that there is power for good that we can access from a consciousness beyond ourselves.

For me, to publicly share my work with the unseen is the ultimate in coming out of the closet. Were I not so sure of the accessibility of these healing powers to everyone, I would keep silent and quietly use what I know, as have so many down through centuries. But I am not uniquely gifted, and we need all the help we can get in these parlous times! I would have a bad conscience if I did not risk sharing what I have learned, so I push my own boundaries and speak out.

Although I disclaim knowledge of how all this works, I have of course created mind maps of the realms in which I have been playing. I never can resist the urge to create theories and models. But even in nonesoteric realms, I hold all maps and theories lightly, consciously making room for mystery and for doubt. Because I am a hopeful person, I have asked how my little dance with the unseen might point toward ways through the dilemmas and uncertainties with which we are faced in this difficult and dangerous time for humankind. I am intrigued by the possibilities that come up for me, and I offer my musings here.

We have learned to unleash great power through science, but our power has outrun our knowing. Even when we sincerely try to care for and heal the environment, our actions have unintended consequences, and our good intentions are often frustrated. There are too many variables, too many connections for us ever to manage nature or control the environment. We can't even understand and control human organizations. What chance have we to manage, let alone heal, the planet? Yet we have to try, because our power is killing the Earth.

What if there are angels, nature spirits, and the like, intelligences who have the task of caring for the Earth and for all of life? What if our creative insights and intuitive flashes are nudges and hints from these intelligences? Perhaps they are willing and able to offer us help and guidance when we ask for it, but perhaps they cannot intervene without permission, because to do so would violate our free will. Perhaps what we need to do to heal our relationship with the Earth is to test our thinking and judgment at every turn by asking, "What is for the highest good here? Which of the actions we might take at this time will bring us into closer harmony and balance with nature and all of life?" Perhaps by listening to and acting on the answers we receive, we can enter into a partnership with nature, in which the powers that we have unleashed through science can come into harmony with the needs of all of life. Then we could thrive in partnership with the Earth, instead of despoiling it and damaging its ability to support us.

Maybe not. Perhaps this is a delusion born of desperation, in the same class as fantasies of benevolent aliens watching over us in UFOs, ready to pull our chestnuts out of the fire at the penultimate moment, just before we destroy ourselves. I prefer my fantasy because it is testable. I can submit my dilemmas and uncertainties to guidance, and use kinesiology or a pendulum to get yes or no answers to the questions I pose. I can act on the guidance, and record the results. Or I can act contrary to guidance, and record the results of that.

It does work for me, and so I sometimes have this vision of the board of directors of a company in a strategic planning session. They spend a few moments attuning themselves to the overlighting spirit of their business, and then, after the staff presentations, followed by full discussion of each issue, they ask for guidance on the different aspects of their strategic plan. In my fantasy, they are sitting around the conference table with their pendulums out, asking, "Is it for the highest good for us to downsize our business this year? Is it for the highest good for us to merge with one of our competitors?" and so on, with each person swinging his or her pendulum and reading the yes or no answers. When they do not agree, they attune more deeply and try again. At the end of the day, off they go to their homes, secure in the knowledge that they have used *all* the resources available to them, seen and unseen, human and angelic, to ensure the future well-being of their business and of the Earth.

Oh, well, it's just a fantasy. And still, . . .

Prospects in Perspective

As I view the current scene, I begin to see potential healing for our organizational insanities, although not yet with clarity. As I look back down the road now behind me, there have been dramatic changes over the years in what clients wanted and needed from OD consultants. Usually, our offerings shifted less rapidly than clients' needs, and that lag continues today. I have written at length about my thoughts and perceptions as a consultant in the paper "Whither OD?" which opens the companion volume (Harrison, 1995) to *Consultant's Journey*. Here, I want to deal with the future in a more personal way, befitting an autobiography.

As I look to the future, nothing is certain, either in the worlds in which I work or in my personal and professional life. I know that I am more oriented toward the spiritual and the personal as I become older. Developing my relationship with the divine has a strong pull for me. I am drawn in my spiritual search to create a deeper connection with nature, to cooperate and communicate actively with her. My recent marriage to Margaret Harris is a milestone on the path to my life goal of building a true co-creative relationship with a woman. The process of dialogue that I began in T-groups, deep and intimate exchange of feelings and thoughts, still has life and excitement for me. So does the co-creative process of community life and collaborative work. I enjoy mentoring and shadow consulting for the joy of seeing others grow in understanding and for the excitement of unraveling knots of organizational complexity. But these preoccupations have the quality for me of interests, not yet of mission. I have a sense now of having been prepared, along with many others, for a great work that is to be done in healing the Earth and the life upon it. Everything I have done and am doing now is either training and spiritual preparation, or perhaps just waiting, until my assignment in that work is given. I look forward to that work with a mixture of awe and willingness, confident that my own assignment will not be beyond what is possible for me and hopeful of the outcome for all of life.

I wrote those last words about a year and a half ago in my first draft of *Consultant's Journey*. I wrote "Whither OD" at about the same time. When it came time to write the final draft of the closing paragraphs of my story, I thought that perhaps, over time, my vision would have clarified and that I would have more to say to other consultants about how they and I might best focus our energies in the future. I spent much time pondering the question, but I did not receive much illumination. Then I sought higher guidance, with better results. Before sharing the result of my enquiry, I shall describe the context in which it was undertaken.

When I ask myself Angeles Arrien's great question, "What has heart and meaning for me? (Arrien, 1993), I am aware that I have never been more motivated than I am now to be of service to my organizations, to my fellow beings, and to the Earth. Yet I have found myself recently only mildly interested in consulting work. I have not sought assignments, and I have put most of my energy into speaking and writing. I do not seem to be dispirited or burnt-out, as I have been at times in the past. Instead I have a sense of waiting for something. Sometimes it seems I am waiting for a summons to some great work, as I wrote above in a somewhat romantic vein. In more cynical moments, I feel that I am waiting until my potential clients wake up, until the pain in organizations becomes greater than the forces of denial. My mind asks, "Is it time yet?" My heart replies, "Not yet." I go back to my writing.

Meanwhile, my vision and values are becoming quite clear. It was first articulated in 1982 in "Leadership and Strategy for a New Age" (now republished in Harrison, 1995). That vision as it currently unfolds for me is one of partnership between humankind and nature, a partnership that extends from the physical plane, through the mental, and into realms of spirit. My vision also embraces a much closer integration of the mundane and the spiritual. My spiritual life is more important for me than ever. Over the last three or four years, I have been increasingly able to interweave the spiritual and practical aspects of my life. For me, the place where those worlds intersect is in the partnership I have been evolving with nature. My growing practice of asking at every turn, "What is for the highest good in this situation?" has gradually brought me into greater attunement with spirit. Not that I am continuously conscious of the highest—far from it! But because I frequently tune in to that which is unseen, and because I receive reliable guidance through doing so, my thought and attention is more and more with spirit. I have been aided, too, by living in a community which has supported me in paying attention to spirit, and which has fostered the regular practice of meditation. It is rewarding to find that even someone with as busy a mind as mine can attain a degree of quiet and attunement through long, though not very diligent, practice.

I used to think of nature as insects, animals, fields, flowers, trees, mountains, streams, and weather. To me, nature was all that was not made by humans. Now, however, I find myself thinking of all that is on the physical plane as manifested by nature, including the things we regard as our human creations. A farm, a garden, a city, a business, a machine, a consulting practice, a relationship—all are co-created in partnership with nature, whether we acknowledge that partnership or not.

As I said earlier in my discussion of intuition, I like to imagine that all our activities are watched over by intelligences and powers which are there to help when we ask in search of the highest good. When we do not ask, they respect our free will and do not interfere. I see the world as in a very real sense, a great garden. For good or ill, we are all gardeners. If we would know when and what to plant, how to care for and nurture our growing things, when to prune and when to harvest, we can figure it out through trial and error and experiment, and if we choose, we can also access the "help-line" of higher guidance.

Increasingly I find this practice works for me. At this time, when we are making such a cosmic mess of our global garden, and when it is so difficult to know when help is really helpful, it feels good to me to have access to unseen guidance. The world is too large, too complexly interconnected, and moving too fast for us to fix it alone. Nor can these others fix it for us from another level. Those who wait for divine intervention to save us from ourselves will wait, I fear, in vain.

Our intention, will, and action are needed on here on the physical plane. What can be empowering is the partnership between us here and those others there.

Since I started cooperating with these guides and helpers, the garden of my life has grown with much less agony and effort, and my harvest has been bountiful. Perhaps what is happening for some of us in microcosm may be possible for all of us in the garden of our planet. For me, at this time, it is an avenue well worth exploring. Ours is a civilization of great vitality, power, and energy. If we can surrender to guidance in our quest for the good, miracles of transformation may still be possible in our earthly garden.

Before writing these paragraphs, I asked for guidance as to how best to meet the challenges of the present and future. My question was, "How can I/we consultants best serve the development of wholeness within and between individuals, organizations, and the planet?" Part of the meaning of *wholeness* for me is balance: finding appropriate rhythms between activity and receptivity, being and doing, relatedness and autonomy, cooperation and competition. Above all, though, wholeness to me means the integration of the physical, mental, and spiritual aspects of our lives. It means healing the compartmentalization inside ourselves, which manifests itself in the outer contradictions of our time. By that, I mean that our physical, mental, and spiritual lives are too separate and disconnected, and I believe that disconnection mirrors our inability to address in an integrated way the needs for healing of ourselves, our organizations, our society, and our planet.

I asked for guidance in our outer lives in the world as well as in our inner evolution. Here is what I received, interpreted, and embraced as answers to my question.

> For us to contribute to wholeness, to healing, we consultants are guided to undergo a death of the ego, an initiation in which we let go of our ideas of who we are, what we do, and how we do it. Much of our work in the world is upside down and backwards; it is work for short-term gains that will cost us dearly down the road. Our quest for impact and for our own empowerment does not serve the whole. Our search for recognition and for the power to make a difference is often ego driven and therefore misdirected. In relying less upon the little self, we gain the guidance and support of a higher Self. In relying less upon our own powers, we open ourselves to become instruments of a higher Power.
>
> In our outer work, our talents are greatly needed; our technologies are less so. We shall serve more by listening than by speaking, more by fostering deep reflection and dialogue than by advising, planning, and implementing. Above all, our outer work is to nurture. Body, mind, and spirit cry out for that nurturance. In that work, the Earth, or Gaia, has much to teach us. We can best receive her lessons by listening to our bodies, which are of the Earth. As we learn to recognize our bodies' needs for nurturance and healing, so we shall come into greater attunement with the needs of the Earth, from which our bodies come.

To bring nurturing to individuals and organizations means bringing healing
love and compassion. It means reconnecting people not only with their bodies
and with the Earth but also with one another and with their organizations.

It is important to grow spiritually, but for wholeness, the fruit of that growth
must be a re-spiritualization of the material plane. A first step is to learn to
treat our bodies as sacred temples of the soul. We can also make an important
contribution to healing our relationship with the Earth when we recreate work
as a sacrament and workplaces as sacred space. Through putting our minds in
service to spirit in our work, we contribute to healing the fragmentation in ourselves and in our organizations among body, mind, and soul.

When I asked to be shown the inner side of our work in the world, the feelings and the thought patterns, the message was much the same. Again, there
was an emphasis on letting go, dropping old habits of thought and attitudes. Here
is the message that I accepted.

We are guided to develop ways of knowing the mind and facilitating changes of
mind and heart. When we assist in the transformative process, it is important to
know where we are in it and how we may best assist the process at each stage.
Transformation begins with discomfort and stress, against which we often
struggle. During that period, our attempts to shore up clients' old ways of
thinking and valuing may work against the flow of energy through time and
merely defer the pain. We can contribute more surely by assisting in reflection
and dialogue to uncover the deep sources of clients' discomfort. We can encourage deep learning as an alternative to blame and scapegoating. Helping
our clients to face the shadow and speak the truth about it will serve them best
in this phase. Speaking those truths ourselves may also serve, but less well, and
sometimes at the cost of our longevity in the system.

When an organism ceases to struggle against change, there often follows a
stage of heavy negativity, which must be cleared to make space for new form,
new ways of being and doing. There is a need for purification, in the sense of
cleansing minds of negative thoughts and feelings and of healing polarities and
differences that have arisen during the struggle against change. Forgiveness is a
key to detoxifying individuals and organizations during this phase. Forgiveness
requires that we acknowledge what needs to be purified and then let go of our
attachments to treasured memories and negative feelings and withdraw our energies from them. Negative energies are held in the physical environment, in
our bodies, and in our hearts and minds. We shall need to know how to aid release at all these levels.

Following the release of the past and the negativity associated with it, there is
a period of emptiness, which people are often moved to try to fill with premature activity. The activity may be untimely either because new thought forms
are not yet well established or because will and intention are not yet engaged in

the new forms. When individuals and organizations engage in unfocused activity, we can encourage them to take time to create a common vision and a shared intention to bring the vision into being.

The keys to our participation in transformation, then, are first in the ways we find to aid individuals and groups to face and speak the truth about current reality and to inquire together into the deeper causes of discomfort and stress. Second, they are in our ability to foster forgiveness and the release of negativity. Third, they are in our talents for facilitating the creation of new visions and helping clients focus will and intention in support of practical implementation. The roles we are invited to enact are not especially dramatic, and they are not central to action of the transformation. We are not called to be agents of change but rather midwives. These tasks of midwifery require of us great skill, much courage, and much compassion. Because the forces that are held in tension and then released in transformation are great, there is danger of hurt and harm in the work, both to others and to ourselves. It is not work that I shall wish to do with only my own will, intelligence, and heart as resources. I shall want all the help I can get, and I shall devote myself to gaining ever more facility in attuning myself to guidance, so that I may dance this work to nature's music.

I present the results of my enquiry with no apology, but with some humility. I am clear that the messages I received and accepted and the interpretations I place on them are right for me. They are signs and signals pointing to a future that has heart and meaning for me. They speak of a coherent body of work, some of which I know how to do quite well and some of which I look forward to learning how to do better. I venture to hope that these signs and signals will have interest and meaning for others as well. I should very much like to find companions along the way, on the next stage of my journey!

REFERENCES

Articles that appear in The Collected Papers of Roger Harrison are indicated by (†) following the entry. If the title given to the article in *The Collected Papers* differs from the original title, the revised title follows the †.

Argyris, C. *Interpersonal Competence and Organizational Effectiveness.* Homewood, Ill.: Irwin, 1962.

Arrien, A. *The Four-Fold Way.* San Francisco: HarperSanFrancisco, 1993.

Blake, R. R., and Mouton, J. S. *Solving Costly Organizational Conflicts: Achieving Intergroup Trust, Cooperation, and Teamwork.* San Francisco: Jossey-Bass, 1984.

Blake, R. R., Mouton, J. S., Barnes, L. B., and Greiner, L. E. "Breakthrough in Organization Development." *Harvard Business Review,* Mar.–Apr. 1969. Also reprinted in *Business Classics: Fifteen Key Concepts for Managerial Success.* Boston: Harvard Business School Publishing, 1991.

Block, P. *Flawless Consulting: A Guide to Getting Your Expertise Used.* San Diego, Calif.: Pfeiffer, 1981

Briggs, J. "Dialogue as a Path Toward Wholeness." In M. R. Weisbord and others, *Discovering Common Ground.* San Francisco: Berrett-Koehler, 1993.

Byrd, R. E. "Training in a Non-Group." *Journal of Humanistic Psychology,* 1967, *7*(1), 18–27.

Dobson, T., and Miller, V. *Giving In to Get Your Way.* New York: Delacorte Press, 1978.

Eisler, R. *The Chalice and the Blade: Our History.* San Francisco: HarperCollins, 1987.

Eisler, R., and Loye, D. *The Partnership Way: A Practical Companion for the Chalice and the Blade.* San Francisco: HarperSanFrancisco, 1990.

Fisher, R., Ury, W. L., and Patton, B. (eds.). *Getting to Yes: Negotiating Agreement Without Giving In.* Boston: Houghton Mifflin, 1981.

Fritz, R. *The Path of Least Resistance.* New York: Ballentine Books, 1989.

Gardner, J. *Color and Crystals: A Journey Through the Chakras.* Freedom, Calif.: Crossing Press, 1988.

Graves, T. *Discover Dowsing: Understanding and Using the Power of Divining.* London: Harper/Collins/Aquarian, 1989.

Haberly, H. J. *Reiki: Hawayo Takata's Story.* Olney, Md.: Archedigm, 1990.

Handy, C. *Gods of Management: The Changing Work of Organizations.* (Rev. ed.). London: Pan, 1985.

Harrison, R. "Workers' Perceptions and Job Success." *Personnel Psychology,* 1959, *12,* 619–625.

Harrison, R. "The Impact of the Laboratory on Perceptions of Others by the Experimental Group." In C. Argyris, *Interpersonal Competence and Organizational Effectiveness.* Homewood, Ill: Irwin, 1962.

Harrison, R. "Defenses and the Need to Know." *Human Relations Training News,* 1963, *6*(4), 1–3. (†)

Harrison, R. "Cognitive Models for Interpersonal and Group Behavior: A Theoretical Framework for Research." In *Explorations in Human Relations Training and Research* (entire issue 2). Washington, D.C.: National Training Laboratories, 1965a.

Harrison, R. "Defenses and the Need to Know." In P. R. Lawrence, J. A. Seiler, and others (eds.). *Organizational Behavior and Administration.* Homewood, Ill.: Irwin, 1965b. (†)

Harrison, R. "Cognitive Change and Participation in a Sensitivity Training Laboratory." *Journal of Consulting Psychology,* 1966, *30*(6), 517–520.

Harrison, R. "Classroom Innovation: A Design Primer." In P. J. Runkel, R. Harrison, and M. Runkel, (eds.), *The Changing College Classroom.* San Francisco: Jossey-Bass, 1969. (†)

Harrison, R. "Choosing the Depth of Organizational Intervention." *Journal of Applied Behavioral Science,* 1970, *6*(2), 189–202. (†)

Harrison, R. "Developing Autonomy, Initiative and Risk-Taking Through a Laboratory Design." *European Training,* 1972a, *2,* 100–116. (†)

Harrison, R. "Role Negotiation: A Tough-Minded Approach to Team Development." In W. W. Burke and H. A. Hornstein (eds.), *The Social Technology of Organization Development.* La Jolla, Calif.: University Associates, 1972b. (†"Role Negotiation")

Harrison, R. "Strategy Guidelines for an Internal Organization Development Unit." *The OD Practitioner,* 1972c. (†)

Harrison, R. "Understanding Your Organization's Character." *Harvard Business Review,* 1972d, *50*(3), 119–128. (†)

Harrison, R. "When Power Conflicts Trigger Team Spirit." *European Training,* 1972e, *2,* 57–71. (†"Role Negotiation")

Harrison, R., "Self-Directed Learning: A Radical Approach to Educational Design." *Simulation and Games,* 1977, *8*(1), 73–94. (†)

Harrison, R., "A Practical Model of Motivation and Character Development." In J. E. Jones and J. W. Pfeiffer (eds.), The *1979 Annual Handbook for Group Facilitators.* La Jolla, Calif.: University Associates, 1979.

Harrison, R. "Startup: The Care and Feeding of Infant Systems." *Organizational Dynamics,* 1981, *10*(1), 5–29. (†)

Harrison, R. "Leadership and Strategy for a New Age: Lessons from Conscious Evolution." Report to clients of the Values and Lifestyles Program. Palo Alto, Calif.: SRI International, 1982. (†"Leadership and Strategy for a New Age")

Harrison, R. "Strategies for a New Age." *Human Resource Management,* 1983, *22*(3), 209–234. (†"Leadership and Strategy for a New Age")

Harrison, R. "Leadership and Strategy for a New Age." In J. D. Adams (ed.), *Transforming Work.* Alexandria, Va.: Miles River Press, 1984. (†)

Harrison, R. "Harnessing Personal Energy: How Companies Can Inspire Employees." *Organizational Dynamics,* 1987a, *16*(2), 4–20. (†"How to Focus Personal Energy with Organizational Mission Statements")

References **193**

Harrison, R. *Organization Culture and Quality of Service: A Strategy for Releasing Love in the Workplace.* (Ian Cunningham, ed.) London: Association for Management Education and Development, 1987b. (†"Organization Culture and Quality of Service")

Harrison, R. *Building an Organization Vision and Mission Statement.* Clinton, Wash.: Harrison Associates, 1988.

Harrison, R. *Culture and Levels of Consciousness in Organizations.* Clinton, Wash.: Harrison Associates, 1990. (†)

Harrison, R. *Towards the Learning Organization—Promises and Pitfalls.* Clinton, Wash.: Harrison Associates, 1992.

Harrison, R. *The Collected Papers of Roger Harrison.* San Francisco: Jossey-Bass, 1995.

Harrison, R., Cooper, J., and Dawes, G. *Humanizing Change: Matching Interventions to Organizational Realities.* Clinton, Wash.: Harrison Associates, 1991.

Harrison, R., and Hopkins, R. L. "The Design of Cross-Cultural Training: An Alternative to the University Model." *Journal of Applied Behavioral Science,* 1967, *3*, 431–460. (†)

Harrison, R., and Kouzes, J. "The Power Potential of Organization Development." *Training and Development Journal,* Apr. 1980, pp. 43–47. (†"Personal Power and Influence in Organization Development")

Harrison, R., and Oshry, B. I. "Laboratory Training in Human Relations and Organisational Behaviour." *European Training,* 1972, *2*, 189–199.

Harrison, R., and Stokes, H. *Diagnosing Organization Culture.* La Jolla, Calif.: Pfeiffer, 1992.

Harvey, O. J., Hunt, D. E., and Schroeder, H. M. *Conceptual Systems and Personality Organization.* New York: Wiley, 1961.

Hawley, J. A., *Reawakening the Spirit in Work: The Power of Dharmic Management.* San Francisco: Berrett-Koehler, 1993.

Kelly, G. A. *The Psychology of Personal Constructs, Vol. 1: A Theory of Personality.* New York: W.W. Norton, 1955.

Kidder, T. *The Soul of a New Machine.* Boston: Little, Brown, 1981.

Korda, M. *Power! How to Get It, How to Use It.* New York: Random House, 1975.

Kubler-Ross, E. *On Death and Dying.* New York: Macmillan, 1969.

LeGuin, U. *A Wizard of Earthsea.* Berkeley, Calif.: Parnassus Press, 1968.

Louis, A. M. "They're Striking Some Strange Bargains at Diamond Shamrock." *Fortune,* Jan. 1976, pp. 142–156.

McClelland, D. C. *The Achievement Motive.* New York: Appleton-Century-Crofts, 1953.

McGregor. D. *The Human Side of Enterprise.* New York: McGraw-Hill, 1960.

Mao Tse-Tung. *Quotations from Chairman Mao Tse-Tung.* Peking: Foreign Language Press, 1967.

May, R. *Love and Will.* New York: W.W. Norton, 1969.

Noer, D. M. *Healing the Wounds: Overcoming the Trauma of Layoffs and Revitalizing Downsized Organizations.* San Francisco: Jossey-Bass, 1993.

Peters, T. J., and Austin, N. K. *A Passion for Excellence: The Leadership Difference.* New York: Random House, 1985.

Pfeiffer, J. W., and Jones, J. E. (eds.) *A Handbook of Structured Experiences for Human Relations Training,* Vols. I, II, and III. Iowa City, Iowa: University Associates, 1969–1971.

Ringer, R. J. *Winning Through Intimidation.* Los Angeles: Los Angeles Book Publishers, 1974.

Ringer, R. J. *Looking Out for Number One.* New York: Funk & Wagnalls, 1977.

Schein, E. H. *Process Consultation: Its Role in Organization Development.* Reading, Mass.: Addison-Wesley, 1969.

Schein, E. H., and Bennis, W. G. *Personal and Organizational Change Through Group Methods: The Laboratory Approach.* New York: Wiley, 1965.

Schein, E. H., with Scheier, I., and Barker, C. H. *Coercive Persuasion.* New York: W.W. Norton, 1961.

Senge, P. *The Fifth Discipline: The Art and Practice of the Learning Organization.* New York: Double-day/Currency, 1990.

Speer, A. *Inside the Third Reich.* New York: Macmillan, 1981.

Tillich, P. *The Courage to Be.* New Haven, Conn.: Yale University Press, 1952.

Vaill, P. *Managing as a Performing Art: New Ideas for a World of Chaotic Change.* San Francisco: Jossey-Bass, 1989.

Weisbord, M. R., and others. *Discovering Common Ground.* San Francisco: Berrett-Koehler, 1993.

Weisbord, M. R., and Janoff, S. V. *Future Search.* San Francisco: Berrett-Koehler, 1995.

Wheatley, M. *Leadership and the New Science.* San Francisco: Berrett-Koehler, 1993.

Witkin, H. A., and others. *Psychological Differentiation.* New York: Wiley, 1962.

Wright, M. S. *Perelandra Garden Workbook II: Co-Creative Energy Processes for Gardening, Agriculture and Life.* Warrenton, Va.: Perelandra, 1990.

Wright, M. S. *Perelandra Garden Workbook: A Complete Guide to Gardening with Nature Intelligences.* (2nd ed.) Warrenton, Va.: Perelandra, 1993.

Wright, M. S. *M A P: The Co-Creative White Brotherhood Medical Assistance Program.* (2nd ed.) Warrenton, Va.: Perelandra, 1994.

INDEX

A

Achievement culture, 114, 123
Action research: as model for T-group, 26; need for, to link information and action, 19; in new plant startup, 55
Addiction: to chaos and crisis, in high-tech companies, 57; to work, 73–74
Affirmation, laws for working with, 144–146
Aikido, 176
Alignment culture, 139, 157, 158
Alignment: as daimonic, 99–100, 158; and health, 101; priority of, in evolution of business organizations, 123
Ananda Community, 152–155
Angel of Findhorn, 139
Angels, 171, 184
Appreciation, of connections: in attunement, 100; in mutuality culture, 159
Argyris, C., 20, 22, 24–25, 37, 47, 172–173
Arica Institute, 88
Armstrong, A., 180
Armstrong, J., 180
Arrien, A., 185
Assertive persuasion influence style, 80

Attunement: in community culture model, 139–140; in evolution of business organizations, 123
Australia, 166
Authority, 44, 45
Autonomy Laboratory, 62, 64–65, 70
Autonomy and initiative, 63

B

Barker, C., 33
Bay of Pigs (Cuba), 99
Bennis, W., 20, 54
Benson, R., 115
Berlew, D., 78–80, 86, 90, 92–93, 103, 119, 159
Berry, D., 60
Betrayal: between individuals and organizations, 162; and empowerment, 27
Birla Group, 149
Blake, R., 50, 55–56
Block, P., 125, 172
Blocks to creativity, 64
Blume, G., 96, 104–105
Bohm, D., 57
Bradford, L., 42, 43, 58
Britain, organization development in, 58–59
British, communication with, 58–59
Brown, J., 107–108

Bryson, J., 165
Business as a Learning Community (conference), 146, 148
Business training: formula for success in, 91–93; pitfalls in, 93–94
Byrd, R., 64

C

Campbell, S., 97
Castle and battlefield: metaphor, 166; model, 33
Change: comprehensive model of, 164–165; congruence between strategy of, and vision for, 127; difficulties in achieving, in bureaucratic organizations, 116; mandated, trauma of, 165–167; minimizing resistance to, 39–40; model of unfreeze, change, refreeze, 54; organizations' readiness for, 39–40, 175; project in research and development company, 123–134; projects, need for working with whole system, 120, 133–134; resources for, collecting and focusing, 61–62; self-managing process of, 174; strategy, 133, 149
Chaos, as disempowering, 178–179
Chinese Communists, 62